Literature as Discourse

PARALLAX RE-VISIONS OF CULTURE AND SOCIETY

Stephen G. Nichols, Gerald Prince, and Wendy Steiner,
Series Editors

Literature as Discourse

Textual Strategies in English and History

Robert Hodge

The Johns Hopkins University Press
Baltimore

First published 1990 by The Johns Hopkins University Press
701 West 40th Street, Baltimore, Maryland 21211

Library of Congress Cataloging-in-Publication Data

Hodge, Bob (Robert Ian Vere)
    Literature as discourse: textual strategies in English and
history / Robert Hodge.
        p.   cm.—(Parallax)
    Includes bibliographical references.
    ISBN 0-8018-4056-2
    1. English literature—History and criticism—Theory, etc.
2. Semiotics and literature—Social aspects.   3. Discourse analysis.
Literary.   4. Literature and history.   5. Historicism.   I. Title.
II. Series: Parallax (Baltimore, Md.)
PR25.H64   1990
801'.4—dc20   89-77606 CIP

Contents

Preface

In the past thirty years the academic study of the subject 'English' has been transformed in Britain and the USA and the English-speaking world. These far-reaching changes have been part of a groundswell of changes that have profoundly affected all disciplines in the social sciences and humanities. The 'traditional' form of these disciplines emphasized the autonomy of each discipline, the purity of its object, the self-evidence of its founding premises and its independence from contemporary social issues and concerns. In discipline after discipline these assumptions have been challenged, under the banners of interdisciplinarity and critical theory.

Thirty years on, the situation in a subject like English presents a complex picture. On the one hand a wide-ranging series of critiques of the practices of the older forms of the subject has challenged their very legitimacy, and the potential scope of the subject has been transformed. But the new has not simply replaced the old. The two forms sit alongside each other in the education system as a whole in an uneasy coexistence. This is a political problem, not just an academic one. If the field of English is partitioned between traditionalists and progressives, each trying to overcome or marginalize the other, then the resulting polarization and division will weaken the field, at a time when there are many attacks on the continuing existence of critical research in the humanities.

This book was written as an intervention in just such a situation. It aims to construct alliances, not to further the existing divisions: to point out routes that link the old and the new, so that practitioners of each do not feel they must define themselves in opposition to those of the other in ways that would constrain and weaken both. I should stress that I do not wish to be seen as even-handed in this enterprise. I do not aspire to turn the clock back half-way, so that the subject can exist in a twilight world between the old and the new. The genuine advances of the new are too important to be compromised with in any way. But those advances are not themselves beyond critique, especially where they have adopted a polemical one-sidedness which was necessary in a time of struggle but which will become increasingly inconvenient if it hardens into a new orthodoxy.

In the new construction of 'English', a decisive move has been the decentring of the category of 'literature' and the challenge to the primacy of the text as the organizing principle of the English curriculum. Instead, literature is seen as a social construct, sustained at particular times by particular groups to serve particular interests: an ideological machine concerned with legitimation and control, working through a system that excludes or privileges certain kinds of text (literary texts and the 'canon') and specific readings and modes of reading (literary criticism and its exemplary works). When literature is seen as a contingent phenomenon produced in and by discourse, then a whole set of new objects and connections becomes immediately and directly available for study: social processes that flow through and irresistibly connect 'literary' texts with many other kinds of texts, and social meanings that are produced in different ways from many social sites. The single term that best encapsulates this sense of the object of study is 'discourse'. This concept, following Foucault's influential usage, emphasizes literature as a process rather than simply a set of products; a process which is intrinsically social, connected at every point with mechanisms and institutions that mediate and control the flow of knowledge and power in a community.

But the notion of literature as discourse does not dispense with the category of the literary nor with the importance of text. On the contrary, what is involved is a new theorization of the literary, and a new strategy for dealing with text. Text and discourse in practice form an inseparable pair, because discourse is only available for study in so far as it leaves traces in text. The theorization of text and the development of textual strategies for the study of literature as discourse is therefore one of the main aims of this book: not only because it is important, but also because I see this as the one area which practitioners of the new have culpably neglected, in the heady fascination with contextualism and the open fields of the extra-textual.

The new forms of 'English' need to go beyond their critique of existing methods and strategies of textual analysis. Otherwise there will be nothing to prevent the old methods from continuing to determine critical practice for want of a clear and viable alternative. But the problem is made more confusing because there is not just an absence here. Interdisciplinarity has made available an open-ended set of possible methods, complete with their own difficult terminologies and agendas. This openness can be liberating for readers constrained by the tyranny of a single method, but beyond a certain point it can become another form of oppression, if it becomes a requirement that all these methods and concepts be fully assimilated by anyone who presumes to speak with authority about texts of any kind.

To meet this problem I have adopted the strategy of drawing primarily on the terms and methods of social semiotics, as described in *Social Semiotics* (Hodge and Kress 1988). *Social Semiotics* provides a coherent and useable framework that is relevant to the present task. It is a synthesis of methods and concepts from a range of disciplines (semiotics, linguistics, psychology, sociology and others), each of which is or ought to be concerned with some aspect of the social production of meaning. *Social Semiotics* attempted to bring these into a single coherent scheme and set of terms. The present book aims to make this body of ideas more accessible, especially for readers whose background is in 'English'. It concentrates on a small core of terms and concepts, explaining and illustrating each of them, and positioning them explicitly against familiar ideas from literary criticism. I have introduced a small number of specialist terms, but I have kept these to a minimum: nine only, not (I hope) an insuperable burden for the reader.

It might be appropriate here to summarize what a 'social semiotic' approach entails, before it is expounded at greater length in the book that follows. At the centre is the search for a textual strategy that goes beyond assumptions of an isolated text and a self-contained language system. The social study of text cannot stay within the category of text as it is normally understood, because social forces and agents and processes all exist outside specific texts and yet are decisive components of their social meaning. But texts are the material carriers of meaning and thus are indispensable objects for the study of social meaning. To neglect or disvalue the search for more powerful analysis of text in the name of a concern for the social, as some have done, is perverse. Instead, social semiotics expands the scope of what it treats as text, including contexts, purposes, agents and their activities as socially organized structures of meaning, text-like objects which are themselves mediated by other texts if they are to be available for any kind of study. Instead of an opposition between a close but asocial reading of a specific class of texts ('literature') and a socially oriented refusal to be entrapped by specific reading strategies, social semiotics looks for strategies of reading that are more intensive, more flexible, more comprehensive and more committed to the study of the social.

One class of meanings involved in the production and reception of text is especially likely to be misunderstood in this context. This is the meaning inscribed in the rule systems that govern literary production itself (reading and writing), the forms and conventions so beloved by formalist writers. From the perspective that sees literature as discourse, these rules are quintessentially social, since the systems of control are implicated in broader mechanisms which provide the context and resources for their operation. This quality of rules affects important categories like 'genre', which are crucial, in addition, to the study of individual texts. Literary conventions and genres are often treated as abstract and formal but not especially social categories. Yet they always operate as part of a social process, and it is these processes and their agents, as material social beings and events, that are the primary objects for social analysis, not rule systems or structures of meaning in isolation. Social semiotics distinguishes sharply between the rule systems or regimes and what these project on the one hand, and the complex and contradictory structures of meaning produced by actual readers and writers, who are no less social for having a material existence, on the other.

There are three crucial aspects of textual processes that are so important that this book devotes a chapter to each. One is the social meanings and functions of style. Style is a distinguishing mark of aesthetic forms of discourse and a decisive component in the construction of literariness, but the aesthetic is commonly used to neutralize connections with social meanings and purposes. This is itself a potent social fact: but social semiotics seeks to go beyond deconstructing it to a thoroughgoing and precise strategy for reading the social meanings of style.

Another important concept is transformation. A theory of transformation is ultimately a theory of how and why change occurs or is resisted. Such a theory is essential in the study of social forces and processes in literature, the key to methods of interpretation that try to track meanings as they pass from text to text or disappear from the surviving record. At the same time a transformational theory brings out the basic truth that all textual production is implicated in a series of histories, so that all reading is a form of historical inquiry, on whatever scale.

A final integrating concern is with the category of modality, i.e. the set of ways that the meanings of texts are keyed in to structures of meanings outside them in such a way as to command or disclaim belief. In this way 'reality' itself is constructed as an effect of texts. This problematic relationship of texts to reality and truth has been at the core of debates about the nature and functions of literature for millennia. It is a problem that is by no means confined to literature, but is a crucial issue with every major form of text, from propaganda and advertising to the cooler descriptions of science and history.

So far I have mostly enclosed 'English' in warning apostrophes. As a term it is no longer appropriate to any of the forms of pedagogic practice that currently go under that name, and it is especially misleading for the enterprise that I describe in this book. It is a pun that is constantly shifting its ground, but always exerting a reactionary semantic–ideological pull. There are real disadvantages with the word and I wish I could use another, but at the moment it has overwhelming currency as a hegemonic term. I make no attempt to use it consistently because I have no wish to pretend or construct a consistency which it lacks in general use. I use it rather to invoke a recognizable but confused and unstable area of the curriculum, not a single, unitary and eternal object. In this area, at present, 'literature' looms large as a defining object, so I follow this assumption too, trusting that this usage will enable me to be understood but not defined.

So the content of 'English', for the purposes of this book, opens out in two directions. One can be described under the rubric of 'culture'; the other under that of 'communication'. Traditionally English stayed within the boundaries of high culture, focusing specifically on literary texts. The complex cultural forms of contemporary stratified societies include 'popular culture' as well as prestige forms. They span different media (written, spoken, print, film, art, TV) across time. This book assumes a scope for English that incorporates new objects without jettisoning the objects which constituted the old territory. I have sometimes aspired to be conservative in the choice of texts and issues to study, including the old-fashioned as well as the familiar, but always dealing with them in relation to strategically selected themes or texts or issues that in different ways point to new possibilities and new uses for English.

English is also traditionally concerned with language: with the systems producing social meaning in all genres, for all purposes, for all groups in English-speaking societies. But the specificity of English language and culture can only be properly understood through a comparative approach. So this book includes examples in a range of other languages: European, both ancient (Greek and Latin) and contemporary (French and German), and non-European (Japanese and Aboriginal Australian). Since the book is intended for students of English, the discussions assume no prior knowledge of these particular languages, but at the same time this approach clearly announces the premise that exclusive attention to English texts and the English language is not enough.

Though the book is primarily addressed to students of 'English' at tertiary level, across the spectrum of the varieties of that discipline, I also have two other kinds of reader in mind. One is the classroom teacher of 'English', trained in one set of knowledges and required to be proficient in another; at the leading edge of change in the subject but disvalued and ignored by those who assert leadership in the field. This book does not try to describe the practices of English at primary or secondary school levels, but it does attempt to establish a form of the subject that would help to restore the unity of the subject at all levels, and be of interest and use to all its practitioners.

Another kind of reader I address more tentatively is the historian. In the interdisciplinary movement of the 1960s, the link that seemed most obvious for English was with History. My own early efforts to forge this link from a base in English proved a salutary experience for me, because it looked so promising yet was so difficult to achieve in practice. Part of my problem was that I had misconstrued the relationship between the two disciplines. Initially I supposed that because English was a different and generally bigger subject in the curriculum, then these were different disciplines on the same level, with English perhaps the more comprehensive. I came to see that English should be regarded as part of History (though the kinds of history taught in Britain and American universities were themselves only different fragments of this single overarching discipline). So the concept of interdisciplinarity in fact serves to reify an existing arbitrary organization of knowledges within academic institutions. But that organization is sustained by economic and political forces that make it extremely difficult to redraw the academic map. So there is a subtext to this book: the conviction that the relation between English and History is not an optional extra but involves the reconstitution of a single enterprise. However, I also recognize the power of the institutional forces that work in the other direction. So this book is not exactly addressed to historians, so much as written to be overheard by them, in hopes that some will be persuaded to allow their own disciplinary projects to be illuminated by a social semiotic approach. And perhaps some day they will welcome their by then eager English colleagues into the capacious arms of a reconstituted practice of history.

A final comment is in order about the strategy and organization of the book. The overall principle of organization is an exposition of the concepts and methods of social semiotics. But even though a concern with method was the motivating principle for the book, I would also stress that method should be seen as immanent in the practice of criticism. So each chapter is concerned with specific points of method, but devotes more space to particular analysis than to formal exposition. The chapters explore issues and texts that were of interest and importance to me. They develop specific arguments, less conclusively than if that were their only aim, but in greater depth than a mere illustration of method would have required: because any method will only seem worthwhile if it can produce original, convincing, important and useable readings.

This book, like every other, owes a great deal to many people. Although I have not done full justice in the text to all those whose writings have stimulated and influenced me, I will not try to correct specific omissions here. More important is to acknowledge individuals who in various informal discursive modes have given me invaluable criticism and support. First of these and on a special level is Gunther Kress, with whom I have worked so closely over the last fifteen years, developing different aspects of a common project. Bill Green's comments and perspective proved a decisive influence at a crucial stage. David Birch, Michael O'Toole, John Frow, Vijay Mishra, Horst Ruthrof and Geoffrey Bolton provided helpful comments on various chapters. John Thompson's comments on the final draft were acute and encouraging, and Julia Swindells and Stephen Cox also provided salutary critiques, just in time for me to benefit from them. Pam Cox's influence is pervasive. She has provided provocation and criticism, materials and orientations on a scale that is beyond mere acknowledgement.

Acknowledgements

The author and publishers wish to thank the following for permission to use copyright material:

J. M. Dent & Sons Ltd for 'To Lucasta, going to the wars' by Richard Lovelace from Poems: *Poets of the seventeenth Century* ed. R. Howarth, 1931.

Grafton Books and Liveright Publishing Corporation for an extract from 'i was considering how' from *Tulips and Chimneys* by e. e. cummings, edited by George James Firmage. Copyright © 1923, 1925 and renewed 1951, 1953 by e. e. cummings, 1973, 1976 by the Trustees for the e. e. cummings Trust. Copyright © 1973, 1976 by George James Firmage.

Olwyn Hughes Literary Agency and Harper & Row Publishers, Inc. for excerpts from 'Lady Lazarus' from *Collected Poems of Sylvia Plath* by Sylvia Plath, Faber and Faber. Poems copyright © 1960, 1965, 1971, 1981 by the Estate of Sylvia Plath. Copyright © 1960, 1963, 1972 by Ted Hughes. Editorial copyright © 1981 by Ted Hughes.

Methuen, London, for material from *The Brand New Monty Python Book* by Chapman, Graham et al., 1973.

Penguin Books Ltd for extract from *Understanding and Helping the Schizophrenic: A Guide for Family and Friends* by Silvano Arieti, Penguin Books, 1981, pp 74–5. Copyright © 1979 by Silvano Arieti.

SBK Songs Ltd. for 'Let it Be' by Lennon / McCartney. Copyright © 1970 by Northern Songs under licence to SBK Songs Ltd.

Warner Chappell Music Ltd. and Warner / Chappell Music, Inc. for an extract from 'Hard Rain's Gonna Fall' by Bob Dylan. Copyright © 1963 by Warner Bros. Inc.

1

Social Semiotics and the Crisis in Literary Studies

The terms 'crisis' and 'revolution' are liable to rhetorical overkill, but there is a precise sense of these terms that provides an illuminating description of the current situation in the subject/discipline of English. In his theory of revolutions in science, T. S. Kuhn (1962) describes a typical pattern of periods of 'normal' scientific practices broken up by periods of 'crisis' and 'revolution'. In the crisis stage, the taken for granted authority of the single presiding scheme, which he calls a paradigm, is weakened, and the field is left open for competing protoparadigms to assert their supremacy, engaging in radical critique and the generation of genuinely new theories and practices. In a revolution, in this account, one paradigm achieves dominance, and then proceeds to establish its adequacy over the whole range of the previous paradigm, incorporating most of its objects plus the new ones that signal its own explanatory power.

In these terms, 'English' is still at the crisis stage. 'Traditional' literary criticism, the centrepiece of the subject, is in disarray, following a powerful and convincing assault on its assumptions from a variety of perspectives, which can be labelled Marxist, structuralist and post-structuralist. Even so, departments with the name English or English Literature still dominate the academic landscape at all levels of the curriculum, and will do so for many years to come. And the central reading practice of 'traditional' literary criticism, often called simply 'practical criticism', has only been discredited by these assaults, not replaced. There is as yet no widely recognized alternative form of practical criticism which will allow a new paradigm to carry out the range of explanatory tasks that is implicit in its critique of the old and its hopes for the new. This requires strategies of 'close reading' even more powerful than those on which the previous paradigm prided itself, without the narrowness and limitations that provoked objection, along with equally powerful strategies of 'distant reading', able to make sense of objects as large as genres, periods and disciplines. In this book I hope to contribute to this particular paradigm-forming enterprise.

Traditional criticism revisited

In addressing this urgent task of critique and incorporation of the previous paradigm, it is important to deconstruct the unity of 'traditional'. Not only were there regional differences between the two dominant national systems, British and American; even more significant were differences between levels of each system. When undergraduate English was dominated by the New Criticism in USA and Leavisite practical criticism in Britain, doctorates were still a passport to positions of authority in the academic hierarchy, and doctoral theses assumed competence in a particular reading regime, that of 'literary scholarship'. Lower down in the education system, the rigours of 'practical criticism' had to be considerably adapted to the different conditions of the secondary level classroom.

So 'practical criticism' in its two closely related regional forms was always in some degree oppositional and marginalized within the full set of reading practices of the 'traditional' paradigm, whose repertoire was therefore never either a single monolithic practice or a happy pluralism. Rather, it was constituted by a single functional set of different reading regimes, held together by a set of discursive rules that controlled all contradictions so tightly that they were invisible to practitioners. But the contradictions remained, ready to be mobilized once the dominance of the 'traditional' paradigm was shaken. The new paradigm should not ignore the possibilities thrown up by these contradictions. Nor can it expect to be without a similar structure of contradictions of its own.

In the USA the paradigm options for undergraduate reading practices developed a dual form, deriving from the 'New Critics' and from Northrop Frye, whose *Anatomy of Criticism* (1957) offered complementary strategies of 'distant reading'. In Britain there was not this choice, so dominant was the model built around the practical criticism of F. R. Leavis and his followers. The case of Leavis repays closer scrutiny, as a particularly clear and influential instance of the contradictions to be found in paradigm-creators. Between 1930 and 1960, Leavisites filled chairs and lectureships throughout Britain and the Empire and Commonwealth, and generations of English teachers in schools were profoundly influenced by his work. Leavis himself was regarded as a master of practical criticism, unerring in his grasp of the language of literary texts, and indomitable in his defence of high literary standards against the threats of mass culture. And last but not least, his form of criticism was highly compatible with the needs and values of classroom teachers of English of the time, who found the Leavis approach eminently usable. Yet in spite of such success and influence, he was personally excluded by the literary establishment of his day. At Cambridge, where he taught for most of his academic life, he never got a chair, and he saw opponents appointed to chairs partly in order to oppose him. On the other hand leading critics in British versions of the new paradigm, such as Raymond Williams, acknowledge the role of Leavis in their own intellectual formation. It is clear that in announcing the triumph of the new paradigm we need to recognize the continuities with the old, built out of contradictions in it which proved points of transition and growth, in spite of their declared hostilities and oppositions.

As an example of Leavis's actual practice as a critic, consider the following discussion of the poet William Blake:

> The measure of social collaboration and support represented by the English language didn't make Blake prosperously self-sufficient. He needed more – something that he didn't get. This is apparent in a peculiar kind of difficulty that his work offers to the critic. I am thinking of the difficulty one so often has in deciding what kind of thing it is one has before one.
>
> > A petty sneaking knave I knew –
> > O! Mr Cromek, how do ye do?
>
> – that is clearly a private blow-off. *The Tyger* is clearly a poem (in spite of the bluffed-out defeat in the third stanza). But again and again one comes on the thing that seems to be neither wholly private nor wholly a poem. It seems not to know what it is or where it belongs and one suspects that Blake didn't know. What he did know – and know deep down in himself – was that he had no public: he very early gave up publishing in any serious sense. (Leavis 1952: 187)

This piece of criticism takes for granted aestheticism (in its confident distinction between a poem and a non-poem) and elitism (Blake is being weighed carefully and found somewhat wanting). Language is deferred to, as the primary object of literary judgement, but interestingly the language is not itself analysed or treated as needing analysis. The qualities are so 'clearly' present that no further discussion is required. What he is diagnosing here, in Blake's case, is what would later be labelled cultural deficit theory in sociolinguistics, where it is used to explain the supposed intellectual and scholastic inadequacies of working-class and black students (cf. Bernstein 1971, Labov 1969). Although texts are quoted or alluded to, the focus is not on the texts as such, but on the processes of their production and reception. These processes are represented as intrinsically social, determining the forms of the text and their 'literary' values. And his own text draws attention to its discursive nature, as the dynamic product of a discursive subject whose discursive processes (e.g. 'I am thinking of the difficulty') are themselves part of his meaning.

In this performance it is significant that Leavis is not doing everything he claims to be (e.g. he takes for granted a precise but controversial sociolinguistic history of English and implies methods of linguistic analysis that he never demonstrates). It is equally significant that he carries out an analysis of the conditions of production of literary meaning that he doesn't see fit to theorize or substantiate, coexisting with the critical programme that he does exemplify: that is to say, there is one programme (a sociolinguistics of literary language) that he privileges but cannot engage in, and another (a discourse analysis of conditions of literary production) that he deploys but cannot theorize or justify. Yet these are two decisive developments that are foregrounded in what I have called the new paradigm and which I try to address in this book.

In the same period in the USA, the New Criticism shared a similar set of strategies and assumptions – unsurprisingly, given many common intellectual roots and a common set of pedagogic needs. As an instance, here is a comment by Cleanth Brooks and Robert Penn Warren, discussing a similar kind of text by Blake in their influential undergraduate textbook *Understanding Poetry*. They quote the whole of a twelve-line poem by Blake, 'The Scoffers' ('Mock on, mock on, Voltaire, Rousseau') and then offer this analysis:

> The speaker begins abruptly by addressing two of the Scoffers, Voltaire and Rousseau. (It does not matter, insofar as the merit of the poem is concerned, whether or not we regard the historical Voltaire and Rousseau . . . as really scoffers against the things of the spirit. The important matter is that Blake should have felt them to be so and should have been able to make poetry out of his indignation against them.) (Brooks and Warren 1976: 329)

This comment takes for granted the self-evidence of the category of 'poetry,' and the centrality of the function of evaluating a poem's 'merit'. We can also see very clearly the pedagogic concern that students should get the correct meaning, and the confidence that ultimately there is a single correct meaning. But we also note the equivocal role of history in establishing the credentials of a reading. It doesn't matter, it seems, what the historical Voltaire and Rousseau 'really' thought, though we are also given to understand that Brooks and Warren do know. It does matter, however, what Blake really thought and that he was sincere in thinking it. Yet there are no markers of sincerity pointed to in the text, and no strategies for an undergraduate reader of the poem to draw on to test this sincerity. Instead, literary scholarship, available to pedagogues but not to students, serves as the basis for an absolute ruling on the truth of history.

We can see here, crossing all that is common to Leavis and the New Criticism, traces of the different orientations of these two forms of the traditional paradigm. The New Criticism shows a greater concern with intellectual history than with social history and the social context of literature. It also shows a keener sense of the gap between the writer (Blake) as constructed in and by the text (the 'speaker') and his material social existence. A form of the same difference still distinguishes the dominant American and British forms of the new paradigm, in spite of all they have in common. This small instance shows what is also true on a broader scale. The new paradigm is not simply a repudiation of the former paradigm. Its break from the past follows lines of cleavage in that past, and is created out of the contradictions within its practices. So we can see a kind of continuity between the new and the old paradigms, so close that in a sense the new paradigm can be seen as a necessary development of the old. But that is not to say that the break was not real, and difficult, and important.

Key concepts in social semiotics

This book uses social semiotics as a framework for studying literature as discourse, and literary criticism itself as constituted through discursive processes. Here I will use Blake and his critics as a source of examples to illustrate some of the key concepts and terms of social semiotics. One of the most basic concepts is structure. Many forms of structuralism have been formalist and indifferent to social context and process, but this need not be the case, and the sheer obviousness of the basic kinds of semiotic structure is what makes them such powerful categories for the study of social meanings.

A semiotic structure is a significant relationship between two or more elements. There are two basic kinds of semiotic structure: *syntagmatic* (syntactic) structures, and *paradigmatic* structures. A syntagmatic structure is a structure consisting of two or more elements in space or time. 'I knew', for instance, combines a subject 'I' and a verb 'knew' to produce its meaning. Paradigmatic structures are organized sets of alternatives. Such structures determine the meaning of the choice of any element. For instance, Leavis uses both 'I' and 'one' to describe himself in the text I have quoted: these two terms form a paradigmatic set, either member of which Leavis could choose. The meaning of the choice of either is to be found in the terms of the choice itself. In the case of 'I' or 'one', one criterion is clearly the difference between personal ('I') and impersonal ('one'). In this instance, Leavis chooses both, at different times, but this does not cancel the significance of the choice. On the contrary, it signifies an important confusion in his construction of his role as a critic, as paradigm shaper and marginalized voice.

Choice, of itself, does not confer a social meaning. It is only when the terms of the choice are understood by reference to social structures that the resulting meaning is social. In this case, the opposition between 'I' and 'one' is structured by the status of the user or the situation. 'One' is a formal use, marking the speaker as of high status (members of the British royal family, for instance, are fond of 'one') or the context as formal. 'I' is direct and relatively informal. By his use of both, Leavis is signalling an ambiguity in either his status or his sense of the occasion. Brooks and Warren in contrast use 'we', which has an ambiguity of a different kind. It is a single word that functions in at least three different paradigms, constructing three different kinds of relationships: 'we' as a single plural ego, i.e. Brooks and Warren; 'we' as a pedagogic plural, incorporating the student reader into their 'regard'; and 'we' as the pronoun of power, used by kings, editors and writers – singular or plural – of textbooks. Ambiguity, we see, does not always signify insecurity.

The social meaning of a syntagm is dependent on the social meaning of the paradigmatic choices that constitute it. A syntagm is not necessarily composed of word-plus-word. Brooks and Warren's text at this point quotes the complete poem by Blake, then adds a three-paragraph commentary, then four questions. These three elements, poem plus commentary plus questions, form a syntagm, a pedagogic syntagm which affects each component. The historical unreliability of Blake's views in the poem, for instance, becomes a problem which the rest of the syntagm exists to neutralize. Leavis has constructed his text as a different kind of syntagm. His whole text, as quoted here, forms a syntagm with Blake's couplet. Part of its social meaning is the juxtaposition of Blake's meaning with Leavis's, poet with critic, dead working-class writer with living middle-class critic. Another part of that meaning is the dominance of critic over poet (though there are other critics who would not even quote at this length). We could add that the poem Leavis quotes is not classified, by him, as really a poem, while 'The Tyger' which is 'clearly a poem' is not quoted. Similarly, Blake's two lines together form a syntagm, juxtaposing a line of poetic discourse ('A petty sneaking knave I knew') with a line of non-poetic everyday discourse ('O! Mr Cromek, how do ye do?'). The social meaning of this as a syntagm is both opposition (between the confident poet–critic and the social being who is represented as addressing Mr Cromek) and identity, since Blake is the source of both elements. But Leavis seems not to have noticed this social contradiction as part of the meaning of this poem: a fact that becomes especially interesting, since he also seems not to have noticed a similar split in his own discourse.

Brooks and Warren and Leavis and Blake have all produced text. That is to say, they have engaged in *semiosic acts*, the social production of meaning, where 'semiosic' derives from *semiosis*, the process of constructing (producing, interpreting) meaning. (In this book, 'semiosis' is distinguished from 'semiotics', which refers to the discipline and its objects.) In each case, the text has a *mimetic* function, that is, it claims to represent part of reality, e.g. Blake's beliefs (Brooks and Warren), Blake as poet (Leavis), and Mr Cromek as knave (Blake). But each text also signifies something of its semiosic context, i.e. the conditions under which it was produced; and that is an important part of its social meaning. This doesn't mean that this kind of meaning is necessarily true. The semiosic event 'O! Mr Cromek' is presented as a fiction within the discourse of the poem, though something like it may in fact have occurred. The text itself semiosically exists as a poem written by a poet, not as an authentic social interaction. Blake's text, that is, constructs a pseudo-situation as part of its own mimetic function. Brooks and Warren do the same thing, with their vivid, dramatic opening words: 'The speaker begins abruptly.'

Blake's poem, though brief, does a lot of semiosic work, constructing a complex set of authors/speakers and readers/hearers, together with the relationships that link them. His first line constructs one situation, the second another. The verb in the first is in the past tense, indicating an event not in the present, on which the speaker reflects for the benefit of someone else. The generalized description ('a petty sneaking knave') reinforces this construction of the semiosic context as a general reflection on life, communicated to a distant non-interacting hearer in some private place (or possibly the poet talking to himself). The second line, however, is offered as a greeting, as though the speaker has just come across Mr Cromek. The exclamation links speaker and Cromek in an immediate social bond.

But the two utterances combine to form a complex new whole. Mr Cromek, we assume, is the 'sneaking knave' of the first line. But in spite of this connection there are still two utterances, two voices, two contexts. In one the speaker is a lucid, trenchant critic of the Cromeks of this world. In the other he respects social conventions in greeting the contemptible Cromek. But the social meaning of this is still unclear, because it is completed by the role of the hearer in the exchange. One kind of hearer of Blake's greeting might not know of his real opinion of Cromek, and would read it simply as an act of politeness. Those who heard the greeting and had also heard the first utterance could still come to very different judgements, depending on their alignment to Blake (as speaker). If they are expected to know Blake's real views, they may see a subtext in his greeting, one which turns a polite greeting into an insult of which Cromek will be unaware. But if they do not feel complicit with Blake in this insult, they may see the discrepancy as a mark of social hypocrisy: it is Blake, then, as much as Mr Cromek who is a 'petty, sneaking knave'. Even if he is seen to be successfully insulting Cromek in public and getting away with it, that triumph is 'petty' and 'sneaking'.

This social meaning projected by the play of semiosic work is clearly an important level of the meaning of Blake's text. Without it, Blake would have been open to the accusation that he's just being rude about Cromek. With it, he is implying a subtle critique of his own social performance as well as of Cromek's character. But to read the social meaning of exchange-syntagms, we need to know the paradigmatic values of the participants. This is where the issue of material social reality comes in. Up to a point we can describe the contexts and roles constructed by the text, but this process quickly loses any explanatory power unless we try to label the actual participants. One is Blake, whom we may think we know, since he is a recognized poet in the English literary canon. Robert Cromek, publisher of some of Blake's engravings, has disappeared from history, though in the early nineteenth century he was probably no less well known than Blake. We quickly recognize that the meanings of the participants which seemed transparent in fact rested on a fairly unexamined version of social history, whose dubious assumptions need to be tested against better informed and more scrupulous historical sources.

But this still provisional version of history doesn't function as truth. What it does is to feed into the analysis of semiosic meanings, in so far as it underpins a simple set of paradigmatic categories. Applying this structure, we can read a further dimension of the social meaning of this text. Cromek stands for a class of entrepreneur which exploits artists like Blake (in another poem he is called 'Bob Screwmuch'). The interaction that Blake signifies in his poem then will have a further meaning: the dependence and servility forced on artists and artisans by those who control the publishing process, and the covert hostility and anger of both parties. But we need to be very clear about how this supposed 'reality' functions semiotically. It is based on the assumption that Blake and Cromek had a real material existence, in an England of the eighteenth and nineteenth century which was itself a concrete social and material reality semiosically organized by paradigmatic structures similar to those we have deployed. If we were to find proof that Blake, or Cromek, didn't in fact exist in this way at this time (for instance that Cromek *was* Blake and himself wrote this couplet) then our interpretation would be significantly altered.

But 'reality' can only affect meaning in so far as it is mediated by texts, although those texts are constrained in many ways by the material conditions that give rise to them. If we think we know that Blake did exist and was a major poet, we only know that through a series of texts. We may forget this textual process and suppose that Blake *is* a major poet, that this is raw 'reality' itself. But in Cromek's day that 'fact' was not known and therefore did not exist, since it could only exist as a specific construction by a social group. In our own day, that 'fact' can also be deconstructed: but it could not have come to exist if an actual person ('Blake') had not written poems which survive. Similarly, the semiosic meaning of Blake's poem is partly his own work, images of himself and Cromek which he has constructed. However, those images can be juxtaposed with others by a reader, to form a syntagm in the normal way, but a syntagm whose author is not Blake, but Blake-plus-the-reader. For instance, if readers discover evidence that Cromek was more sincere and hard pressed than Blake believed, the overall meaning of the poem alters, incorporating the hysteria of Blake (the poet) as a component of his critical judgement.

So far I have written somewhat uneasily of 'reality', putting it in inverted commas to indicate the difficulties surrounding the term. The problem with reality in social semiotics, as in philosophy or literary criticism or everyday life, is that it is usually both essential and unavailable in an absolute form. An act of semiosis is incomprehensible and useless unless it can be matched up against some part of reality, yet semiosis typically constructs its own version of reality. This second kind of reality is not entirely to be trusted, yet without some measure of trust the semiosic process breaks down. To understand how reality is mediated in semiosic practice I will use the term *modality*. The modality of a semiosic act is the claimed or imputed relationship between reality and mimetic content. So modality is a claim or judgement about mimetic structures and how much they can be relied on, but the claims or judgements themselves take place on the semiosic plane, and hence are highly sensitive to social pressures and meanings. Modality is different from honesty, or reality; it is always at best motivated honesty, concerned with constructed schemes of reality. And because it always refers to an action performed by producers or receivers of text, it also always expresses semiosic meanings which are essentially social: e.g. solidarity and trust, authority and power, diffidence and suspicion.

A good illustration of how modality works is the inverted commas I put around 'reality'. These are modality markers. They signify my recognition that 'reality' is only what people claim it to be, that it does not have absolute status. But I don't actually have a total doubt about the knowability of reality. I don't put 'Brooks and Warren' or 'Blake' in inverted commas, even though logically a doubt about 'reality' must include a doubt about the reality of Brooks and Warren and Blake, especially since I believe that the Brooks and Warren and Blake I write about are constructs which are the products of a number of texts. But by putting inverted commas around reality I signify how scrupulous I am about reality-judgements, hoping to acquire credibility from my readers (which I lose as I talk about it). I don't write 'Brooks and Warren' because that degree of self-doubt would seem like overkill and therefore might discredit my judgement. It may seem paradoxical that a marker of uncertainty can be used both to achieve trust and to lose it (and conversely, that markers of certainty can reinforce trust and cast doubt on it). But this complexity arises because modality is interpreted semiosically not mimetically; by reference to context and use, not simply by measuring texts against reality.

Many aspects of a text have a modality function. Critics and others who try to persuade naturally develop skilful patterns of modality which reveal where they are trying to buttress their reality, and where therefore they need to be scrutinized most carefully. The Brooks and Warren text begins with the modality of total confidence. The 'simple present' tense ('begins') has the highest modality value of any tense in English: the modality of universal truth offered as direct perception. The next two sentences then bristle with markers of modality. The effect of such profusion is always to weaken the modality, even when the apparent aim is to strengthen it. By the time Brooks and Warren reach their strong assertion 'the important matter is', we may wonder how far we can trust this protestation. The two sentences on this topic are enclosed by brackets, which are also modality-markers. The bracket signals that this section is relatively speaking not true or not relevant to the main argument, but is sufficiently true in its own terms to need saying. The device serves both to mark and to contain a contradiction (or to be more precise, a nested set of contradictions).

So when we turn back and look again at what kind of statement Brooks and Warren accord the modality of absolute certainty, and what they are much less certain about, it is surprising to find that it almost exactly contradicts the dogmas of the New Criticism. 'The Heresy of Paraphrase' was the trenchant title of one of Brook's best known expositions of his doctrine (in Brooks 1968), but here we see that paraphrase is in practice the critical act that he is most confident about. Conversely, the careful separation of Blake-as-narrator from the historical Blake is surrounded by markers of uncertainty.

To illustrate the complex operations of modality we can look at what seems like a broadly similar structure in Leavis's last two sentences. As we have just seen, the present tense normally has a higher modality than the past. So 'one suspects' has a higher modality than 'Blake didn't know'. But 'one suspects' itself has a modality function, signifying doubt. So the whole phrase surrounds Blake knowing or not knowing with Leavis's present certainty that he isn't certain of Blake's past slightly-uncertain not-knowing. This ought to undercut the sentence totally, but that is not its actual effect. What it does instead is to establish Leavis's credentials for his next sentence: 'What he did know.' This is not simply past, but past emphatic: a tense signifying that Leavis is really certain about this one, though if we look carefully at the statement we can't see why he should be so much more certain about it. Perhaps Leavis is sure that Blake in fact didn't have a public, but one suspects that deep down in himself Leavis doesn't really know what Blake knew about the matter. Leavis's modality markers show us what he wants us to believe, more than what he 'actually' does believe. Our own modality judgements, as readers, may accept his modality claims at their face value, or not. So the same text may not have the same modality for reader and writer, or for different readers. This indeterminacy may be regarded as a nuisance, at times, but it reflects the very great contribution of modality to the effect of texts, literary or otherwise.

A useful way of seeing the relationship of Blake's text to reality is through the key notion of *transformation*. A transformation refers to structural change. If we start from a text, like Blake's, which projects a version of reality, we can follow that work of projection by tracing the transformations of which it consists. Transformational analysis, then, tries to fill in gaps, more or less as we have done. But the text we are presented with is itself the product of transformational work which had a material reality and worked with a real series of material texts. Transformational analysis needs to be able to work from both directions. In each case analysis needs to specify the agent of transformation and the purpose of the transformational work as a social act.

To illustrate one kind of transformational analysis I will take one phrase from Leavis's text: 'Social collaboration and support represented by the English language'. In interpreting this, we can project a chain of transformations as follows:

1   social collaboration and support

⇑

2   (a) [*x*] collaborates [with *y*] social[/*y*]
    (b) [*x*₁] supports [*y*] social[/*y*]

In trying to decode this further we then run into problems. Who are *x* and *x*₁? It seems to be the English language which is supporting Blake, in 2(b), but how could the English language 'collaborate' with him in 2(a)? Presumably others, or society itself, collaborate(s) with him (and others) through the English language?

This analysis could be pushed into much greater detail, but the main point is clear enough. Leavis's sentence seems to be offered as a transformation of the fuller statements which it implies, but when we try to reverse these transformations we do not get a simple clear prior text. On the contrary, we get a tangle of unclear and inconsistent utterances. Overall, they do make a kind of sense. They imply a social world of mutual collaboration and support, acting in some way through language as its medium and guarantee. This 'sense' is heavily ideological. In this case our analysis can also name the ideologue: Leavis. It is Leavis who both invokes and masks this image of a harmonious and seemingly benign social order. But Leavis in the same text also implicitly rejects this ideology. Blake, he points out, was *not* supported sufficiently by his society or his public. Because Blake struck out on his own against this social collective, Leavis calls him a 'genius' (1952: 186). But because he lacked this support and rejected it, he is hardly even a poet, or not an assured one, according to Leavis.

I have brought out this contradiction starkly because it helps us to see the function of Leavis's transformational work in 'social collaboration'. He projects an ideology of conformism so unclearly because he is also committed to its opposite. Both ideologies coexist within a page, in relation to the very same poet – just as they both together describe the contradictions in his own position, as upholder of traditional literary values and leader of an influential school of criticism, and as a radical, marginalized voice excluded by the British literary establishment.

Logonomic systems and the institution of literature

Both critical traditions take for granted a self-evident and foundational distinction between 'poem' and 'non-poem'. Behind this distinction there are two more important distinctions, between literature and non-literature, and between art and non-art. This set of distinctions is decisive in defining the object of literary studies, yet is also by definition outside it, since it must be taken for granted for literary studies to have an object to work with. But for the social semiotic project, this kind of distinction is highly significant and needs to be made available as an object of study to all students of English. Institutions that exercise control of and through discourse do so through rules that prescribe or exclude classes of speakers, topics and occasions. To understand how this process works, I will use the concept of *logonomic system*. 'Logonomic' comes from two Greek words: *nomos* meaning a rule or system of regulations, and *logos* meaning both word or speech (as in 'dialogue') and ideas or body of thought (as in 'logic' or 'geology'). The double meaning, which no single English word exactly conveys, is important, because logonomic systems typically control both forms of thought and forms of language and discourse, indeed, control each through the other. Logonomic systems arise to maintain relations of power and cohesion within groups or institutions. Since groups are held together by a sense of common purpose and values, as mediated by discourse, the tendency for individuals to develop divergent ideas and experience must be held in check by some means, and logonomic systems meet this need.

The discipline of literary criticism is a good example of logonomic systems at work. Literary criticism refers to an institutionalized practice at a given time, within a specific society, of an accredited group of practitioners working in agreed ways with a recognizable body of texts which constitute 'literature'. Without a reasonable measure of agreement as to what 'literature' is, the discipline could not exist. But 'literature', understood as the object of literary criticism, is not a universal category. The word only acquired its modern sense in English during the nineteenth century (Williams 1986). It is no coincidence that the development of English Literature departments followed on later, flowering towards the middle of the twentieth century. The history and definition of 'literature' is inescapably bound to the history of the subject 'English', itself embedded in a history of pedagogy and strategies of cultural reproduction.

Logonomic systems organize groups by controlling semiosis: who can think and say what to whom in what way, and who or what is excluded from discourse and knowledge. This control is exercised by rules, implicit or explicit, concerning the major elements of the semiosic process: producers and receivers, texts and topics. Rules concerned with these can be termed *production regimes, reception regimes, genre regimes* and *noetic regimes* respectively. ('Noetic' here refers to objects of knowledge as divided up and organized into systems of thought.) Since these regimes together make up a logonomic system they obviously overlap. They are often presented separately, as though they had different contents and functions, but the real difference is strategic. It's important to emphasize that these regimes exist as a set of prescriptions constraining meaning, but that in practice they produce only the specifications for 'correct' meanings, which are not to be confused with the meanings actually or even typically produced.

The poem/non-poem distinction draws on a genre regime. The genre regime of literature classifies texts: as literature and non-literature, as poem, novel, play, short story, etc. As a strategy of control it has the advantage of seeming objective and asocial. Brooks coauthored companion volumes to *Understanding Poetry* and called them *Understanding Fiction* and *Understanding Drama*, thus comprehending and compartmentalizing the whole field of literature in a way that appeared neutral and unproblematic. Genres can be defined in formal terms, through a set of observable properties of texts. However, that apparent merit becomes a disadvantage in the light of the overall purpose of a genre regime, which is to organize behaviour and thought, not simply to classify existing texts. The rules of a genre become rules for authors and readers as to how to write and read, and what they should write and read about. They thus become a covert vehicle for production and reception and noetic regimes. Genre regimes as the organizing principle of a curriculum mesh well with text-based pedagogies such as 'English' has been in the past. However, the notion of genre becomes problematic when 'literacy', i.e. the production and reception regimes of the written code, is foregrounded. Genre has had to be substantially retheorized before being used for this purpose in English classes (see Kress 1982).

We can see the pedagogic use of 'genre' as an organizing category underlying Leavis's use of the poem/non-poem distinction. Blake's poem has metre and rhyme, so we might think it should be classified as a poem on purely formal grounds. But it's not, by Leavis: it's a 'private blow-off'. 'Private' indicates among other things the production regime that Blake, in Leavis's view, doesn't observe. There is a poetic manner – elevated, dignified, and above all public – which Blake doesn't adopt in this poem (though 'The Tyger' passes the test). We may note in passing that Leavis elsewhere criticizes excessively elevated diction, as in Milton – there isn't necessarily a single consistent principle here. The topic also seems unsuitable for poetry, as Leavis understands it, though he doesn't expand the point. Because Blake doesn't complete his part of the contract, Leavis can't read it 'as a poem'. So the necessary reception regimes can't begin to operate. But if Leavis can't read it 'as a poem', he doesn't know how else to read it. As he puts it graphically, 'It seems not to know what it is or where it belongs,' as though texts themselves can feel alienated and socially insecure. Leavis then blames Blake for not knowing and Blake's public for not telling him, leaving his own sense of inadequacy as a critic unstated and unexamined.

It is interesting to recognize that although Brooks and Warren work with the same broad distinction between literary and non-literary, they apply it differently, less harshly. They are not concerned about Blake's colloquial tone in the poem they discuss here, and elsewhere in their book they analyse popular songs and ballads with only a slightly patronizing tone. Again, we see slight differences within or between two closely cognate forms of the 'traditional' paradigm which were to loom larger in the new paradigm.

There is a further factor that influences what each critic can and does say: that is the context in which they produce their text. Brooks and Warren were writing an undergraduate textbook, constrained by the requirements of that social space. Leavis's text was produced under less typical conditions: a speech to the Students' Union of the London School of Economics and Political Science, an audience who, like Blake's public, might not have quite known what they should expect from an eminent but controversial literary critic. At issue in both cases is a generalized body of knowledge which is used to interpret the social meaning of contexts. The object of this knowledge is a linkage of orders of space (categories of place) and knowledge into what I will call a structure of *domains*.

Blake's piece does have some of the markers of poetry, as we have noted earlier. It has both rhyme and metre, two of the best known formal markers of poetic status. It is printed with space to the left and an unjustified right margin – another sign of poetry in a print format. This kind of sign is often called a convention. It might be asked, what do these conventions have to do with the nature of 'poetry'? The question brings us to an important principle of classification of all kinds of sign. The linguist Saussure, writing in the early twentieth century, divided signs into two broad classes (Saussure 1974). One he called 'motivated'. These were signs in which the signifier or carrier of meaning had a clear or natural connection with the signified or meaning. The stylized pictures of men and women used to signify men's and women's toilets would be an example. Other signs Saussure called 'arbitrary' or 'conventional', because the link between signified and signifier was 'arbitrary' (the product of a social will which took no account of how things really are) or 'conventional' (because this link was maintained purely by a convention or agreement of a group that the link should hold). Saussure regarded words, the primary medium of literature, as arbitrary or conventional signs, though he also acknowledged that some aspects of verbal language, such as word order, could be 'motivated' signs.

A distinction like this needs to be seen as relative, not absolute. It is a continuum along which different kinds of signs can be ranged, not two boxes into which all kinds of signs can be put. But the distinction needs to be seen as relative in other ways too. The crucial issue concerns whether the link between signifier and signified is clearly perceptible or not. If it is, we can call the signifier a *transparent* sign, because the signified is relatively clearly visible beneath the signifier – visible for some semiosic agents, though not necessarily for others. The opposite to a transparent sign is an *opaque* sign, one where the link is not easily seen or understood. This is different from 'conventional' or 'arbitrary', since a transparent sign might also be strongly supported by conventional agreement, as much as an opaque sign. Saussure's distinction opposes 'nature' to 'society', as though the social must be against nature, and the natural must be antisocial. In practice this assumption is too simple. The social is a specific appropriation of the natural, and even the antisocial is a specific product of the social. With signs and meanings it is always important to be able to recognize specific social determinants even in the most 'natural' signs and meanings, and conversely, we must always be able to track back the most thoroughly worked-over sign to its intersection with objects and processes of material social reality.

One illustration of these terms is to be found in two words Leavis uses: 'private' and 'blow-off'. 'Private' is a word from a high status vocabulary; 'blow-off' is vulgar, whatever its meaning. From one point of view, Saussure would be right to insist that 'private' seems to have no connection, as a series of sounds, with the concept of privacy. However, 'blow-off' as a series of sounds is closer to its signified. The initial sound 'b' is technically called a plosive. There are many ways of saying the word, but the vulgar can really explode it, and finish with an emphatic 'ff', a fricative which mirrors the opening 'b', but in a less vehement form, like a hiss of escaping air. 'Scoffers' from Blake's poem as quoted by Brooks and Warren has a similar quality, and it stands out for this reason in its context as they use it: 'as really *scoffers* against the spirit'.

Readers of poetry will perhaps recognize here the quality called 'onomatopoeia', or 'sound echoing sense' – a quality that is, interestingly, seen as typically poetic yet not greatly admired in Western academic criticism. But as 'blow-off' shows, it is even more strongly marked as low status, because there is an equally widespread recognition that transparent signifiers are typical of low-class discourse (or conversely, that opaque signifiers are a marker of high-class discourse). So the quality of transparency is itself a signifier, as is opacity. We could take as another example Leavis's phrase 'the measure of social collaboration and support'. This is the impressive language of academic discourse. We also saw that it is heavily transformed and only loosely connected to any meaning. It is an opaque signifier in every respect. But far from being a weakness, the opacity is a strength (in academic discourse). It is words as clear and direct as 'private blow-off' that are risky, risking precisely the label of 'non-academic' and low status.

There is a good reason why the quality of opacity in signifiers should itself be a transparent signifier of high status. If it is difficult to connect signifiers and signifieds, this difficulty, seen as a transparent signifier of skill in both writer and reader, establishes the status of small elite groups of those who are trained to do such work. Literary critics are not necessarily more opaque than other academics (though the proponents of the new paradigm are often criticized for being more opaque than either Brooks or Leavis). But the opacity is not only a transparent sign: it is also strongly conventional, in the sense that strong conventions exist at the logonomic level requiring such a display of opacity.

Returning to rhyme and metre, then, we can say that these have been among the most salient markers of the poetic, certainly in the English tradition from the seventeenth century to the nineteenth. But these two features are themselves transparent signifiers. Both refer to qualities of sound, and therefore signify the oral dimension, poetry as primarily an oral not a written form, in spite of the fact that the term 'literature' literally signifies writing and the written medium. Paradoxically, then, it seems that the most prestigious form of literature within the discipline of 'English' declares its status as not really 'literature' at all (not written), though of course it is only studied in its printed and published form. But both rhyme and metre are built on regularity, repetition and control. These are transparent signifiers of conformity and suppression of sponta-neous, natural speech. So these markers of poetry as transparent signifiers communicate a complex and contradictory message about poetry. The complexity is added to when we see what a poet like Blake can do with it. His first line is in impeccable metre, an iambic tetrameter, each stress falling exactly where it ought. His second line, however, is conversational, with stresses and intonation patterns that fight against the neat pattern of metre (to get it right, you have to stress it 'how *do* ye *do*', instead of the more natural '*how* d'ye *do*', and it still doesn't sound very 'poetic'). And 'knew' is not an exact rhyme with 'do' in the standard English pronuncia-tion that determined poetic diction in Blake's time. Blake is able to use a conventional expectation that poetry will signify a high status orderliness as a means to signify his own repudiation of that status and that order, though in doing so he ran the risk of being dismissed as not a 'poet': or he would have, if he had ever tried to publish this as a poem.

Built into the markers of poetry, then, is an ideological scheme, by which I mean a coercive version of the social world: in this case the notion of the poet as outside the culture of the written word but expressing obedience and conformity to an external set of rules. But in this scheme, as in the critical position of both Leavis and the New Critics, what we are struck by is not consistency but *contradiction*. So endemic is this quality in ideological performances that we need to accept that it is functional and systematic. So instead of the notion of ideology as a fixed but distorted version of the social world, we will use the notion of an *ideological complex*, a functional set of ideological schemes or versions of social reality contradictory in themselves but serving the interests of a specific class or group.

For many theorists, the group that is the source of ideology must by definition be the dominant class in society (e.g. Thompson 1986). Although there is much to be said for this more restricted definition, I prefer not to use it in this book. This is because similar forms can be used by non-dominant groups as strategies of resistance, which are no more (and no less) compromised by this similarity than is the case with ideological complexes in the discourse of the dominant. Blake's version of the hypocrisy of social life expresses contempt at the whole charade, or anger at his hopeless complicity, or perhaps both. He used a rough and truncated form of the satiric couplet, and left the text hidden in his notebook. Brooks and Warren, in contrast, although clearly allied with pedagogic authority, celebrate Blake's heroic 'indignation' against Voltaire and Rousseau, in the same kind of educational context that would not praise a student's equally sincere 'indignation' against a literary classic like Wordsworth or Austen. If the same text or topic can have such ambiguous or different ideological meanings and effects depending on the play of forces in their semiosic context, then we clearly cannot assume a single automatic value of 'dominant' or 'resistant' for any ideological form. Instead, we need to accept contradiction and instability as the typical features of ideology as it appears in discourse, in criticism as in literature.

New lamps or new bulbs:? literary criticism and social semiotics

Both literary criticism and writing refer to a range of different practices with their own histories, which have been shaped by specific social forces: so definitions of what literature is or what a poem is cannot be absolute or fixed. Those definitions have force only at a particular time for a particular social formation. But if they cannot be accepted as absolute truths, at least they can be usefully studied as social facts. The current Kuhnian 'crisis' offers a rare pedagogic opportunity which should not be missed: to incorporate the processes by which a 'discipline' is constructed and challenged as themselves an important object of study, building in the provisionality of disciplinary knowledge as one of its founding premises.

In this situation the project of social semiotics would by no means advocate elimination of the previous canon of authors or texts, so that poets like Blake (or Milton or Shakespeare) should no longer be read by the post-Beatles generation. On the contrary, it now becomes possible to read these writers more productively, attending to parts of their work or their meaning that were rendered illegible and illegitimate by earlier reception regimes – as well as giving them bedfellows that would have made traditional critics feel distinctly uneasy. Even a shift away from a text-based pedagogy to an orientation towards semiosic processes does not dispense with categories of text or genre. Rather, it opens the issue of textualist strategies to scrutiny and debate.

In this chapter I have deliberately avoided coming to summatory conclusions about the Anglo-American tradition(s) of practical criticism. Instead, I have tried to illustrate an analytic practice that is strategically concerned with heterogeneity and contradiction as well as norms and continuities. The ritual act of burning effigies of ancestors is a normal practice for upholders of new paradigms. It is no more illuminating than the earlier phase of uncritical worship, or the alternative stance of bland neglect.

The currently fashionable slogan of 'post-modernism' has been used by some to justify an indifference to history that is as old as pre-history itself. My concern has not been to remain fixated with figures or struggles from the past, nor to encapsulate them in tidy formulae to eliminate or control their potency. Rather, I have wished to establish a broader discursive space for the object 'literary criticism'. If a new generation of students is tacitly excluded from the discourse out of which and in reaction to which contemporary criticism has grown, they will find much of it mysterious and unchallengeable, constrained and unproductive. For a social semiotics approach the discourses of 'criticism' (including not only high theory but other kinds of discourse, in classroom and coffee shop as well as in articles and books) are intrinsic to the object of study, in many respects the most important dimension. The new object is no longer the meaning(s) of literary texts as such, but the processes by which meaning is produced and renegotiated and circulated around literary and other texts which perform analogous functions in contemporary culture. This may seem a sharp break with the concepts of traditional criticism, and in many ways it is, though it is not so far from the rhetorical claims made by 'traditional' critics on behalf of their vision of 'English'.

SOURCES AND CONTEXTS

The debate about the scope of 'English' and its future in the curriculum is still heated and unresolved. An authoritative statement of the core premises of the new paradigm is Williams, *Marxism and Literature*, 1977; see also Eagleton, *Literary Theory: An Introduction*, 1983. The Methuen series '*New Accents*' edited by Hawkes has published a range of accessible texts that have helped to establish the teachability of the new paradigm, and engaged in a polemic with the old. Some books that have contributed to this function have been Belsey, *Critical Practice*, 1980, Widdowson, *Re-reading English*, 1982, and Batsleer and others, *Re-writing English: Cultural Politics of Gender and Class*, 1985. See also Green, *Broadening the Context: English and Cultural Studies*, 1987. For a more pessimistic view of strategies and possibilities for radical change, see King, 'Changing the Curriculum: The Place of Film in English Departments', 1983.

For an American perspective, see Scholes, *Textual Power*, 1985. Slevin in 'Connecting English Studies', 1986 sees the subject at college level as a loose federation, not a single coherent discipline. On English at the secondary level, see Griffiths, *Literary Theory and English Teaching*, 1987 and Corcoran and Evans, *Readers, Texts, Teachers*, 1987. Peacock and Scarratt in 'Changing Literature at A-level', 1987, argue that in Britain it is comprehensive schools that are the main site of change. For an Australian contribution to this pedagogic development, see Reid, *The Making of Literature*, 1984.

On uses of a Kuhnian framework for the social sciences and cultural studies, see Barnes, *T. S. Kuhn and Social Science*, 1982, and Hodge and Tripp, *Children and Television*, 1986. For an application to 'paradigm shifts' in the subject English see Green, 'Literature as Curriculum Frame', 1988. This article specifically addresses the core paradigm-role of literature within the discipline of English, and the consequences of its decentring and displacement. For representative arguments for that centrality see Rosenblatt, *Literature as Exploration*, 1970 and Dixon, *Growth through English*, 1967, and for a recent restatement Martin, 'The Place of Literature in the "Universe of Discourse" ', 1983.

For other frameworks for understanding the functions of English as a discipline, see Young, *Knowledge and Control*, 1971 and Bernstein's concepts of classification and frame in *Class, Codes and Control*, 1971. Althusser's theory of ideological state apparatuses in *Lenin and Philosophy*, 1971 has been productively applied to the analysis of classroom discourse by Silverman and Torode, *The Material Word*, 1980. Foucault's *Discipline and Punish*, 1979, provides a historical framework for understanding the emergence of a set of disciplinary practices, including education and the teaching of techniques of literacy.

The theory and antecedents of social semiotics are set out fully in Hodge and Kress, *Social Semiotics*, 1988. See also Kress and Hodge, *Language as Ideology*, 1979, and references throughout the present book. For the basic terms of structuralist semiotics, see Saussure, *Course in General Linguistics*, 1974 and Barthes, *Elements of Semiology*, 1968. On logonomic systems, see Peirce's concept of 'leading principles', 1949, and Foucault on 'discursive regularities' in *The Archaeology of Knowledge*, 1972. On 'transformations' and 'modality' as used in this book see chapters 5 and 6 respectively.

Leavis's programmatic views on the discipline of English are expressed at greatest length in *Education and The University*, 1948. A polemic on the role of literature and literary training in contemporary culture is developed more fully in *Nor Shall My Sword*, 1972, which also contains a more sympathetic view of Blake's poetry as social criticism. An influential statement on Leavis's influence, even within the British Left, was Anderson's 'Components of a National Culture', 1968. See also Pechey, '*Scrutiny*, English Marxism and the work of Raymond Williams', 1985, arguing that there are still accounts to be settled. But Bowen, in 'Practical Criticism, Critical Practice', 1986, contests the exclusive focus on Leavis and Cambridge, stressing the heterogeneity of the different sites and kinds of English at this formative period in the paradigm.

A major formulation of the scope of the discipline of literary criticism, especially for America, was Wellek and Warren, *Theory of Literature*, 1949. There have been many studies of the New Criticism which demonstrate its heterogeneity even at the height of its influence. There is a ready consensus on how potent it was and how quickly it died: it is equally a commonplace that it still lives on, modishly disguised as Deconstructionism. Lentricchia's *After the New Criticism*, 1980, traces many of these connections. Watkins, 'Conflict and Consensus in the History of Recent Criticism', 1981, looks at the condition of criticism in the USA after the self-evident demise of the New Criticism. Said questions the radical credentials of various protagonists of the 'old' and 'new' New Criticism in 'American "Left" Literary Criticism', 1983. Cain's *The Crisis in Criticism*, 1984, situates New Criticism pedagogically both in its radical and its institutionalized form. The journal *New Literary History* has been an influential force in constructing and disseminating the 'new historicism', a theoretically informed reconstitution of the historical dimension of literary studies.

For other strands or schools within the old paradigm see individual chapters below: genre, period and language studies (chapter 2); New Criticism and literary history (chapter 3); stylistics and comparative literature (chapter 4); Freudian criticism (chapter 5); drama and theatre criticism (chapter 6); narrative and the analysis of myth (chapter 7); and the study of Classics (chapter 7).

The discipline called History currently faces the same sense of crisis as English, for much the same reasons. Cannadine in 'British History: Past, Present – and Future?', 1987, argues that the profession is currently in a state of crisis, after a 'golden age' that lasted from the 1940s to the early 1970s. From the Left in America, Blake asks 'Where are the Young Left Historians?', 1984, and gives a sombre answer. Steedman in 'Battlegrounds: History in Primary Schools', 1984, criticizes the effects of 'progressive' methods of teaching history, in similar terms to radical critics of the dominant pedagogy of 'English and Growth' in English. But Hill in 'Agendas for Radical History', 1986, warns that in the crisis that already exists, it is the new history of all forms that will be threatened, and the 'stodgy' will remain. Beattie, from the Right, in *History in Peril: May Parents Preserve It*, 1987, seeks to ensure that Hill is right.

On interdisciplinarity and possible relations between History and English, see especially chapter 8, but it is also a recurrent theme throughout the book.

2

Genre and Domain

There is something very persuasive about the division between 'literary' and 'non-literary', and the same is true about basic divisions within literature, into the genres of poetry, drama, novel and short story. It seems so obvious that these are different kinds of thing, and the terms seem simply to acknowledge that difference in a way that is helpful and uncontentious and not worth talking about. But from the point of view of social semiotics, the construction of a system of genres is not at all simple or unproblematic. A system of genres is the product of an act of classification, and classification is always a strategy of control. What is classified and controlled is not just texts. The classifications of texts are also classifications of people – readers and writers – and of what they write or read about and what they should think and mean. Clearly the concept of genre is crucial in understanding how literature is implicated in basic systems of social control.

The word 'genre' has an interesting history and connections. It derives from the Latin *genus*, which itself is derived from a word meaning 'to give birth to'. So originally 'genre' referred to people, not texts: people classified according to class ('genus' often meant 'high class') and race. It then became a term in logic meaning a general class which was then subdivided into 'species'. Somewhat later, 'gender' branched off, referring first to different 'kinds' of entity in general, then to the world classified by language according to sex: male, female and neuter. The history shows how a seemingly neutral, logical category had its origins in social categories of class, race and gender.

The term 'genre' is currently used about art and popular culture as well as literature, where its usage reveals something of the dynamics that underlie the term. Genre paintings are paintings which have a strictly defined subject and style. A major part of their social meaning is precisely this obedience to a set of prescriptions. Where art (or literature or anything else) is subdivided into a large number of distinct genres or categories, that is a transparent signifier of meticulous control. The role of 'genre' in popular culture points to another aspect of the system. Through genre categories like 'Western', 'SF', 'Romance' etc. those in control of modes of production (publishers, media companies etc.) can promise to deliver a familiar set of meanings to groups of readers and thus deliver those readers to authors and publishers. Because of the power of this promise they can then exert control over the production of those authors.

'Genre' thus refers to systems of classifications of types of texts. Genre classifications are part of a broader social system of classifications, not all of which use the term 'genre', but which have the same essential characteristics and functions. Genres (or types of text) are classified in terms of both the semiosic dimension (primarily conditions of production and reception, matching kinds of author and writing to kinds of reader and reading) and the mimetic dimension (primarily what topics, themes or meanings will be included and what will be excluded, and their modality, i.e. how they are understood to relate to the real world). Sometimes the mimetic dimension is emphasized in a definition, as for example with the Romance genre, but the kind of modality (e.g. fantasy), the implied class of reader (e.g. female, adolescent, working-class) and the relation of reader with writer (e.g. high complicity) are all also understood in the full formula for the genre. Sometimes the semiosic dimension is emphasized, as in the mega-genre of 'poetry', but then kinds of content and modality will also be recognized as 'unpoetic' as we saw with the Blake poem. Sometimes the group that produces and/or consumes a genre is its marker, as in black literature or children's literature.

But genres have a double face depending on their orientation, whether to controllers or to those who are controlled. As an instrument of control, a genre limits meanings. But for those who write or read texts within a genre, it enables a specific plenitude of meanings. So a generic label, such as 'Romance', may be sufficient to allow a superior critic to dismiss out of hand every work that conforms to the Romance formula, whereas for the 'fan' of Romance, each new text can be positioned and evaluated against other texts and authors in the genre, producing a wealth of implicit meanings that are invisible to the non-fan. Students of literature are usually aware that outsiders (e.g. historians, scientists, etc.) see only limiting meanings in literature ('oh that's just fictional', or 'that's a bit poetic') whereas they can see the complex pattern of interrelations and differences within the field of literature. They often don't recognize that the same is true for despised (non-literary) readers or consumers of despised (sub-literary, popular) genres. In both cases there is the same dialectic between an emptying-out of content in the interests of simplicity and control, and a counter-movement in the direction of diversity and richness.

Parallel to genre systems or social classifications of types of text, there is also always a social classification of types of context and types of content or topic appropriate to those contexts. Communication is always dependent on context, as we all recognize effortlessly in our own communication. We do not say the same things in the same way in private as in public; among friends in a pub or coffee shop as at the workplace etc. Different societies at different times operate with different logonomic systems that divide contexts up into categories of place associated with kinds of meaning and kinds of semiosic agent. We will call these *domains*. Like genres, domains are part of a system of control. Heavy sanctions are brought to bear on someone who 'speaks out of place', and socialization processes that train people not to offend in this way are so effective that it often becomes like second nature to speak or write appropriately. But again like genres, domains can also become the site of resistance, if oppositional groups lay too strong a claim to a particular domain to be fully controlled. So teachers and pupils both recognize that what can be said by pupils in the playground is fuller in many ways than in classrooms, though more constrained in other ways (e.g. not normally including displays of scholarship), while what can be said by teachers there is more constrained.

Just as physical space is subdivided and assigned to specific functions and 'owners', so aspects of the 'field of knowledge' are also subdivided and organized by noetic regimes under the control of particular groups and owners. So we can use the same term 'domain' for products of the territorialization of knowledge, especially since the domain of knowledge is typically associated with specific physical spaces which are sites of dominance of the owners of that knowledge (e.g. hospitals as site and guarantor of medical knowledge, churches as the site of religious knowledge, etc.).

There is a complex relationship between texts and contexts, genres and domains, because texts can originate in one domain and then pass into others. Literary studies are built on a complex play of genres and domains. Most literary genres were originally produced for consumption in the relatively private domains associated with leisure. When they are studied in educational contexts, they undergo a domain-shift, in terms of which one crucial type of meaning (pleasure) which is legitimate in these private domains becomes marginalized, along with the kinds of semiosic relations that predominate in those domains (solidarity, equality, spontaneity). But literature is studied in educational contexts precisely because it comes from these alien domains. Something of the energy associated with these domains is essential to the ideological function of English, even though the aims of educational domains seem so opposed to it. The result is a contradiction at the core of literary studies, pivoting around notions of public and private, pleasure and morality. This contradiction is not simple nor stable, nor is it in a state of balance. On the contrary, it is the result of a transformational process which is designed to be continually at risk, though not always to the same degree. Literature is meant to be enjoyable, but not too enjoyable, and the pedagogic practices of English are designed to both incorporate and transform the pleasures of the text. It is because of this that the fundamental issue raised by popular literature and popular culture in the literary curriculum is not new, but in one form or another has been at the core of the whole enterprise for centuries. In its own way the preceding paradigm, Classics, played the same dangerous game with pleasure and the popular, risking Homer and Virgil, Aristophanes and Ovid alongside Caesar and Cicero.

A popular theory of genre and domain

Theories of genre are well developed within literary studies, though this is not so true of the category of domain. But it's important to recognize that this knowledge is not the specialist preserve of a trained critic, but some-thing that is and must be far more widespread, a system that is deployed with great complexity and precision across the whole of a culture. To illustrate this fundamental point, we will look at plate 1, which shows a comic strip from 'The Perishers', written by Maurice Dodd. Maurice Dodd is writing here in a particular genre, the comic strip, so we can make some preliminary comments on this genre. It's a popular form, designed for a mass readership, readers of newspapers. This fact constrains features of its form (e.g. four frames, fitting a set column-width, self-contained story with continuity of characters across the series to build up a readership, etc.). The drawing style is simple and linear, appropriate to its popular audience and context. But the point of the joke is a complex reflection on genres and domains: in effect, the Dodd theory of genre, worthy to place alongside scholarly treatises on the subject, yet clearly assuming an immediate recognition among its readers of a particular system of genres.

Maisie is depicted in the first two frames reading out a nursery rhyme to Baby Grumpling, who is sitting at her feet threading Christmas decora-tions. At first he looks astonished. Then he gives a parody of literary cri-ticism, at first year university level or beyond, attacking it essentially on two points, its cohesion and its credibility. He gives it a genre label, 'doggerel', which combines a judgement with a description. (It could equally be labelled 'nursery rhyme' or 'folk rhyme', which would imply different judgements, and different expectations.) Maisie counterattacks, reverting as she usually does to physical violence, but Baby Grumpling moves off, and in the last frame the power relationships are inverted, literally in Maisie's case.

What Dodd is doing is 'making strange' both nursery rhymes and literary criticism. Baby Grumpling is right, of course. The nursery rhyme doesn't cohere, it doesn't make sense, and it is archaic and out of date.

Plate 1 Popular culture as metacriticism. *The Perishers* by Maurice Dodd © the *Daily Mirror* 1987, permission of Syndication International Ltd.

But nursery rhymes are like that, and they are normally protected by their generic status from such inappropriate judgements. This is an oral form, which makes sense in terms of a specific customary practice, and it records a different monetary system. But it becomes nonsense when it is transferred from this domain to a new domain, the private domain of the nursery or bedroom where a parent reads it as a 'nursery rhyme' to a child. Dodd then doubles the nonsense-factor by giving a response from another domain, university level literary studies.

But Dodd doesn't represent any of these domains directly. In his strip he has transformed the mother–child relationship into one between a girl with a formidable will to power and a baby with an equally extraordinary intellectual capacity. Who is he to talk of credibility? we may ask. But of course, readers of comic strips know the kind of reality to expect in this genre, with such certainty that they normally don't pause to question it. They also recognize that though this particular exchange is impossible and unreal, the different genres and domains do exist with their own autonomy and different kinds of truth. By bringing them together in a way that is labelled as unreal, Dodd can imply both that they normally do not make contact in everyday life, and that this separation is essential for them to seem normal and sensible and unproblematic.

This is a sophisticated point, worthy of Baby Grumpling at his most pretentious. And we note that it's made in a text designed for popular consumption. It's an accident (from Dodd's point of view) that it has wandered into this present book, which is situated firmly in an academic domain. But it's not an accident that Dodd can produce a sophisticated meaning of this kind in a humble comic strip. Schulz, Feiffer, Leunig and many others do so regularly in this genre. Sometimes the label 'popular' has the same function as Baby Grumpling's contemptuous 'doggerel', to pre-empt any serious attention to a whole class of texts. Genres in popular culture can undoubtedly produce complex and sophisticated ideas, showing that this kind of knowledge is a widespread social fact, not a monopoly of literary critics. But it's also true that only in an educational domain would a discussion like this present one occur.

Text, genre and domain

Genres and domains are fundamentally different kinds of object from texts. Texts have a material existence, but genres and domains do not exist in the same direct material form. They are a construct, a projection from specific rules and regularities, themselves produced and maintained by specific agents through specific practices that constrain or enable the production of meaning. As a consequence, genres and domains can seem peculiarly invisible and inaccessible to study. The kind of knowledge at issue is typically not in the text itself, but is implicit in the tendencies of many texts. In so far as genre and domain entail specific production and reception regimes which control interpretation of texts, it is these categories rather than individual texts which can seem decisive for the study of social meaning. This has a number of implications for methods of interpreting texts. With texts from other periods or cultures, however, our contemporary background knowledge for these other texts will correspondingly seem as difficult for outsiders as it is or was effortless and inevitable for insiders. The result is a paradox for English in its role as a kind of historical enterprise. Texts from the past become problematic and unreliable, requiring a knowledge of historical rules of genre and domain which seems difficult to acquire and impossible to demonstrate. Texts survive but are meaningless: assumptions of genre and domain are the key to meaning but do not survive. A genuinely historical inquiry thus is made to seem both essential and impossible.

The solution to this problem is to restate its terms, to reconnect them to a set of practices which are so functional and so widespread that they must be relatively easy to understand and grasp. The starting point for the study of genre and domain must be with texts from the knowable present, so the relations between the interpretation of texts on the one hand and structures of genre and domain on the other can be articulated in all their complexity.

There are a number of propositions that can guide a historical study of genre and domain:

1   Genre and domain encode rules that constrain the legitimate production and reception of meaning, what meanings are allowed or required to be produced in specific texts in specific conditions. They do not present the only meanings of texts. Meanings so constrained are neither inevitable nor always the most significant or highly valued at the period.

2   Genre and domain encode rules and knowledges that are important social facts, which must be communicated with massive redundancy if they are to have the force they do, through a large number of meta-texts (commentaries, etc., like Dodd).

3   Individual texts typically encode instructions as to how they should be read, and these instructions include prescriptions of genre and domain. These instructions are normally rudimentary, skewed and compressed, so that more than one text is needed to reconstruct an outline of the operative rules of genre and domain. But these rules do not pre-exist the act of interpretation as a single, taken-for-granted body of knowledge. On the contrary they are always provisional, never unproblematic, and never the only meaning of a text.

To illustrate these propositions I will begin with a text from contemporary popular culture, since the relevant background knowledges are still

accessible and available for study. The song 'Let It Be' was first recorded by
the Beatles in 1971, and released in an album of that name.

> *John Lennon*: (*in falsetto voice*): And now we do our Hark the herald angels
>   coom
> (*Instrumental, piano*)
> *Paul McCartney*: (*piano accompaniment*)
> When I find myself in times of trouble
> Mother Mary comes to me
> Speaking words of wisdom
> Let it be
> And in my hour of darkness
> She is standing right in front of me
> Speaking words of wisdom
> Let it be
> Let it be (*x 4, light drum, instrumental and vocal backing*)
> Whisper words of wisdom
> Let it be.

As an initial genre label, 'pop song' here seems obvious and
uncontentious. The Beatles in general and this song in particular were very
popular, and both the group and the song would figure in any history of
British pop song. The judgement, and the history, would be part of a
consensus social knowledge, certainly for a large group of contemporary
English-speaking people. But the same consensus would agree that no
history of English literature should mention them at all. We should note,
as Stephen Cox has kindly pointed out to me, that the Beatles (alone of all
contemporary popular music groups) did rate fifteen lines in Margaret
Drabble's Fifth Edition of the *Oxford Companion to English Literature* of
1985. 'Companion' status is not full membership, but this is one of the
signs of a fundamental shift in the genre rules that organize the field of
'English'. This exception, isolated and ambiguous as it may be at the
moment, shows the important fact that these rules are not immutable. In
its time, English vernacular literature itself was excluded from classrooms,
but has now replaced the Latin texts that once kept it out. But we need to
recognize that currently the weight of social authority still overwhelmingly
supports the consensus system of classifications. Mere popularity on its
own, on whatever scale, would be insufficient to trouble this system.
Demonstrations of 'profundity' or 'seriousness' can be dismissed with
surprising ease as beside the point. This is popular song: therefore it is not
literature. And with this goes exclusion from the subjects 'English' or
'English Literature'. We can see clearly how the category of genre works as
an instrument of social control, allied with a system of domains, which
keeps items from the domain of entertainment from the educational
domain.

John Lennon's opening words, not strictly part of the song but part of the experience of listening to it, point to fissures and complexities in the song with relation to its genre, as we can see if we attend to the play of genres and domains that cross his brief text. These words come from the genre of 'introduction', a genre from the domain of live performances. But this genre contrasts with song, as speech versus music, everyday discourse versus art. Lennon increases the tension between the two genres by speaking in a mocking falsetto. The paradigmatic opposition this invokes is between 'silly' and 'sensible', with 'silly' signified by a non-adult non-male pitch. That is, he is assigning the phrase to a female and/or childish viewpoint which is labelled by that fact as unacceptable.

The sentence itself then splits off into three distinct domains. 'And now we do our' is the language of the travelling entertainer, a representation of a popular folk tradition. 'Hark the herald angels' quotes a well known hymn, and in the process also quotes the genre (hymn) and the domain (religion). 'Coom' replaces 'sing' in the hymn title. It is said with an exaggerated working-class accent, which comes from a different domain again. It may also have a vulgar sexual meaning, implying a masturbatory fantasy. The juxtaposition of genres and domains, along with the impression of conflict between them, implies a complex social meaning behind the critical judgement: the song that is to follow is a childish (and/or effeminate) lapse into a vulgar form of simplistic or popular religious sentimentality. The sexism and elitism in this judgement, incidentally, clashes with the common ideological meaning of John Lennon and the Beatles as pop stars. It also clashes directly in an unmediated way with the values of the song that is to follow.

In its written form, the song has some of the markers of poetry – rhyme, metre and variable line-length. But it has other characteristics which point strongly away from poetry and the written mode, towards song and the oral dimension. The most obvious marker of song is the repetition. 'Let it be' is repeated seven times (and thirty-one times in the song as a whole). Other phrases are repeated with slight variation, and there is also structural repetition between the first four lines and the second four, and from verse to verse, in the full song. Such extensive repetition is an embarrassment in the written mode. 'Let it be' seems simple enough on first hearing, and by its thirty-first appearance, surely the listener must have got the point. Baby Grumpling would not approve.

But of course, this is an inappropriate response to repetition in song. The genre specifies not simply textual forms but also reception regimes (ways of reading) and semiosic conditions, as part of a single functional complex, though it still remains possible to read a genre in different ways, under different conditions and constraints. Repetition makes the task of singer and listener more manageable, easing the burdens of memory for the one and comprehension for the other. A key phrase like 'Let it be' becomes highly memorable. For many hearers, it may be all that they are sure they remember from the song. But the simplicity of the phrase is deceptive, with oral modes of reception. It is repeated, but in different frames and contexts, and its apparent simplicity allows it to accrete more meaning, not less. The phrase is either spoken by Mary, her 'words of wisdom', or it is said by the speaker in some kind of response to Mary's words: sometimes 'spoken', sometimes 'whispered'. 'Let it be' has either a positive meaning – 'Allow it to exist' – or a negative one 'Leave it alone'. It may trigger off allusions to two other very famous phrases: Shakespeare/Hamlet's 'To be or not to be' and God's 'Let there be light' from the Book of Genesis. Sometimes the musical tone is optimistic ('Yeah let it be'), sometimes melancholy or pessimistic. And 'it', as so often in English, gestures vaguely at a multiplicity of possible objects: e.g. life; some kind of trouble (e.g. the break-up of the Beatles, which was imminent when the song was being recorded); or some other hope for the future, or resignation towards the past. The phrase, precisely because it has such syntagmatic and paradigmatic simplicity, acquires an inexhaustible syntagmatic and paradigmatic density as a result of repetition in different frames which mobilize different paradigmatic categories. The reception-regime of popular song requires no constraints on ambiguity (as would the regimes of science, for instance) nor even the obligation to produce acceptable text about the meanings of the song (as in the regimes of English pedagogy).

Another important and related property of the genre of song, as legitimated by specific regimes, is a kind of multiple and unresolved ambiguity. The way the words of songs are overlaid by tune and the distortions of singing style allows a kind of indeterminacy of meaning in a song, and a toleration of contradiction and irrationality in its reception. One crucial indeterminacy in this song revolves around the identity of 'Mother Mary'. This could refer to the Virgin Mary, Mother of God, a very significant figure in McCartney's Catholic background. It was also the name of McCartney's dead mother. Lennon's sneer at the 'herald angels' who 'coom' does not resolve the ambiguity either, as to whether the mother is the Virgin herself (mother to Christ-Paul) or Paul's angelic mother, or both.

The ambiguity does not simply concern one word. It affects genre, and through this, domain and the organizing noetic regimes (the set of objects of knowledge and discourse). As a genre, pop songs exclude as subjects both religious sentiments and personal feelings towards named individuals, especially dead mothers. There are exceptions to both these exclusions: the point is not that these topics never occur or never achieve popularity but that they are marked, so that if an exception happens it is marked as exceptional, as a transgression – as Lennon labelled this song, though he himself transgressed in both these respects in his own songs.

Genres do not only define a homogeneous set of meanings. A genre also establishes the basis for significant differences, through paradigmatic sets of categories defined against the norms of the genre. Differences of song style and performance style, for instance, can carry importantly different social meanings. Singing is always different from speaking, but sometimes the difference is more marked. McCartney's voice in 'Let It Be' is mellifluous and unspeechlike, signifying a disengagement from the world of everyday speech, and a conformity to the requirements of song. He sings the song solo, a transparent signifier of isolation and individualism, as opposed to the harmonies of the early Beatles. It has a regular rhythm, but no regular or insistent drumbeat, so that it does not connect with physical action and dance. Repetition I have said is typical of song, but this song has more of it than many, and therefore signifies strongly the meanings of repetition; a non-linear view of the world, and a solidarity between singer and listener based on the recurrence of the familiar.

The overall meaning of this song – or more exactly, the 1971 Beatles version of this song – thus includes a complex made up of many particular components, which operate against an understood base-line established by the genre. This illustrates nicely the double function of both genre and domain: as systems of control which limit semiosis and the free production of meaning, while at the same time protecting and enhancing, within those limits, the semiosic power and productivity of those who respect them. Or more precisely, they allow oppositional impulses to produce a contained resistance, a delusory plenitude, or that is what they are meant to do, from the point of view of the logonomic system. In practice they may become, under some circumstances, for some people or groups of people, the site of genuine resistance and a powerful extension of meaning.

Genre and control

The use of popular song as an instance of genre may give a misleading impression about the function of genre in broader systems of classification and control. The classification of popular music as non-literature does have significant social effects, but it can be objected that pop singers still do quite nicely. We will now turn to a pair of texts where the system of classification at issue clearly has powerful sanctions and effects.

'I love,' said Susan, 'and I hate. I desire one thing only. My eyes are hard. Jinny's eyes break into a thousand lights. Rhoda's are like those pale flowers into which moths come in the evening. Yours grow full and brim and never break. But I am already set on my pursuit. I see insects in the grass. Though my mother still knits white socks for me and hems pinafores and I am a child, I love and hate'.

'But when we sit together, close,' said Bernard, 'we melt into each other with phrases. We are edged with mist. We make an unsubstantial territory'.
'I see the beetle,' said Susan. 'It is black, I see; it is green, I see; I am tied down with single words. But you wander off; you slip away; you rise up higher, with words and words in phrases.' (Virginia Woolf, *The Waves*, 1931)

Dear Dr Arieti, It Is Because I Am So
Passionate That They Brought Me Here.
Dr Webster Asked Me Why I Was Brought Here. And I
Couldn't Answer Without A Certain Hesitation, But Now
I Know, I Know Now:
I'm Too Passionate.
That's Why I Can't Get A Job.
You Had The Wrong Diagnosis.
Take This For Instance.
Look Up The Word Passion In The Encyclopedia
(A Masterpiece Of A Word) And In The Dictionaries.
Don't Get Cerebral Meningitis In Your Studies.
But You Will Find That There Is A Difference
Between The Passions Of Jesus Of Bethlehem And
The Passions of Bluebeard.
Between The Passion Of Misplaced Sympathies And The
Passions Of Suicidal Thoughts.
Are You Passionately In Sympathy With Your Great Poet
Dante, Dr Arieti?
And I Am In Passionate Admiration Of The Works Of
Molière, The French Troubadour.
And There Is The Passion Flower.
And The Passion Plays Of Oberammergau.
(Letter From Margaret, a schizophrenic patient quoted in
Arieti 1981)

Literary critics and psychiatrists of all factions like to think that their judgements are objective ones based purely on the evidence before them: that is, ultimately on kinds of text. However, it is important to insist that not all the differences are 'in the text'. Nor are they controlled by genre. Many of them are constructed by the reading regimes of the different domains. If a text is read as a symptom, in the medical domain, it is read in a specific way, with important consequences. Similar textual qualities can be read as literature, in either educational or leisure domains, with very different consequences and judgements. It then becomes illuminating to follow the 'Perishers' strategy, and read texts 'against the grain', in this case treating literary texts as symptoms and symptoms as literature, precisely to reveal the nature and power of the reception regimes that operate in the two domains.

Both texts we will look at were written by women, both of whom were certified insane at various points of their life. Virginia Woolf suicided ten years after she published *The Waves*. Margaret's fate is not known. Both these passages were published, but this is where difference begins. *The Waves* is regarded as a literary masterpiece, as its dust jacket claims: 'Virginia Woolf's greatest achievement' (Stephen Spender). Margaret's letter to her psychiatrist was published by him to illustrate the symptoms of schizophrenia. 'At the time Margaret wrote this letter, she was in a fairly advanced regression. She had been hospitalized for a few years and gave the impression of being apathetic or at least emotionally shallow' (Arieti, p. 75).

Before we begin, I will set out in schematic form some of the most salient aspects of the different reception regimes in the two genres (literary text and symptom) and the two domains (literature and psychiatry).

	Literature	Psychiatry
1 Role relations (reading regime)	Reader–writer bond (+ solidarity) Reader respects writer (– power)	Reader–writer opposition (– solidarity) Reader determines meanings (+ power)
2 Topics (noetic regime)	art / literature included subjectivity of subject everyday life excluded	art / literature excluded subjectivity as object everyday life excluded

We will begin our double reading with Virginia Woolf's text. The two speakers are children at this point, early in the book. Susan's language uses simple sentences, which may imply her childishness, but if we give a symptomatic reading, these are not the sentence forms of a child. They are more like the careful simplicities of Margaret's 'schizophrenic' writing. Susan's simple sentences don't connect. She claims to be talking about intense emotions, love and hate, but does so in a style that is highly controlled, which in a psychiatric domain might risk giving 'the impression of being apathetic or at least emotionally shallow'.

If we read it as symptom, we don't expect the text to make much more sense than this: we've got enough for a diagnosis and that's all we need. But if we read from within a literary regime, which expects major works of literature to make profound sense, we will stay with the text till that happens. The 'insects' Susan sees in the grass, for instance, can be equated with children, people. The beetle that is black and green is like Bernard, and other people she loves and hates. She compartmentalizes the emotions as she separates them out into fixed words. Her image becomes a reflection on language and feelings, or two kinds of language (hers and Bernard's) and two kinds of feeling.

Margaret also reflects on language, on the inability of single words to express complex or ambivalent feelings. Her example is 'passion(s)', which includes love and death, and a range of feelings. She instructs her psychiatrist to look the word up in an encyclopedia, implying that he doesn't know the meaning of the word that is at the centre of her self-diagnosis, probably picking up something Arieti had said. Just as Susan implies something of the hostility in her relationship with Bernard the insect, so Margaret implies antagonism towards Dr Arieti her psychiatrist, which he chooses not to notice in his own analysis. In many other ways she can be seen to be constructing a covert relationship with her psychiatrist. One way (which seems not to have worked) is through literary allusions: to Arieti's claimed (and undercut) love ('passionately in sympathy') for Dante, who was notable for his descent into hell (like her) and his pure adoration of Beatrice, and also to Margaret's own 'passionate admiration' for Molière. She describes Molière as a 'French troubadour', whereas the literary student will know that Molière, though French, was not a troubadour or love poet, but a satirist. Exactly what her allusion refers to isn't clear. Perhaps she has in mind Molière's *Don Juan*, or his *L'amour médecin*. Certainly it must contain a satiric hit at doctors and sexuality, coded in a literary allusion which excludes the psychiatrist.

Margaret also demonstrates her lack of sanity by disobeying genre rules: in this case writing a letter which does not conform to the rules of letter writing, or not to the rules for letters to psychiatrists. Arieti, however, is treating it as a different genre again, one that Margaret did not suppose she was writing in, the genre of symptom (though long-term psychiatric patients do learn the genre of symptom and can produce symptomatic texts at will). Margaret also departs from the conventions of written prose, by capitalizing every word – another symptom, from the point of view of a psychiatrist. But this formal device separates out every word, breaking up the flow of language in a way that expresses something very similar to Susan's condition: 'I am tied down with single words.' Emily Dickinson is a greatly admired American poet who used a similar convention. So did William Blake, in his engraved versions of his poems. Formal innovation can be a mark of literary genius, or of psychopathology, depending on the reception regime that is brought to bear.

We have so far stayed with Susan as though she was a real person, like Margaret. In fact, as a literary critic would want to point out, she is only *a character* created by Virginia Woolf in a novel. But from a symptomatic point of view we could ask: what kind of novel is this? Susan and Bernard are totally implausible as children discoursing. The relationship constructed by their juxtaposed speeches is equally implausible. The 'novel' as a whole is constructed in the same way: increasingly long speeches by one or other of its six main characters, juxtaposed alongside each other with no linking narrative, with virtually no interaction, no plot, no setting. As kinds of subjectivity, the characters are indistinguishable from each other and from Virginia Woolf. Symptomatically, we could say that

Virginia Woolf's writing here shows her own inability to distinguish herself from her novelistic creations, or to imagine any kind of social interaction outside her own obsessions. Another way of putting it would be to
say that just as Margaret's symptom is that she can't write a proper letter,
so Virginia Woolf can't write a proper novel.

But of course, from the point of view of literary criticism Virginia Woolf
is writing a legitimate genre: a modernist novel. The genre she is signally
failing to write is the realist novel. The notion of genre both overlaps with
domain but also subdivides it into different spaces which operate according to different rules. 'Modernism' as a genre label hasn't in fact always
existed. In the nineteenth century, *The Waves* would have been classified
as symptom not literature, and not been published. The emergence of
modernism in all mega-genres (poetry, novel, drama) as well as in art and
music had the effect of incorporating something of what would previously
have been regarded as non-literary into literature, though only under
certain conditions. Conversely, a faction within psychiatry ('Anti-
psychiatry') has emerged which refuses to accept that the label of 'mad'
should be attached to people or texts, and insists on seeing the sense in
psychiatric symptoms. Arieti in his discussion of Margaret is influenced by
this tradition, and although he sees her as not fully in control of her
meaning processes ('at best her knowledge reaches an unclear form of
consciousness', p. 76) he acknowledges that her text does have meaning:
'No matter how disconnected, the letter conveys a tone, an atmosphere,
what at times is called a *sphere of meaning.*' 'Tone' and 'atmosphere' are
terms from literary criticism, not from psychiatry, and 'sphere of meaning'
is both a crucial term for Arieti (he italicizes it) and also problematic
(hedged by the tentative modalities of 'what at times is called'). The terms
and devices act as the channel through which comes an alternative way of
reading the text and an alternative way of constructing relations between
writer (patient), reader (psychiatrist) and text (symptom/work of art).
Literature and education are not the only domains which have a great need
for the controlled incorporation of what they ostensibly exclude.

The aim of this discussion is not to certify Virginia or nominate
Margaret for a Nobel Prize. The point is to show how structures of genre
and domain are unclear and unstable in strictly textual terms, and rest
ultimately on issues of power and its maintenance or resistance. There are
no neat formal definitions that distinguish literary texts from symptoms.
Classification systems serve particular interests in a process of negotiation.
Crossing genres or domains is always an intervention at a certain point in
the system, which reveals something of the dynamics of the system itself.
So a 'literary' reading of a schizophrenic text challenges what will count as
a meaning or as a reading of that text. It also challenges the power relations
within that domain, in particular the asymmetrical power of psychiatrists
over patients. It gives some power as well as some meaning back to the

patient. It also offers the possibility of a coalition within the domain: power need not operate uncontested.

A 'symptomatic' reading of a literary text similarly challenges the power of literary critics in their own domain. For this reason, Freudians are viewed with great suspicion by most literary critics. But a contrast with psychiatric regimes brings out an important function of literary regimes and literary genres. If psychiatry disempowers writers, literature adds to their stature. It does so partly by refusing a connection between literary meanings and judgements, and everyday meanings and judgements, but this sacrifice of meanings is designed to protect and legitimate those meanings within their own sphere. It defends authors (some authors) against negative judgements, not only from psychiatry but also from the 'normal' community, or from the 'normal' community against its own abnormality. The boundaries around genres may control authors but they also defend them. That is why authors and readers have a vested interest in genres, even though they may also work to subvert them. A system of genres, including literature itself as a kind of genre, does not make sense purely as a fixed tidy system imposed by lawgivers from above. Genres are fluid, untidy products of processes of negotiation and struggle whose outcome is not always certain or predictable.

Genre, domain and history

The rules and meanings of genres and domains are important social facts for any society at any specific time. So it is useful to distinguish two problems of an historical inquiry that makes use of texts from the past. One line of questioning would ask: what was the meaning of this text for its original community? How was it intended to be read? This line of inquiry typically invokes a theory of genres and domains in what seems a scrupulously historical form of inquiry, but in practice confuses the set of competing meanings that intersected in specific texts with the set of rules that existed to limit and control that plenitude. In this section I will ask the more limited question: what traces of systems of genre and domain are legible in specific texts from the past, and how can these be read against patterns in a broader social history?

The text I will take is a medieval 'poem'/song. The first stanza is as follows:

[Song to Mary]

Of one that is so fair and bright
Velut maris stella [like the star of the sea]
Brighter than the day is light
Parens et puella [parent and girl]

I cry to thee, thou see to me
Lady pray thy son for me
Tam pia [so pious]
That I mote come to thee
Maria.

As a start towards reading traces of genre and domain in such a text, there are two useful strategies. One is to attend to highly salient features and systems of transparent signifiers, since the 'obviousness' of these aspects of the text is likely to have been functional at the time, serving to anchor the system for its users. The other is to establish simple paradigmatic sets linking aspects of language to major social classes. The social meanings that this method gives rise to will be crude and unnuanced, perhaps, but they lay a sound basis for more sophisticated analyses.

In this case, the text has been altered somewhat by its modern editor, Dame Helen Gardner, who has modernized the spelling. Even so it has one immediately striking feature: four of its nine lines are in Latin (my own translations are in brackets alongside, which will be discussed later). The obvious question to ask is: what was the meaning of the two languages for its hearers? The date is important: around 1250, about 100 years before the birth of Chaucer, who is widely regarded as the first major poet in English, the architect of English as a literary language. At this time, 200 years after the Norman Conquest, Latin was the language of the Church, French was still the language of the Court, and English was the low-prestige vernacular, the main medium of everyday speech but only just beginning to be written down and used as a medium for literature. The social meaning of the two languages, Latin and English, is clear, then. Each signified a radically different and opposed domain: religion and the world of public affairs and the low-status domain of private life. But the poet stitches these together within the same syntactic frame, a syntax which is determined by English not Latin. Latin and English are kept within separate lines, a transparent signifier of difference, but the syntax and sense flow on, signifying an overall unity. And the site of the unity is in English not Latin, signifying a vernacular English consciousness confidently including fragments of Latin/religion, not vice versa.

The modern feeling that Latin and English must be distinct kinds of language is not an inappropriate starting point for an inquiry into what the thirteenth-century meanings of the two languages were. Similarly the text in its Latin and English parts suggests broad differences of domain that guide and repay further inquiry. The phrase *Tam pia* ('so pious, virtuous') is a meaning from the centre of the domain of religion, then as now. *Parens et puella* conveys a meaning that seems to come from religious doctrine, Mary as Mother of God (Christ) but daughter of God (the Father), the same paradox as is contained in the formula 'virgin' mother.

But this phrase has a different twist; *puella* literally means 'girl'. It can mean 'daughter'. It can mean something like 'virgin' but it can also refer to a girl-friend, a lover or even a young wife. The paradox juxtaposes not simply ages (young/old) but also kinds of meaning, kinds of domain, leading to a religious paradox or an erotic conflation.

The English text is composed of the same two strands. 'Of one that is so fair and bright' establishes an erotic relationship with Mary, emphasizing her beauty not her sanctity. 'Lady, pray thy son for me', however, is more distant, more respectful, more devotional, like *Tam pia*, 'so pious'. But his prayer is that he come to her, not to Christ, and the stanza ends with the single word *Maria*, as object of desire and reverence, thus conflating religious and erotic feelings, and the domains of religion and personal life.

This account of the operative structures of genre and domain is clearly incomplete. It has drawn on a rudimentary history of the English language of the kind that a non-specialist could consult, but most such histories leave out the political and social dynamics of linguistic conflict and linguistic change. It has produced a complex specification of genre and domain which invites questions, sending the non-expert this time to standard literary histories to look for answers. From these we can learn that in the thirteenth century there was a 'genre' of mystical poetry that mixed religious and erotic feeling in much the same way as this song does, but that was normally in Latin and was marked as religious. There were a number of genres in the vernacular, including songs and carols, which often linked Christian and pre-Christian themes and motifs in a syncretic mix. But the form of this song, with its regular metre, its complex stanza scheme marked by rhymes and different line lengths, and its elegant movement within this complex form, all signify a third kind of genre, the courtly poetry of the troubadours, which was more commonly composed in a form of French rather than in English or Latin. The themes of the troubadours were erotic and secular, although drawing on religious motifs and images. This poem's subject comes from the religious domain, though its form comes from a secular domain, and its language is poised between a high status public form and a more intimate and private one. It builds up its meaning by a play of genres which repeats and amplifies the meaning of its dialectic of domains. That meaning, however, is fundamentally ambiguous, since at its core is a contradiction between disparity and reconciliation, smoothness and disjunction.

The category of genre is often used as an a historical category, to put texts from very different periods and societies alongside each other, as though the category of history is eliminated by the category of genre. But genre can also be used as an instrument of historical analysis. Out of the comparison of two texts as far apart in time as 'Let It Be' and 'Mary', read against a background knowledge of genre and domain, can come a pattern of similarities and differences that can be acknowledged and read in a thoroughly historical way, assimilated into a systematically historical account. Both 'Let It Be' and the 'Mary' song deal with the same broad set of anomalies, but Christianity and Catholicism, religion and the secular, Latin and English all have a different value in the twentieth century. So 'Let It Be' is open to the charge of being nostalgic and reactionary (as Lennon thought), whereas 'Mary', it could be claimed, acts to decentre the dominant religious tradition from within. In formal terms 'Let It Be' does look backward, although it is also a moment in the Beatles' musical history, which saw a major transformation of the genre itself. The 'Mary' song, written in the middle of the thirteenth century, was a very early work in the creation of English as a literary language, and even its seeming compromises (with Latin and court poetry) were strategic innovations. Some of the points of greatest resemblance turn out to be major points of difference between the two songs, given a fuller historical context. But one quality they initially had in common now divides them. Both originally were popular songs, marginalized by the dominant logonomic systems of their day. The 'Mary' song has lost its tune and its popular status, and now can be classified as a poem, as literature, worthy to be studied not listened to or sung. It would be interesting to see what will happen to 'Let It Be'.

The world turned upside down: ideological complexes and the functions of genre

In a striking and famous image for ideology, Marx and Engels claimed that it was like a 'camera obscura' that showed reality but in an inverted form. The image contains an important but partial truth about ideological forms. Ideology includes more than a single representation, whichever way up. It refracts different aspects of reality in different ways, ranging from negation and inversion through different degrees of displacement to a more or less direct reflection. It may combine these contradictory schemes into a single functional whole, an ideological complex. But this mimetic complex only operates and makes sense in terms of the semiosic plane. Here a decisive role is played by modality systems, which label and orient the various components to reality. Modality itself acts primarily as a form of negation or inversion. So modality systems can invert the inversions of an ideological schema, giving them a masked kind of truth, or they can subvert the seeming truth of an ideological representation and neutralize it. Modality systems act as a control on ideology. But modality operates partly through genre systems. Genres have built-in modality-values which are carried by the genre and therefore do not always have to be overtly marked. For this reason they are unusually potent, unconscious and invisible in their role in determining ideological effects.

To illustrate the complex and contradictory positionings of texts to reality as mediated through genre, we will look at a short poem by Richard Lovelace.

Song
To Lucasta, going to the wars

Tell me not, sweet, I am unkind,
    That from the nunnery
Of thy chaste breast and quiet mind,
    To war and arms I fly.

True, a new mistress now I chase,
    The first foe in the field;
And with a stronger faith embrace
    A sword, a horse, a shield.

Yet this inconstancy is such
    As you too shall adore;
I could not love thee, dear, so much,
    Lov'd I not Honour more.

First I will sketch in something of the background to indicate the 'reality' this poem is positioned against. It was published in 1649 as part of a volume of poems by Colonel Richard Lovelace, aged thirty-one, an officer in the defeated Royalist army of Charles I, who was executed that year. Paralleling this military defeat was a defeat in the propaganda war. In the 1630s Charles had constructed a persuasive image of the ideal Court and Courtier, through the art of van Dyke and through Court poets such as Carew, Davenant, Suckling and Waller. But the Puritan ideological counter-offensive had successfully represented the Court as a centre of licence and amorality, opposed by the moral righteousness of the Puritans.

Lovelace's poetry was published at the Royalist's lowest moment. But the Royalist's own ideological counter-offensive was itself gathering momentum. Charles the 'Royal King and Martyr' was being constructed as a potent focus for religious feeling, so persuasively that no less a champion than Milton was assigned the task of attacking the royal icon. Lovelace's book of poems, supported by prefatory poems by other Royalists, helped to construct a new image of the Cavalier as a figure who combined virtue with pathos and elegance.

The genre of the poem is announced in its title, 'Song'. As in the thirteenth century, 'song' is opposed to 'hymn', but both genres have shifted their positions and meaning. 'Song' signifies secular and courtly, as opposed to the bourgeois religious affiliations of 'hymns', though it still implies the popular, a possible alliance between the Court and folk traditions that the Puritans recognized and fiercely opposed. The genre built in a number of specifications of theme and modality. 'To Lucasta', in the title, is a compressed signifier of many of them. It is the name of a woman, thus constructing a semiosic indicator of male – female erotic address, an ideology of the sexes which represents passionate and sophisticated men seducing literate and sexy women. But 'Lucasta' is a made-up name, a coinage derived from Latin, probably a combination of *lux* – 'light' and *casta* – 'chaste'. Latin was not a language in everyday life in seventeenth-century England, and use of Latin thus had a modality-effect, distancing the woman, making her less real, as well as signifying her as a high-status object, suitable for a high-status lover. And in practice the Lucastas, Celias etc. of this genre of song had no individual reality guaranteed to them, even if sometimes the poet did have a particular woman in mind. And even if a song was about a real woman, it was not addressed to one in its originating semiosic act. These were written by males for male approval, with a female pseudo-hearer. So the male readers were constructed as voyeurs of the singer's erotic adventures and also as their feminine recipient. This double position gave these male readers a double source of pleasure, which had the further merit of being invisible to them, protected by its generic status.

Within this frame, a staple set of meanings acquired a characteristic modality-value. Ostensibly, these songs could seem to celebrate uninhibited libertines and fickle or despised women, but this stance was neutralized and confined by the genre modality, with its guarantee that this was just a posture of male to male, a fiction – even though erotic relations in Charles's Court often did involve infidelity and double standards, and contempt and fear towards women. It is not so much that this ideological image was untrue as that it was implicitly labelled as not trying to be true, and hence its truths and misrepresentations both became more permissible.

The genre included topics from three broad domains: love, war and religion. But the modality it assigned to the three topics was different. Although love in this genre is modalized as we have seen, it is still real love that is fictionalized. War, however, generated endless metaphors whose function in context was to negate the reality of war. The 'battle of the sexes', for instance, was conducted as a war which was an alternative to actual fighting. To keep war unreal in the metaphors of this genre, the signifiers of a contemporary war were banned (at this time, cannons and muskets, troop movements, problems of organization, provision and discipline etc.) in favour of archaic weapons (swords, shields) and an abstract version of combat. Religion similarly is invoked in a deliberately distanced, low-modality form, not the specific religious beliefs and practices which provoked war and inhibited love at that period, but an unreal religiosity which could absorb pagan gods alongside the Christian God. Thus the genre was able to offer a contradiction, between love, war and religion, and also resolve it, by modality operations that neutralized and inverted the reality of war and religion.

Lovelace's poem is immediately recognizable as an example of this genre. At first glance it might seem slight and banal, with its implausibly noble conclusion, 'Loved I not Honour more'. Yet this poem was not only very popular in its day, it has continued to be anthologized. And the reasons for its success have a lot to do with its skilful use of the themes and modality structures of the genre. Its subject, Lucasta, is the subject of twenty-six poems by Lovelace, though he addressed a few to other aliases (Althea, Aramantha, Gratiana and others). The name is a coinage, which suggests a little thought on Lovelace's part. Lovelace never married, and the identity of Lucasta is not known, though it is assumed that she did exist. One Lucy Sacheverell is mentioned as a main candidate, though nothing much is known of her that would add to the poem.

But more real, in this poem, are the 'war and arms' to which Lovelace says he flies, because it was well known that Lovelace did fly to war and arms. Between 1640 and 1649 he fought and worked on behalf of the king, and raised a regiment at his own expense (using up his whole inheritance to do so, it is said). So Lovelace uses the vague language of the genre ('war', 'arms', 'sword', 'shield' etc.) but the context relabels its modality, so that the war is more not less real than he is claiming. Similarly, chastity is a recurrent theme of this genre, as the resistance to be overcome. Lovelace connects it to a specific religious institution, the nunnery, absent from England for 100 years when he wrote, but still an important institution in continental Catholicism. And Catholicism was a real issue in the Civil War, as the religion of the hated Queen, Henrietta Maria, with a strong following in the Court, and among Puritan England's enemies in Scotland and Ireland and in France and Spain. Lovelace's poem affirms the Catholic institution yet also rejects it – in favour of war not sexuality, not vice versa. War is represented as an erotic experience of a curious kind. His mistress is not an abstraction (loyalty, England etc.) but 'the first foe in the field', which if taken at its face value implies an aggressive form of homosexuality.

The conclusion, for all its seeming platitudinousness, is very complex. It both opposes Love and Honour, yet claims to have resolved this opposition (because the more he chooses Honour the more he claims he is loving Lucasta). But 'Honour' itself conflates two different domains of discourse and two different value systems. Within the Puritan discourse of the family, 'Honour' was the possession of women, equivalent to chastity and to be guarded with their life. Within the discourse of the Court, Puritan 'Honour' was mocked but 'Honour' as the secular reward for duty was highly valued. Lovelace's 'Honour' is both the Court's Honour (duty to the king) and the Puritans' Honour (chastity, his and hers). This reconciliation of Puritan and courtier is both opposed to and guarantee of his

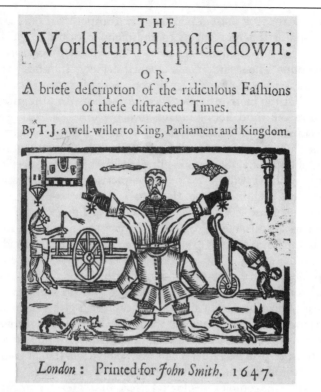

THE
World turn'd upſide down:

O R,
A briefe deſcription of the ridiculous Faſhions
of theſe diſtracted Times.

By T. J. a well-willer to King, Parliament and Kingdom.

London : Printed for *John Smith*. 1 6 4 7.

A seventeenth-century version of the motif of inverted worlds

The genre (woodcut) is marked by 'crude' technique, which carries low modality − 'reality' is not expected or required, the joins are allowed to show. But 'crudity' itself is a signifier of the popular, a transparent signifier of concern for meaning overriding attention to style (the opposite of the Cavalier obsession with style over function), constructing and defining a popular community and its values (simple sincerity, plainspoken honesty). The message seems conservative, invoking natural laws of physics and ethology (the law of gravity, the proper roles of fishes to swim, horses to be ridden, rabbits to be hunted) on behalf of a 'natural' social order. But at the centre of the picture is the centre of the problem − the mixed-up Cavalier as a concentration of absurdities. He has a Puritan's head on an inverted and fragmented Cavalier body, and he sees with his ears (trusts what he hears not what he sees). So the yardstick of a world the right way up is used to critique all orders in society, not just the lower orders. The blame is heaviest on the failure of the rulers to live up to their role. T. J. critiques actual Cavaliers in the name of an impeccable aristocratic ideal − as did many others who fought for 'King and Parliament' against the actual king. Against this tactic, the Royalists had great need of a respectable Cavalier.

Christopher Hill used the phrase 'The World turned upside down' as the title for his major book on radical traditions in the English Civil War − a radical historian quoting and inverting the conservative inversion of popular radicalism.

Plate 2 Ideological inversions. *The World Turn'd Upside Down* (The British Library).

love for Lucasta. It is both inconstancy (the courtier's vice) and loyalty to a cause. And at this moment of commitment to principle, he addresses Lucasta more directly than ever before. In seventeenth-century English, the pronouns 'Thou' and 'You' signalled degrees of intimacy very sensitively. Lucasta has the more formal 'you' in the first two lines of the last couplet, but the more intimate 'thee' in the last. And the smooth song rhythm of the third line is broken into by 'dear', a term of intimate address in everyday life which is so strong that it is a marked form in song. (Lovelace himself addresses no one else as 'dear', not even Lucasta, in all the rest of his poetry.) So this song breaks with the genre expectations that everyday intimacy will be excluded, at precisely the point where he is rejecting love itself in favour of 'Honour'.

At the mimetic level, then, this poem is a fine example of contradictions in an ideological complex, serving the conflicting ideological needs of the Royalist cause to an exceptional degree. But contradiction on its own is not enough. The ideological effectiveness of this poem rests on its control of modality, both the modality of 'song', which allows it to touch lightly on the contentious components of the complex, and also Lovelace's departures from song modality, which give greater weight to some components, while keeping the protective screen of the genre. It is no accident that of Lovelace's one hundred and eight published poems, which pursued different aspects of his Cavalier ideological programme in a variety of forms, his three most famous works were all songs.

In reading the complex ideological effects of this text, an understanding of contemporary structures of genre and domain has an important role to play. The generalized modality-value of song and the specific value of its components are crucial in controlling reception regimes, providing cover for the ideologue. But ultimately this knowledge shows the poem's cunning not its content, and to appreciate both we need to draw on political and social histories that situate the specific ideological problems that Lovelace was addressing. Traditional literary histories are actively misleading because of their characteristic use of genre attributes in their own reception regimes. Here as an instance is the authoritative commentary on Lovelace and 'Lucasta' by Professor Douglas Bush in the Oxford History of English Literature:

> For us, to think of the cavalier spirit is to think first of Richard Lovelace (1618–56/57) . . . His poems display the extreme unevenness of a gentleman amateur, and fame has rightly fixed upon the few lyrics in which he struck a simple, sincere, and perfect attitude; in these, with pure and exalted idealism, he enshrined the cavalier trinity, beauty, love and loyal honour. 'To Lucasta, Going to the wars', which states a chivalric theme far older than its century, is Jonsonian in its logical beauty and completeness: we may remember, by the way, that Lovelace was the last literal translator of the terse Catullus (to use Herrick's epithet). (Bush 1962: 122)

Here the political category (Royalist) has been transformed to the literary category 'Cavalier', used as a generic label (Cavalier lyric). Then it is linked to 'spirit' to purify it of specific political allegiances or programmes; or more precisely, to remove it from serious political scrutiny, so that its ideological force can work uncontested. The category of genre (including literature as a mega-genre) legitimates a reception regime that connects Lovelace to Jonson, to chivalric romance, and (more enigmatically) to the Roman poet Catullus, and not to contemporary Court ideologues like Laud, Clarendon or the author of *Eikon Basilike*. This is the typical use made of the category of genre in the discipline of English. It endorses specific ideological performances while removing them from history and from criticism. It attributes truth to the inverted modalities of literary genres, and transmits ideology as a higher truth (as a vulnerable but untarnished and timeless 'ideal'). It is not simply unhistorical, it is antihistorical. A social theory of genre and domain, then, has a double function: to attempt to recover active components of production and reception regimes from the past as from the present, and to deconstruct modern reading strategies in which tacit claims about genre and domain have a central role.

SOURCES AND CONTEXTS

The use of genre as an organizing principle of sets of texts goes very far back in the Western tradition: see Fowler, *Kinds of Literature: an Introduction to the Theory of Genres and Modes*, 1982, and Rosmarin, *The Power of Genre*, 1985. An influential use of genre theory has been Frye's ambitious taxonomy in *Anatomy of Criticism*, 1957. Propp's classic *Morphology of the Folk Tale*, 1968, demonstrated the explanatory power of structuralist method deployed on a corpus within a specific genre. Genre theory has also been usefully deployed in popular culture, especially film (see Neal, *Genre*, 1980). But Derrida's deconstruction game with genre in 'The Law of Genre', 1977, has been well received perhaps partly because it confirms the traditional assumptions about genre, that it is something that the cultured individual knows about but is above.

Within the teaching of reading and writing, the concept of genre has been given prominence in the work of language theorists in the Hallidayan tradition: see especially Kress, *Learning to Write*, 1982, and for discussion and critique, Reid, *The Place of Genre in Learning*, 1987.

On the linguistic strategies of the taxonomic mind see Kress and Hodge, *Language as Ideology*, 1979, and Marcuse, *One Dimensional Man*, 1964. On the history of classification schemas in European thought, see Foucault, *The Order of Things*, 1973. With specific reference to classification and control in education, see Bernstein 1971.

The term 'genre' is not greatly used or theorized in History, but in practice systems of genre are used to distinguish History from non-History (e.g. English, organized around literary texts, Archeology organized around material texts; cf. Goody and Watt 1968 on literacy as the precondition for History). Different kinds of History are also tacitly based on the recognition that different kinds of text require different modes of interpretation. See e.g. the debate between Fogel and Elton, *Which Road to the Past?*, 1983, on 'Cliometrics' and its strategies of reading quantitative texts, as against the reading strategies and kinds of text of traditional 'empirical' historians. Even within a single branch of History, historians recognize the different evidential value of different genres of documents: e.g. speeches, public records, diaries. There is a great need within History for an adequate theory of genres.

Halliday's concept of 'register' (1978) influentially incorporated a theory of genres as text-types within a functional theory that linked topics, contexts and rules of style, positing that knowledge of a set of 'registers' was an important component of normal sociolinguistic competence. Hymes 1968 developed the related notion of 'communicative competence', which includes rules of appropriacy of use in specific contexts as well as general rules of grammatical correctness. Earlier thinkers who contributed to a theory of domains are Schutz 1970–3, in his concept of 'provinces of meaning', and Malinowski's 1965 emphasis on the role of context in language form and function. The *Journal of Pragmatics* publishes a range of articles on this theme.

The relation between gender and genre has been extensively explored. For useful recent discussions, see Batsleer et al. 1985 and A. Kuhn, 'Women's Genres', 1984. Woolf's *A Room of Ones Own*, 1929, influentially drew feminists' attention to the issues of gender and domain. On the extension of a gendered structure of domains to organize relations in the work place, see Game and Pringle, *Gender at Work*, 1983.

On popular song, see Hodge, 'Song as Discourse', 1986, and Barthes on 'the Grain of the Voice' in *Image-Music-Text*, 1977. For a recent review of studies of popular culture within History, see Merrick, 'Rethinking Popular Culture', 1988. On medieval lyrics see Pearsall, *Old English and Middle English Poetry*, 1977. For a useful collection of texts for the seventeenth century, including a range of materials on the construction of 'Cavaliers' and 'Roundheads', see Lamont and Oldfield, *Politics, Religion and Literature in the 17th Century*, 1975.

The study of the English language until recently has not used tools of analysis that were politically, socially or even linguistically sophisticated. Authoritative works in this vein are Strang, *A History of English*, 1970, and Samuels, *Linguistic Evolution*, 1972. Leith's *A Social History of English*, 1983, is the best introduction that draws on contemporary work on the politics and sociology of language to inform its account of the history of the language, and its present worldwide diversity. See also Burke and Porter, *The Social History of Language*, 1987. For an introduction to work in France, see Achard, 'History and the Politics of Language in France', 1980. Briggs in his 1986 review of Leith and other books on the social history of language argues that this ought to be a significant component of social history. Williams, *Keywords*, 1986, gives a social history of the key terms in cultural studies that is a model for this particular enterprise, as well as being an invaluable tool for research in English and History. See also Hodge, 'Historical Semantics and the Meaning of ''Discourse'' ', 1984.

On changing constructions of madness see Foucault, *Madness and Civilization*,

1967. On the 'sense' of schizophrenics see Bateson, 1971, and Laing and Esterson, *Sanity, Madness and the Family*, 1973. On the label of insanity used as part of a system of control exercised on women see Matthews, *Good and Mad Women*, 1984. On the 'madness' of Woolf and other women writers see Rigney, *Madness and Sexual Politics in the Feminist Novel*, 1978.

3
Readers, Writers and Roles

I will start from what seems obvious. In order for literature to exist as a social practice there must be writers and readers and texts. But slightly less obviously, these three indispensable elements do not normally exist in the same time and place. Writers do not know most of their readers. 'Dead' writers live on in their works in much the same way as do the living. Texts themselves survive in memories, transformed by imagination or other processes of the mind, recreated or alluded to in other texts. Material readers, writers and texts are indispensable, but not enough to account for everything that makes up literary semiosis. Each of these positions is a site where versions of the semiosic plane intersect, and this play of semiosic meanings greatly complicates the status of the three primary categories.

If we look closely at the material processes of literary production we can see further possibilities for complexity. Writers normally write for some kind of readership, whose presumed interests as real readers affect that writing. At the same time a writer may try to coerce or model these readers into appropriate attitudes and orientations. Writing (and reading) occur within logonomic systems which constrain and determine meanings. Rules of genre and domain restrict the autonomy of writers and readers alike. And writers and readers both draw on other texts which they incorporate into their own construction of meaning. Writers are co-authors of their texts, part of a complex structure of agency which can take many different forms. Individual readers form part of a stratified and open-ended complex, as unpredictable new kinds of reader enter to add new possibilities of meaning.

In sorting through these complexities, in literature and other media, it is important to be clear about the distinction between material agents, objects and processes of semiosis and the meanings constructed by or about them, precisely because the distinction is so difficult in practice. The meanings of the semiosic plane (e.g. the author or audience) are a very important aspect of the social meanings of literature. They imply versions of social relations which serve a crucial ideological function, especially persuasive because they often remain outside that particular text, beyond scrutiny. These versions of society can therefore seem like social facts, but they are always meanings, built up out of syntagms like any other kind of message. These *semiosic syntagms*, messages about elements, processes and relationships in the semiosic plane, have both a mimetic content (their version of society) and a semiosic content (sources and effects within a specific semiosic situation). The semiosic plane is organized by this set of messages, but because of the different interests of participants and sources (authors) of these meanings there is not necessarily a single set of meanings about the semiosic plane. On the contrary, there is normally an inconsistent set of competing semiosic syntagms, different versions of such key elements as 'author' and 'reader'.

In this bewildering flux of semiosic syntagms there are two kinds which play an important role. One is the *semiosic effect*, semiosic syntagms which are inscribed into or interpreted from a text by authors or readers (e.g. authors addressing/constructing a 'dear reader' to whom they are of course a dear friend). The other is the *semiosic specification*. These are meanings assigned to various elements of the semiosic plane (e.g. the construction of an author in prefaces, publishers' blurbs, critical articles etc). Semiosic specifications are constructed by texts, but that fact is often forgotten, because so many texts so long ago may have contributed to the process. But though both these semiosic syntagms are meanings, not social reality itself, they are not dissociated from material determinations. Semiosic effects construct versions of semiosis but they are always measured against other versions by active participants who have their own interests and experience to draw on. Semiosic specifications attach themselves to material agents and objects which nonetheless still have an independent existence. The fact that semiosic specifications can be lies, forgeries or mistakes (e.g. claims to 'discover' a new Shakespearean sonnet) only illustrates the point, because such claims can be tested by appeals to other texts (e.g. those establishing dates of paper, provenance, and other surviving texts from the period).

Semiosic effects and the 'New Criticism'

Literary studies since Aristotle has incorporated some recognition of semiosic processes and meanings. At one time it attributed great strategic importance to the concept of author (Shakespeare, Dickens etc.) as the basis of the literary curriculum. This provided a point of anchorage between literature and life, literary studies and history. However, the simplistic and unexamined concept of author couldn't perform its task, and a kind of revolution occurred within literary studies that adopted the drastic step of eliminating the author. This step was associated with a movement that labelled itself 'New Criticism' in the 1950s, and for two decades dominated the undergraduate teaching of literature, especially in America. Although the label 'New' now looks somewhat shop-worn, this school opened up a line of semiotic analysis which is still influential and productive, continuing now under the equally forward-looking label of 'post-structuralism'.

Two concepts played a crucial role in the ideological formation of New Criticism: the 'international fallacy' and the 'affective fallacy'. These terms were put into circulation by the American critics W. Wimsatt and M. Beardsley. They opposed the intentional fallacy for the following reason:

> The design or intention of the author is neither available nor desirable as a standard for judging the success of a work of literary art. (Wimsatt 1970: 3)

The affective fallacy is similar in tendency:

> The Affective fallacy is a confusion between the poem and its results (what it *is* and what it *does*) . . . It begins by trying to derive the standard of criticism from the psychological effects of the poem, and ends in impressionism and relativism. (Wimsatt 1970: 16)

The term 'fallacy' comes from logic, where arguments can be ruled as right or wrong. This is clearly part of an authoritarian strategy. It dogmatically rules out any appeal outside the approved body of texts, and seems to declare the study of semiosic processes as illegitimate. But Wimsatt and Beardsley are not simply making a semiotic mistake, which we in turn can label the 'textualist fallacy'. They were successful ideologues, not failed semioticians. They were declaring the main premises for a reception regime that has proved potent and enforceable, and one which has its own contribution to the theory of social semiotics. On the one hand it has neatly severed the difficult links between literature and history. On the other hand it has drawn attention to the existence of semiosic effects, to the process whereby texts imply or construct semiosic syntagms, projecting a phantom society that can act as a surrogate for actual societies, ancient and contemporary. Following this line, critics have produced an elaborate set of terms to describe different kinds of semiosic effect; 'implied authors', 'points of view', 'narrator', 'ideal reader', or 'dominant/ privileged reading'.

But the precise study of these semiosic effects has not gone along with an equivalent attention to the material processes of semiosis, and has ignored the organization of this dimension as itself a set of meanings. Real readers were treated as pre-emptorily as real writers by New Criticism, though in this ideology some readers are less real than others. The target of the 'affective fallacy' is the reader who does too much work, and who has access to an uncontrolled set of texts: who can say 'I don't like that' of a 'masterpiece', and dare to claim that they like 'trash'. This way of reading is a radical challenge to a reception regime that is concerned to reproduce a single 'standard' of judgement that is to be controlled by literary teachers/ critics as arbiters of taste. It constitutes a threat not because it inevitably remains a private fact about individual psychology but because if taken seriously it might open up the social fact of a structured and stratified readership, with its own significant differences and disputes. An interest in semiosic effects should not be seen as opposed to a concern with semiosic specification and the material processes of semiosis. On the contrary, each of these is an indispensable aspect of the study of the social meanings of literature.

A final effect of the ideology of New Criticism concerns its relationship to what were and in many cases still are the dominant practices in teaching the skills of 'literacy' lower down in the curriculum. New Criticism annulled the material existence of students as reading and writing bodies and minds, struggling to express meanings, experiences and purposes of their own. It replaced their self-meanings and sense of agency with a set of legitimate semiosic effects that were entirely in the control of the teacher. The classroom practice organized around literature in this practice seemed to emphasize reading over writing, but what was actually involved was a specific reading regime constantly monitored by a writing regime, which operated to banish uncontrolled intentions and affects. Janet Emig described the typical effects of this kind of emphasis on this kind of reading: 'being asked to stay inside the constraints of another's text, or at least a single interpretation of that text, can perhaps be a training in docility that can well serve any religious, political or aesthetic majority' (Emig 1983: 174). Most writing in school, in English and in History and in other subjects, then becomes a means of demonstrating successful docility to the teacher as the sole material reader of all these school-based genres (cf. Applebee 1981). The plenitude of semiosic syntagms specified or allowed by these various genres is thus anchored, in the conditions of the classroom, to the overriding meanings constituted by the teacher's response ('good work', '65%').

Authors, narrators and the society of the novel

In some respects, literary criticism has been at the forefront of social semiotics in its sophisticated study of complex structures of implied authors, narrators and readers, and other kinds of historian and social theorist have something to learn from literary critics here. But traditional literary criticism stopped short of the analytic power it might have had, by its indifference to social forces and meanings whose source is outside literary texts and literary criticism. As an example of the potential of this critical tradition as a tool for a genuinely historical inquiry I will take a classic essay by Mark Schorer which was contemporary with Wimsatt and Beardsley's work: 'Technique as Discovery', published in 1949. In this article, Schorer distinguishes between 'content' or 'subject matter', and 'art' or as he prefers to call it 'technique'. 'Modern criticism', he insists, 'has shown us that to speak of content as such is not to speak of art at all, but of experience' (1972: 66).

One text he discusses in this framework is Emily Brontë's *Wuthering Heights*. The 'content' of this book he is entirely contemptuous of: 'We can assume, without at all becoming involved in the author's life but merely from the tone of somnambulistic excess which is generated by the writing itself, that this world of monstrous passion, of dark and gigantic emotional and nervous energy, is for the author, or was in the first place, a world of ideal value: and that the book sets out to persuade us of the moral magnificence of such unmoral passion' (1972: 69). 'Brontë' and her intentions are here mostly an effect of the text, but even this effect can be safely ignored. Schorer sees the value and the values of the novel in the technique, primarily in the construction of the means of narration and points of view. Lockwood is the main narrator, 'a foppish traveller who stumbles into this world of passionate violence'. There is also a person who tells the tale to Lockwood, Nelly Dean, 'the old family retainer who knows everything'. These perspectives represent 'conventional emotion and conventional morality', and since Lockwood and Nelly both live on after the two lovers, Heathcliff and Catherine, are dead, their values prevail, at least in Schorer's view: 'Thus in the end the triumph is all on the side of the cloddish world, which survives.' What doesn't survive is 'a girl's romantic daydreams', whose 'absurdity' is perceived by the 'novelist' in spite of herself, because of her 'technique'.

This analysis is interesting and fruitful precisely because it is so heavily ideological and so exclusively concerned with ideological meanings carried by semiosic syntagms. But to complete his ideological work Schorer needed a real Emily Brontë as a point of anchorage for his interpretation, an Emily split into two: her consciousness that of a sheltered, romantic girl (twenty-nine years old, in fact) and her unconscious, the 'novelist', a degendered technician who upholds conventional emotion and conventional morality. His own gendered position as reader (critic) of this doubled author and doubled narrator is outside his criticism but completes its meaning, strongly endorsing the 'technician' against the self-evident (to him) absurdity of feminine consciousness and 'experience'.

Many readers, especially women, may find Schorer's interpretation outrageous. It elevates the frame over the picture. It assigns immoral passion to the conscious, and conventional morality to the creative unconscious – a neat paradox, but not one that is likely to survive unchallenged. But in many ways Schorer's analysis is an elegant parody of a serious social semiotic analysis. He has sketched out an adequate minimal account of the key semiosic positions. The values he gives these positions are perverse and unexamined, with no consistent attempt to locate them in social structures of past or present, so that his reading is tendentious and unconvincing, as he no doubt (unconsciously) intended. Yet his method needs only to be allied to an adequate social theory to become something of a model for analysis, one which could produce very different readings from what he produced on this occasion.

The potential value of Schorer's approach, when disentangled from some of its limiting assumptions, can be brought out by comparing it with an analysis of Emily Brontë by Philippe Ariès, an important French social and cultural historian (Ariès 1981). Ariès broke new ground as a historian by the semiotic range of the documents he drew on: not simply letters, journals, etc., but also works of art, literature, sculpture and architecture. In his work on Western attitudes to death *The Hour of Our Death*, he located a major shift that he claimed occurred in the nineteenth century. One key document he used to exemplify it was *Wuthering Heights* ('this extraordinary book'), supplemented by Emily Brontë's poems. His discussion (twelve pages in length) shows a subtle understanding of genre, but not an equal concern for semiosic structures and syntagms. In Schorer's terms he goes directly for the 'content', the 'experience', and ignores 'technique', the semiosic syntagms that not only mediate this 'content' but are themselves fraught with important social meanings. This omission in practice strikes at the validity of his project, since he is not concerned exclusively with the history of attitudes to death or about death (mimetic structures) but also with continuities and change in the semiosis of death, the logonomic systems that constrain semiosic practices in the social construction of life and death.

One piece of 'evidence' Ariès uses is Heathcliff's behaviour over Catherine Linton's death:

> The day she was buried there came a fall of snow. In the evening I went to the churchyard . . . being alone, and conscious [that] two yards of loose earth was the sole barrier between us, I said to myself – 'I'll have her in my arms again! If she be cold; I'll think it is this north wind that chills me; and if she be motionless, it is sleep.' I got a spade from the tool-house, and began to delve with all my might – it scraped the coffin; I fell to work with my hands; the wood commenced crackling about the screws; I was on the point of obtaining my object, when it seemed that I heard a sigh from someone above, close at the edge of the grave.

Ariès recognizes the origins of this in Gothic and Sadeian literature. He nonetheless takes seriously the aberrant behaviour and aberrant beliefs of Heathcliff which are represented here, beliefs which Emily Brontë's poems suggest she shared in relation to the deaths of her own sisters. The dead one is the object of erotic obsession, and Heathcliff's desire for union is direct and physical. Grief is not softened by religious constructions of the afterlife, nor is it channelled by rituals designed to control mourning, and to separate the living and the dead. This is a marked departure from the dominant funerary practices of Brontë's time and class. Yet this kind of breakdown in those forms and practices was soon to become itself the dominant pattern in contemporary society, especially marked in Protestant capitalist nations like England and the USA. In this interpretation, Heathcliff is not a product of 'romantic daydreams' of a sheltered girl but an image of the future, situated at the leading edge of a profound cultural change.

This passage, however, is set in a complex nested structure of constructed speakers. At the core is Heathcliff's exclamation 'I'll have her in my arms again!' But this is reported by Heathcliff himself, framed as his fancy. Heathcliff's whole speech is reported by Nelly Dean to Mr Lockwood, who is the overall narrator. The book was originally published under the name of Ellis Bell, Emily Brontë's pseudonym. To illustrate how complex this structure of embedding is, we can set it out as follows:

((((((Heathcliff) – Heathcliff) – Nelly) – Lockwood) – Ellis) – Emily)

This progression becomes significant in terms of the social meaning of each stage, itself considered as a semiosic syntagm. One recurring pattern is an alternation of genders: Heathcliff (male) – Nelly (female) etc., culminating in Brontë's own gender play on the author him/herself. The first sequence, Heathcliff reporting Heathcliff, seems to break the gender pattern, but the innermost Heathcliff has a transformed gender, speaking in the lyrical, fanciful way that Emily herself wrote about her dead sisters. She/he speaks this to a masculine Heathcliff, who knows that this is mere fancy, but then translates its metaphors into direct action.

Schorer has disregarded Emily's attempt to construct a male persona for herself as author, preferring his own distinction between the 'novelist' and the 'girl', though he calls the novelist 'Emily Brontë', thus collapsing the two. In some ways, however, he is right, because the distinction between Ellis and Emily did prove fragile. So are the other distinctions. The narrators in the chain repudiate each other yet also fuse. Heathcliff's literary language is neither speechlike nor lower-class, but is supposedly reported in the speech of the lower-class Nelly Dean, and then (without benefit of tape recorders or transcription) recorded and repeated by the literate middle-class Lockwood, as constructed by Ellis/Emily. The distinctions are maintained only by an elaborate fiction. Without it, the distinct personas would collapse into a single ambiguous persona, oscillating between male and female, middle-class and working-class, oral and literary, though its primary form is female, middle-class and literary.

There are other kinds of 'author' implicated in this text. Ariès draws attention to one kind, the literary traditions Brontë drew on, Gothic and Sadeian fiction. This genre constructed the figure of Heathcliff and the graveyard setting: Heathcliff as a demonic figure indulging in morbid passions. And behind this genre, with its implied meta-author who is literary and masculine, is a set of oral folk traditions with a diffused communal author. The setting is the Yorkshire moors. This landscape is today often called 'Brontë country' and much visited by tourists, as though the Brontës (primarily Emily) were its creator. Yet the Brontës were only honorary co-authors of the Yorkshire moor, whose other author is 'nature' or 'god'. This conception of Emily as co-author of the moors is not a later reinterpretation of her work, either. Charlotte Brontë (as Currer Bell) constructed this meaning in her preface to the second edition: '*Wuthering Heights* was hewn in a wild workshop, with simple tools, out of homely materials. This statuary found a granite block on a solitary moor; gazing thereon, he saw how from the crag might be elicited a head, savage, swart, sinister' (Brontë 1946: xvii). In this, it is the moors themselves which seem to suggest the work, and half write the story, so that the writer ('he') and the head (Heathcliff?) are themselves natural forces, spirits of the landscape who work on and with it.

The action itself, however, which Ariès was most interested in, also has a kind of author. Just as 'God'/Brontë is the author of the moors, 'society' is the author of the funerary practices which Heathcliff is defying. Brontë mimetically constructs both the correct observances for the burial of Catherine, and Heathcliff's anti-ritual, whose meaning derives from its relation to the ritual itself. These funerary customs are Ariès's primary object of study. Traditional funerary practices aimed at the public control of grief and grievers. For individuals, the experience of grief and loss can be intensely painful, but for a social group it is also potentially dangerous, since grievers can break free of social control, ignoring rules of public constraint and order, flagrantly and embarrassingly failing to do the 'right thing'.

Ariès's history describes what I am calling a logonomic regime that was dominant for many centuries up till the nineteenth century. This regime made basic distinctions between life and death, living and dead, private and public, and love and grief, yet also established sites of mediation between them, organized through ritual, which managed both separation and identity within a privileged public time and space, in a set of domains that were controlled primarily by the established Anglo-Catholic Church in England at this period.

Protestantism, especially in its purer forms, is associated with a different regime. It rejected ritual and structures of mediation, and in its oppositional forms it challenged the established Church's control of the domains of death. Instead it posited absolute boundaries and distinctions and a strict separation of the domains of the living and the dead, to be policed by everyone. But where these distinctions failed to work, the result was not controlled mediation but uncontrolled fusion. The 'Puritan way of death' either exaggerated the distinction between life and death, living and dead (e.g. by banishing the business of dying entirely from the domain of the living, confining it as now to sanitized hospital spaces) or turned the dead into the living, through 'lifelike' images of the dead, or obsessive recreations of the dead by the living. Ariès has many fascinating examples from tomb monuments to illustrate the point.

Emily Brontë was in a unique position in relation to the Victorian management of death. In the words of her first publisher, her short life 'was passed almost entirely in the parsonage at Haworth, which looked out over the graveyard, with the Yorkshire moors stretching far around.' The Babbage report of 1850 confirms the impression that Haworth was something of an exemplary necropolis: a death rate of 25.4/1,000 per annum (against 17.6 in a neighbouring hamlet), with 41.6 per cent dying before the age of six. In the view of the commission, Haworth cemetery had done all it could in the interests of death: 'The parish churchyard is so full of graves that no more interments should be allowed.'

We can be more specific about the accredited author of death rituals in the Brontë country. In the vicarage at Haworth, Emily Brontë saw every day the work of an official agent of death rites (her father) through whom the Church spoke its meanings. But as a female she was marginalized in this work, with no public role. She felt at first hand the inadequacies of the Puritan way of death (her aunt/mother was a militant Methodist), surrounded by folk customs which among the Yorkshire people still survived as an alternative tradition. And she was surrounded by death: her two elder sisters, dying before her, her younger sister and her brother close to death when she herself died. There were various constraints on her life, as a female dependant of an impoverished middle-class clergyman. Her scope for loving was largely limited to herself and to forbidden others, her sisters and her brother – like Heathcliff, who passionately loved Cathy, the 'sister' who was not his sister. Such repression of loving was a kind of chronic mourning, just as intense mourning was a kind of loving – precisely the conflation of love and mourning, living and dead that pre-Puritan rituals aimed to defuse, and Puritanism forbade but could not control.

The erotic dilemma that she faced as a function of her gender position fed its forms and energies into a crucial point of instability in the traditional modes of dealing with death. Sexuality was a force which these

customs were specifically designed to control, through gender components of the logonomic system, prescribing specific roles, meanings and
relationships to men and women, living and dead, during the time of
mourning. Emily Brontë's sexuality was deprived of legitimate outlets by
gender rules that were typical for her class and time, and hence it was
available to generate oppositional structures and rituals.

Her example, chosen by Ariès himself, raises the role of gender in this
new set of meanings and practices. Ariès does not theorize gender in his
account, but seemingly coincidentally the two examples he discusses at
greatest length, one French the other English, are both semiosically the
products of women. Similarly, the most striking examples of tomb sculpture he illustrates are produced by or for women. An attention to 'authors'
and roles in semiosis inevitably raises questions about who is producing
the revolutionary new meanings he has isolated, and by what complex
stratagems these new speakers can produce their new meanings.

So we can see how Schorer's concern with semiosic syntagms involving
authors and narrators is complementary to Ariès's concern as a historian
with mimetic structures ('content'). Drawing on both we can recognize
that Heathcliff's attitudes and anti-rituals cannot be dismissed as a girl's
'romantic daydreams'. They are manifestations of a particular kind of
semiosic agent, mourning her/himself and the absence of love, narcissistic,
excessive, repressed; incapable of loving or grieving in socially approved
ways: a casualty not simply of the Puritan way of death but of Victorian
rules of gender. This figure produces a form of ritual that is the repudiation of ritual, collapsing the key distinctions in the dominant logonomic
system, fusing very old forms with emerging forms in a radically new mix.
The semiosic syntagms that Emily Brontë constructs as effects of her text
seem designed to enclose and neutralize the Heathcliff meanings. She
appears to have constructed a structure of narrators like a house of cards,
narrative within narrative, each chained to the other, mimetically constructing a reassuring society of communicators, each numbingly normal
in their inability to comprehend what the novel is about. But the semiosic
excess (two narrators, two novelists) signals the instability of this structure,
which exists to collapse into a significant pattern of ambiguities about
gender and class, love and death. Mimetic and semiosic meanings are
complementary in what they have in common and what is different. A
recognition of this complex pattern adds to the tasks of a reader, whether a
literary critic or a social historian, but the difficulties are not gratuitous or
extrinsic to the value of the text for either. Brontë's novel is no worse a
novel for being so illuminating a document in social history, and it is no
less revealing a document for being acknowledged to be a novel.

Drama, theatre, performance

Of the three main mega-genres of literature, drama has always been an anomaly. The problem is that it isn't really 'literature'. It is characterized by semiosic practices and semiosic syntagms which come from pre-literate modes. It can't therefore be 'read' within the reception regimes of literature: or more exactly, it constantly threatens these reception regimes as they strive to accommodate it. One strategy has been to distinguish 'drama' (consisting of texts which can be read like novels or poems) and 'theatre' (which is gone to, or enjoyed, by people who are that way inclined). The problem of drama/theatre is at its most acute with Shakespeare, who is agreed on all sides to be the 'greatest writer in English literature', but who was a popular playwright whose works were originally theatre, not 'drama'. The existence of the split is acknowledged and controlled by an obligatory section on 'Shakespeare's Theatre' in school texts and by the custom of teachers taking their English class to 'see Shakespeare' (as though he is peculiarly visible in performance). Yet although the performance aspect is institutionalized in various ways, it is still largely excluded from the official literary curriculum, because it is difficult to discuss or examine in distinctively 'literary' ways. The concept of the semiosic syntagm allows us to look at 'drama' and 'theatre' as different orientations to a common object, consisting of meanings that both link and oppose verbal text (script) and performance text (theatrical action).

As an illustration I will take one of the best-known scenes in English theatre: Lear's death scene in Shakespeare's *King Lear*. I will start with Shakespeare's text and Shakespeare's theatre. However, the original performance, even if we could reconstruct it exactly, does not limit or determine the possibilities of performance. Shakespeare was only the co-author of the original performance-text. He was a nodal point of a set of semiosic syntagms, but not their exclusive source. Other performances at other times have no option but to provide their own co-authors (actors, producers, designers etc.) to produce performance texts. These inevitably have their own semiosic meanings, which do not have to be faithful to Shakespeare's theatre, or to their own theatrical conventions. On the contrary, they generate semiosic meanings precisely by a pattern of differences within paradigms of theatrical possibilities. For illustrative purposes, therefore, I will also look at the 1982 Granada television version of the play, produced by Laurence Olivier, who also starred as King Lear.

Albany: All friends shall taste
The wages of their virtue, and all foes
The cup of their deserving. O, see, see!

Lear: And my poor fool is hanged: no, no, no life?
Why should a dog, a horse, a rat, have life,
And thou no breath at all? Thou'lt come no more,
Never, never, never, never, never.
Pray you, undo this button. Thank you, sir.
Do you see this? Look on her. Look, her lips –
Look there, look there. (*He dies.*)

Lear V. iii

The title page of the first quarto of 1608 gives a double context for this play: 'As it was played before the Kings majesty at Whitehall upon St Stephen's night in Christmas holidays. By his majesties servants playing usually at the Globe on the Bankside.' These two theatres were importantly different in terms of some important paradigmatic categories: Court versus city, private (covered) theatre versus public (open air), night performance versus day, winter versus summer.

In this last scene, both theatres would have had similar group of people on stage, giving, mimetically, the semiosic context of those speeches by Lear and Albany. It is almost the entire cast. The King's bad daughters, Goneril and Regan, are dead on the stage (seemingly gratuitously, since they died off-stage and are brought back). Cordelia, the good daughter, is dead, having been carried in by Lear. The surviving aristocracy (the Duke of Albany, the Earl of Kent, the Earl of Gloucester) are all present, as is the former King, Lear. There are also various soldiers, messenger(s) and gentlemen. One important category is living versus dead, with some of the dead ignored (Goneril and Regan) and others the focus of attention (Cordelia then Lear). Shakespeare has represented a stratified state, with aristocrats totally in control, and subordinates present in silent docility and obedience. He has not, however, specified how many attendants there are, how and where they stand, how they react to the scene before them. Shakespeare's text allows a number of possible semiosic statements here, ranging from dignified affirmation of hierarchy and power to a frozen repudiation of the emotional catastrophe.

The original contexts of performance represented a possible text, a possible set of meanings, over which Shakespeare had limited control, his co-authors being institutions of the state. 'His' stage directions (i.e. those included in the early published texts) are another matter. These must be regarded as a distinct text from the speeches, since these are communications to actors and producers, overheard by readers of the play but not by spectators. Shakespeare's directions are typically sparse, which itself is a signifier of his role in relation to other co-authors (actors, producers) as this role is encoded in publishing conventions of the period. In Olivier's *Lear*, adapted to television, we see a number of interventions creating further semiosic syntagms. In the Globe and Whitehall theatres, spectators were positioned by their social and economic status in stratified theatres. The television camera constructs a range of positions which all viewers share, semiosic effects under the control of the producer. In this last scene, in Olivier's production, the camera focused close up on each successive speaker, with no reaction shots. While Albany spoke his head occupied the full frame. He was thus constructed as an isolated individual, speaking his personal meanings directly to each viewer and to each member of the court indistinguishably, all of whom fuse together into a single individual outside any particular space and time.

With Lear's last speech the camera technique was similar. His face is seen close up most of the time. When he dies, his lips are close to Cordelia's; and the camera moves in very close indeed to both, in a three-way intimacy with the double death. Then the camera moves away, first circling around and above the dead pair, then moving back and up, positioning the viewer high above the scene. Here at last can be seen some meanings constructed by the setting for this production. Lear and Cordelia are on an altar, at the middle of Stonehenge, both dressed in white robes as sacrificial victims. Kent is at their head, Edgar standing beside them as though officiating as priest. The rest of the Court stand around in a perfect circle, with no differentiation of rank or status. Without a word they kneel as one. The winter sun appears, in the centre of the screen and exactly between two columns of Stonehenge. Lear and Cordelia are thus constructed as solar deities or sacrifices to a solar deity, and the sun's return is a symbol of hope and regeneration. These effects become part of the mimetic content of the performance text, overwhelming at this point any meaning produced by Shakespeare. Their semiosic effect is to construct the viewer as a privileged, godlike witness of this sacred event.

Albany's speech as I have recorded it is Shakespeare's text, or at least Shakespeare's text as transmitted by the quarto and folio versions. It has meanings conveyed by the words. It also implies some semiosic effects that can be attributed to Shakespeare, and others which are open possibilities which different actors or producers can choose and thus to some extent become authors of. This speech, coming where it does, clashes sharply with what precedes and follows it, a classic instance of 'dramatic irony', a semiosic effect authored by Shakespeare. The words announce the conventional end of a conventional play, in which good triumphs and evil is punished, but these platitudes come to pieces as the action unfolds. The kind of language – generalized, impersonal, symmetrical and conventional – semiosically constructs a kind of speaker, as a public figure combining the wisdoms of religion and state in a seamless exchange of clichés. An actor can use voice, expression and other resources to either reinforce or disrupt the semiosic effects of the words, but those effects remain at least part of the meaning of the play. Likewise the response of others in the scene – deferential acceptance of the platitudes, or anguished disbelief etc. – complete the semiosic effects of this speech.

But Albany's final words 'O, see, see!' come from a completely different semiosic position. This is urgent, direct, personal and involved. It breaks absolutely with the calm impersonality of what he has just said. His public manner has collapsed, leaving him a powerless and involved spectator, bonded much more closely to the constructed audience on stage and any other conceivable audience, seventeeth- or twentieth-century. All this depends though on what he has suddenly seen. Shakespeare's surviving text does not tell us. Lear and Cordelia have been on stage for some time. They could hardly have wandered from view, and now return. It seems that Shakespeare has left it to actors to create an appropriate 'business' to generate Albany's shock.

The Olivier production shows a consistent response to the meanings and difficulties of this speech. It removes the lines up to 'deserving' and transfers the words, 'O, see, see!' to Lear, who mutters them as the introduction to his final speech. The Olivier production thus becomes the author of an absence, an absence whose significance is the meaning of what has been suppressed and the relationship implied by the suppression. One result of this suppression (and others in this scene) is to give the scene more pace and unity. It keeps the focus on Lear/Olivier as star and focus and source of feeling. But it also classifies as irrelevant a semiosic effect that Shakespeare included in his version: the spectacle of Albany the aristocratic moralist being bumbling and emotionally inept even in this highly charged moment. Since the whole play explores the consequences of emotional impoverishment in high (patriarchal) places, this could be seen as a significant meaning to retain in the last scene, even if it gets in the way of a rush of sympathy for Lear. The contrast at this point opposes Shakespeare and Olivier (as semiosic effects) as social critic versus glamorizer of patriarchy. The semiosic syntagm at issue is the relationship between the two, seventeenth-century playwright and twentieth-century actor-producer. But the meaning of this syntagm, although it arises from the semiosic effects of two texts, also comes from the meanings attached to these two persons as putatively real individuals. Semiosic specifications of them are constructed from a number of texts (including the rest of *King Lear*). Their meanings are thus not social facts but a construction of social facts, open to alternative readings and reconstructions.

Lear's final speech, as part of a theatrical performance, can be interpreted in a number of ways (assuming it is not cut, as in this instance it was not). I will look at one particularly problematic line: 'Pray you, undo this button.' Which or whose button? we may ask. Why is he asking this, immediately after the emotional virtuosity of five 'nevers'? Semiosically the contrast between the intensity of grief and the intimate everyday request is as jarring as Albany's 'O, see'.

In performance, actors have to disambiguate mixed cues by inserting 'business', actions which make good sense of Lear's statement, or declare what kind of non-sense it is. If Lear is holding Cordelia in his arms, straining under the burden and about to collapse, then the request would make practical sense, for a sane but exhausted man. Olivier's Lear is kneeling beside Cordelia, with both hands free. He makes this as a polite request to his right, and two hands (probably Kent's) reach out and quickly undo one unnecessary button of Lear's tunic. The semiosic effect of the line in this portrayal is to construct a Lear incapable of carrying out the simplest of everyday acts without the assistance of servants: a lifetime of power leading to total dependence, or a reversion by Lear to a state of childlike helplessness. But another set of effects would arise if this was Cordelia's button, concealing the daughter's breast from the forbidden gaze of the father, who requires another hand to break the taboo, so that he at last can look ('look there, look there') and die. Olivier's Lear does kiss the lips of the dead Cordelia and dies with his head on her (fully clothed) breast: a hint of incestuous feeling, but well within the bounds of decorum.

Actors and producers are of course well aware of their potential role as co-authors of the perfomance text. But traditional literary critics happily offer interpretations of Lear's character or the meaning of the final scene, without recognizing that they are engaged in an analogous practice, reconstructing semiosic effects from clues in Shakespeare's script, as co-authors of their own distinctive text, the 'critical interpretation', where the meaning of their intervention in relation to the dramatist is as significant as that of an actor or producer and in the same way.

Shakespeare is positioned at the site of another fissure within traditional literary studies: between 'criticism' (oriented to the text) and 'history/ scholarship' (oriented to information about authors and readers, texts and contexts). For literary scholarship, 'author' is a crucial category, since it is possible and nicely arduous to assemble information about authors. But from the point of view of traditional literary criticism this kind of information seems irrelevant because it is unassimilable into its reception regime. The 'intentional fallacy' was aimed at precisely this prestigious edifice of information. But it is the indispensable basis for establishing the semiosic syntagms that constituted literary texts as social phenomena, though the 'information' itself must be sorted through very carefully before it is usable, analysed in terms of a political and social framework, which traditional literary scholarship prides itself on not having.

As an illustration, I will look at some of Shakespeare's 'sources' for Lear. Establishing Shakespeare's sources has been a productive industry for centuries. In the case of Lear, it is agreed that the basic plot came from folk tale sources which entered the written record with Geoffrey of Monmouth's twelfth-century 'history' of the kings of Britain, a version of Celtic myths (including the Arthurian cycle) that proved as popular and influential as it was (as now agreed) unhistorical. Over fifty versions of the story survive. Of these, three versions play a significant role: Holinshed's *Chronicles*, an influential moralized history of 1587 which Shakespeare also drew on for other plays; Spenser's *Faerie Queene* of 1590, which adapted Geoffrey of Monmouth's 'history' to the ideological purpose of legitimating Queen Elizabeth's rule; and a popular play, *The True Chronicle History of King Leir*, published in 1605. This information can be elaborated or challenged in detail, but the crucial issue here is: how can information of this kind be used in a study of social meanings of this piece of literature?

The social meaning of the relation between a 'source' and a 'text' is built up by elaborations and specifications of the semiosic syntagms that link them in a pattern of differences and identities. If a text is nearly identical to its sources, part of its semiosic meaning is this identity. In the last scene, however, Shakespeare departs from all known sources. Spenser provided the detail of Cordelia's death by hanging, but in his poem this occurred after she had defeated her sisters and reigned happily for many years. All sources give the story a happy ending. Shakespeare is the sole author of the double death. This ending is thus, among other things, a repudiation of all these sources. That means, in terms of the meanings I have assigned to these sources, a repudiation of history and myth, morality and political ideology. The double death must have seemed to its initial audience brutal and unexpected, deprived of the consolations of religion and morality provided by Tudor history and popular culture. What is left is a savage and pessimistic social critique, directed at the contradictions of patriarchy and its lethal consequences for the sexual life of men and women, a mimetic construct (in this play at this moment in it) which has as its semiosic effect the projection of Shakespeare as social critic challenging the consensus truth of his day. However we should note another Shakespearean innovation which has the opposite tendency. In other sources Albany (= Scotland) is an ambitious and defeated villain. Shakespeare's Albany is a virtuous and moderate ruler, something that James I, himself a Scot, would no doubt have liked.

It is possible to trace the chain of source texts even further back, thus raising new problems of interpretation. Robert Graves (1961), using Geoffrey of Monmouth as data, argued that the original folk tale is a transformation of the Celtic myth of the White Goddess, a fertility goddess who takes three forms. In this myth as he reconstructs it, Lear (or Llyr or Lludd or Nudd) is an aspect of the solar deity who is ritually sacrificed at the end of the old year. The form of the myth is analogous to the Greek myth of the judgement of Paris, who chooses between three goddesses (aspects of the triple goddess), awarding the prize to Aphrodite, goddess of Love, over the goddesses of wisdom and power. Lear is old not young, and though he means to choose love over wisdom and power he rejects the true goddess of love (Cordelia), but these transformations work on a common underlying pattern.

This myth is associated, according to Graves, with common harvest festivals still celebrated in Shakespeare's time. Geoffrey of Monmouth reports a tradition that Cordelia buried her father in a tomb once sacred to Janus, the double-headed god of the new year, and that people of Leicester (Leircestre) annually mourned his death in a solemn festival which Graves plausibly identifies with midsummer festivals or 'wakes', commonly held during that time of the year. The festival known as *Lammas* (1 August) is derived according to Graves from Anglo-Saxon *Lughomass*, mass in honour of Llugh (Llew, Lear). The Celtic year began in late June. Lear, then, is a form of the double-headed god, Janus, looking both ways, god of the old year who is to be sacrificed, and god of the new, his twin, who will succeed him. The god of the old year is associated with the oak and with thunder. The god of the new year, symbol of resurrection, is in festivals the fool.

Even if we accept that Graves's case is in broad outline an accurate enough account of the history of the ritual (festival) text, covering 1,000 years before it entered print, the crucial question to ask is: can we use this information as part of a study of social meanings? The first point to make is that this kind of history has a double face. On the one hand it is an attempt at a history of material semiosic acts, constituted by specific agents, texts etc. This history, however, is the object of reconstructed histories at different times, from specific vantage points (e.g. Shakespeare, or Elizabethan society). This version of history is itself a potent semiosic fact, determined both by the material history of that history (e.g. what documents or material records, including memories, survive) and by the social uses of that history.

Shakespeare's relationship to festival texts (wakes, etc.) provides a nice illustration of what is at issue here. Ancient festivals survived vigorously in Shakespeare's England. As such they were assigned social meanings which served to specify or classify their users, as 'authors' (direct or indirect) of this class of text. The crucial paradigmatic distinction was the opposition between Puritan and Anglo-Catholic. These festivals had been appropriated by the traditional Church in the Middle Ages, officially inscribed in the Book of Common Prayer of 1549, which purged many of the less successfully Christianized instances in response to radical Puritan critiques, but legitimized others. Even this compromise was inadequate for Puritans. The religious controversy had social dimensions. The folk traditions had popular support in rural regions, remote from the metropolis – in Wales and Cornwall, northern England, and parts of Scotland – while the Puritan opposition was most strongly identified with southern England and an emerging class of proto-capitalists. But the traditionalism of traditional festivals also appealed to the monarchy and the traditional ruling class, or those whose position gained legitimacy by appeals to ancient tradition. Festivals thus acquired a double meaning, as authentic popular traditions drawing allegiance from large portions of the rural masses, and as ideological legitimations of monarchy, aristocracy and a hierarchically ordered state.

But festivals did not survive out of attachment to history. They survived because they continued to do semiosic work, serving crucial social functions for small rural communities. Semiosically, they constituted a privileged space for the expression of oppositional meanings, 'midsummer madness,' a time of licence and inversion of hierarchy and constraint. Their mimetic content was a specific conflation of love (celebration, fecundity, abundance) and death (sacrifice, loss and mourning) in a single package with a double meaning and purpose. The image of death followed by love, growth and regeneration was an equally potent 'natural' consolation in times of loss and bereavement, or famine and exploitation. The festival, whether in midwinter or midsummer, spring or autumn, mobilizes the 'natural' meanings of the cycle of the seasons so superbly on behalf of these ideological needs that the state Church under the Tudors was reluctant to renounce it. Even in contemporary urban societies like Britain, politicians can still deploy the rhetoric of 'sacrifice' to unite the nation.

Elizabethan drama had roots in these festivals, just as Greek drama did 2,000 years before. Shakespeare identified himself with these ritual roots more strongly than most of his contemporaries. The title of his early comedy 'A Midsummer Night's Dream' specifically invokes the same kind of festival as Lear's story arose out of. An influential critical work on his comedies is entitled Shakespeare's Festive Comedies (Barber 1959). Another critic, Michael Long (1976), has argued that King Lear displays the same festive pattern as the comedies, as a tragedy of spring and regeneration. Olivier's version of the play invoked an ancient marker of this tradition (Stonehenge), with a winter sun rising to symbolize regeneration and hope. Shakespeare's Lear does incorporate motifs from the festival ritual text which are not in his sources: Lear's madness; the storm scene, where Lear's curse is an anti-king's inversion of a prayer for festivity; the triple-fool (Lear's fool, plus the Earl of Kent and Edgar, Earl of Gloucester, who both disguise themselves as madmen/fools). The first published version of the play specifically noted that its performance, before the king, took place during the Christmas holidays (the midwinter period of licence which still prevails today, even in Antipodean Australia), on St Stephen's Day, the day after Christmas: a day celebrating the death of the first Christian martyr, immediately after the day celebrating the birth of Christ. The crossover from a midsummer to a midwinter festival does not affect the ritual value, since each is built out of the same contradictions, as part of the same ideological system. It would have been no accident that this performance, which declared its affinity with traditional rituals, took place before the King at Whitehall, rather than in front of a city audience at the Globe.

Yet Shakespeare as constructed by this text and its conditions of production has a more complex and contradictory meaning than this account suggests. For he has broken the ritual pattern decisively by representing a double death (both Lear and Cordelia/the fool, old king and successor, past and future), and by incorporating a psychological and social critique of the patriarchal protagonist and his schizoid society. His ending provides no vindication for sexual repression, nor consolation for death. It offers a traditional ending, with virtue rewarded and evil punished, then immediately cancels it. It represents two deaths, and two kinds of incapacity to mourn: Lear's excess of grief, and everyone else's numbed incomprehension. And the play ends with the audience itself unprepared, only fifteen lines after a death whose cause is not explained. He has deliberately removed the essential quality of the festival-text as a provider of consolation, as a training in how to cope with death.

Later ages have re-authored the end of this play in various ways in order to restore this traditional set of meanings. In the eighteenth century, Nahum Tate simply rewrote the end of the play to give it a happy ending, and Dr Johnson strongly approved as literary arbiter of the age. In the twentieth century, Olivier's production emended the text less drastically but to the same effect, adding messages via stage props, music etc., to give the consolation that Shakespeare withheld. A school of Christianizing critics (e.g. Wilson Knight 1957; Danby 1965) has reinterpreted the play to restore the consolatory messages that Shakespeare removed, making it a 'Christian drama of redemption'. Each of these forms a semiosic syntagm which in different ways redefines both the play and Shakespeare, though doing so along lines of cleavage in the original play and its context.

We can understand something of the semiosic status of the original *King Lear*, and of the genre of tragedy of which it is an exemplar, if we situate it in terms of the kind of history of the semiosis of death that Ariès attempts to construct. In Ariès's account, ritual in precapitalist societies such as England played an important role in mediating the death of the other, through funerary rituals and customs. Christianity drew on a number of myths of consolation in order to prepare people beforehand to endorse the rituals. In seventeenth-century England, the death of loved ones – parent, spouse, child – was so endemic that control of grief was a major need and a major industry. Emerging Puritanism, however, had seriously deficient mechanisms for managing grief and providing consolation for death and loss, and its assault on traditional festive rituals, where it was successful, left a gap. But in the new urban environments that developed, representations of death in song, popular literature and theatre (all of which the Puritans disapproved of) grew out of the earlier festival and other texts, and continued and transformed those functions.

In this context, *King Lear* becomes a unique but significant phenomenon: a representation of both death and the inability to mourn, a semiosic event that both substitutes for and repudiates the customary strategies for dealing with grief. An Ariès could use a work like *King Lear* precisely for its significant aberrations, just as he used *Wuthering Heights*. With both texts in both periods, the literary work represents and exemplifies semiosic meanings which have important implications. Conversely, the history of the semiosis of death, like other such histories, has an intrinsic relation to a history of media, with literature an important though changing instance within the semiotic (media) systems of literate cultures.

Semiosis and popular culture

Contemporary popular culture is a rich source of materials for the study of semiosic syntagms, complementing and illuminating the study of both specifically 'literary' texts (novels, poems), and performance texts (theatre). Visual media (film, TV, comics) have developed specialized resources for producing semiosic effects (angles of vision, position of camera etc.). These are usefully concrete instances of the same kind of phenomenon in traditional verbal texts. Popular texts, treated as trivial or worse by traditional literary criticism, show a complex pattern of relationships between visual and verbal semiosic effects. Film and media critics often polemically insist on the uniqueness of these contemporary forms. It is true that technical resources and conditions of semiosis are different enough to reposition concepts from traditional literary criticism such as 'author', since the authorial function in mass media is clearly dispersed among a number of agencies. But part of the difference arises because issues of technical resources and semiosic conditions have been ideologically suppressed in the traditional literary concept of 'author'. A comparative approach across all main media systems opens up the study of the range of practices at issue even within literature itself.

Contemporary popular culture is a convenient site for this study for another reason. Since it is contemporary and appeals to a mass audience, materials exist to reconstruct a dimension which has largely disappeared from history, the response syntagms constructed by different kinds of readers, and the semiosic activities which completed the meanings and effects of texts and genres. With Shakespeare, much of this can only be guessed at. There is still considerable guesswork with contemporary texts, but at least with these we can do more to give the guesses a broader and firmer basis.

For illustrative purposes I will look at one moment in one popular film: the death of Mr Spock in *Star Trek II: the Wrath of Khan*. The film is especially suitable for my purposes for two reasons. It is part of a series (a series of films growing out of a TV series) with a particularly articulate and cohesive group of fans ('Trekkies' as they proudly label themselves). And the scene represents the death of a major character in the series, thus breaking with one of the strongest rules of the series-genre. This will allow us to track the theme of death into modern media and contemporary society.

The analysis will start from the micro level, a stretch of dialogue between Admiral Kirk, the other main character in *Star Trek*, and the dying Mr Spock, his second in-command. Spock sacrifices himself to save the others by entering the lethal anti-matter chamber to restore power to the ship. Although I will start from the micro level, the analysis will make the point that neither this nor any other level is autonomous. On the contrary, different levels allow the coexistence of different mimetic and semiosic meanings: different meanings for different kinds of reader, who construct different relations to different kinds of author with different effects.

At this level, the 'moment', there are two extreme reading positions: the hostile critic, who knows only what I have quoted about the film, and the Trekky, with an extensive knowledge of surrounding levels of text; the film, the series, and the body of ancillary texts that sustains the community of fans. These two positions are abstract specifications, but they serve to establish both the range of interpretations and the meaning of that range. It is admittedly difficult to do equal justice to the two extremes, because hostile critics commonly mark their position by an irresistible silence and refusal of meaning. This kind of production of non-meaning opposes any translation into meaning, whereas fans like Trekkies are endlessly loquacious. In this situation, it is legitimate to take for granted the transparency of the hostile critic's viewpoint (hereinafter HC) and to assume that all readers, Trekkies included, can effortlessly reproduce it.

I will begin with the visual text, attending particularly to a sequence of four frames. These shots mimetically construct the situation which is the semiosic context for the character's speeches. Kirk is on the safe side of a transparent shield, Spock near death, unable to communicate directly either through touch or speech. (The sound comes through an intercom system). For Trekkies, this is a symbol of the relationship the two men have always had, constructed in many instances of the *Star Trek* text: both constrained by their training, status and gender, with Spock the half-human, half-Vulcan especially inhibited. In frame 1 Spock speaks, with difficulty: 'Don't grieve, Admiral. It's logical. "The needs of the many outweigh . . ."' In frame 2 Spock nods as Kirk completes the quotation: ' ". . . the needs of the few . . ."'. In frame 3 Spock raises his head, and adds: ". . . or the one"'. In frame 4, exhausted, his face turns away, as he summons up strength to speak again.

The camera positioning through the exchange constructs specific semiosic effects that interact with these meanings. It is almost fixed throughout the exchange, behind Kirk and to his right, so that the two men are almost in profile, in a close mid shot. The camera does not cut from speaker to speaker or give reaction shots. Thus it constructs a position for the viewer poised between the two, viewing the relationship from outside it, not either man from within it. But the camera does take sides, remaining on the side of the living (Kirk, in sharp focus). It moves very slightly to the right, till the two men are in profile, as though the camera is along the line of the transparent barrier. After the exchange it cuts sharply to a position immediately behind Spock, seeing him clearly just as he becomes unable to see, slipping down into unconsciousness and death, while Kirk looms mistily on the other side of the screen.

The speech exchange draws meanings from the constructed context in ways that are sometimes too obvious to need saying. Its meaning comes not simply from the meaning of the words, but also from the meaning of the speakers in this context – Spock the heroic individual who has sacrificed himself for the greater good, Kirk his best friend. But the very fact that it is so obvious conceals just how open-ended this kind of meaning is, depending on the meanings assigned to Spock, Kirk and their relationship. To HC, Spock's first two sentences will seem conventionally heroic, but on closer inspection and especially for Trekkies they produce a complex set of semiosic effects. 'Don't grieve' is mimetically a repudiation of emotion but semiosically expresses it, said by a dying man in a voice suffused with pain to his best friend. 'Admiral', however, is a formal title, projecting a very different semiosic effect, analogous to a shift in camera position from close up to a mid-shot. For Trekkies the shift in point of view, which defines Spock here as elsewhere in *Star Trek*, signifies his typical repudiation of personal intimacy even at moments (like this) when he feels it most strongly. 'Jim' remains a rare and difficult word for Spock in *Star Trek*. The following sentence, 'It's logical', is similarly incongruent. It is impersonal and not in fact quite logical, since it compresses two different statements: 'It *was* logical (to sacrifice my life)': 'It is *not* logical (to grieve).' In his last moments it seems that Spock is not able to distinguish present from past, or positive from negative, nor recognize the irrelevance of logic to strong emotions like grief and loss.

For Trekkies, both 'Admiral' and 'logical' have a fuller significance, as defining meanings of Spock constructed by many other texts, with many other authors. They are both self-quotations, used so often in the series that they become a shorthand signifier of Spock's contradictory meanings: as human (capable of feelings) and alien (totally rational), stoic but acutely sensitive, and virtuous, with satanic pointed ears. In relation to this set of meanings, Spock's speech at this moment has a further significance: fidelity to his defining contradictions (at a moment that might have allowed him to transcend them), and also a slight displacement from it, under the extreme pressures of the occasion.

At this textual micro level, visual and verbal elements have semiosic effects which have different significant sources ('authors'), both fictive and real, in both the mimetic and semiosic planes. Some are equally available to Trekkies and HC, but they would be blocked by the reading regimes that define the HC position. But other meanings would be inaccessible to HC, since they rely on shared knowledge that effortlessly produces powerful and secret new interpretations that further bond the community of Trekkies.

I will now look at two 'authors'/focuses of meaning from other levels of text, sources of meaning that are available only to Trekkies. Gene Roddenberry was 'Executive Consultant' of this film, which, in the words of the credits, was 'based on STAR TREK created by Gene Roddenberry', and the character Spock was played by Leonard Nimoy. Both Roddenberry and Nimoy existed, and functioned in the overall process that produced the series. Trekkies have access to many texts that provide information about these material processes. They also construct specific meanings, about Roddenberry, Nimoy/Spock and the series, that are constrained to some degree by their knowledge of these texts, but not absolutely, just as the material history of festivals constrains but does not determine the meanings it has for a Shakespeare or Olivier.

For Trekkies, Roddenberry has an important role not as author of individual episodes but as the author/'creator' of the series and its universe.

> Gene created a totally new universe . . . He created an entire galaxy, and an entire rule book for operating within that galaxy, with very specific laws governing behaviour, manners, customs, as well as science and technology. Now that's a hell of a job. He didn't create a show. He created a universe, and it works, and it works well. This was a massive, titanic job of creation. (Gene L. Coon, former producer on *Star Trek*, quoted in Whitfield 1968: 74)

This is a statement by a producer, not a fan, one that is reproduced in the influential *The Making of Star Trek*, which has a high status among fans (it's co-authored by Roddenberry himself). It isolates and assigns a semiosic value to a kind of meaning that is a component of every story, every incident, a value which is intrinsically linked to the meaning it claims for its author, who here is seen as akin to God. The two claims go together. Roddenberry is like God because he has 'created a universe', and it can be classified as a universe because it has its god/creator. This is a very important meaning indeed, repeated and reinforced by each new story: just as Brontë semiosically acquires divine status as 'creator' of (a definitive version of) the Yorkshire moors.

The book *The Making of Star Trek* provides plenty of evidence that Roddenberry did indeed have an important role in the construction of the series. It also shows evidence of a very complex set of other determinants, many of which compete with the dominance of Roddenberry. This kind of contradiction is not a problem for Trekkies. On the contrary, a multiple play of 'authors' is one of the characteristic qualities of the *Star Trek* universe for its fans. The ambiguities at issue can be seen clearly in the pivotal role of Spock. *Star Trek* without Spock is unthinkable. He regularly attracts the bulk of the fan mail, although he is listed second and is second-in-command to William Shatner's Kirk. Who is the author of Spock? Roddenberry describes a dual authorship:

> Although I created the basic Spock, the final fleshing out of the character was a joint endeavour in which Leonard and I worked as co-creators. (p. 214)

But the authorship of Spock was more complex in practice, as described in the book. Roddenberry did invent a character named Spock at the outset, but only as a relatively minor character. The second-in-command at that point was a cool, efficient, highly logical woman, 'Number One'. But NBC, the TV network, rejected the pilot programme constructed with these characters. They were persuaded to reconsider their decision and allowed a second pilot to be made, but they made two stipulations: 'Number One' and Spock both had to go.

Roddenberry agreed to the first, but he not only refused to axe Spock, he promoted him to second-in-command, replacing 'Number One'. It was an interesting move. 'Number One' had ambiguous gender, overtly female but with masculine-gendered qualities of intelligence and rationality, underlying which was female sexuality. Spock in his new role became bi-gendered, too, overtly masculine, highly logical, yet also more sensitive, intuitive and caring than the macho Kirk, as loyal and ultimately passive as an ideal wife to 'his' Captain. The Kirk-Spock relationship thus became a disguised transform of the idealized gender relations within traditional marriage, except that the Spock/wife is physically and intellectually more powerful than the male partner. The original Kirk – 'Number One' relationship worked with similar gender ambiguities. At the time it seemed 'progressive' to Roddenberry, showing a woman as (almost) a commander in the world of the future, though 'Number One' was actually destined to be always Number Two, and always prey to her female sexuality. Spock carried the same ambiguities, but more disguised and able therefore to be more radical and subversive, since he/she is not only more capable than Kirk but also the real 'star' in a way 'Number One' could never have been, combining this with a repressed meaning of homosexuality that is also subversive to the traditional concept of marriage. This stratagem was forced on Roddenberry to evade an overt act of censorship (by NCB), but his solution incorporated that censorship into the final Spock, thus making NCB a co-author of Spock. This chain of events is not inscribed explicitly in Trekkies' construction of Spock, but its end result is, in the form of a conviction that his 'real' meaning has been displaced and disguised.

The stated target of NCB's unease about Spock was his ears: 'Remember, we have a big religious group in this country, and those pointed ears look too much like the devil' (p. 125). Roddenberry was the author of those ears (Nimoy didn't like them either), but NCB correctly read behind them to another 'author' of another category of text. Behind the popular iconography of the devil is the figure of a fertility god (Pan, Silenus, Satyrs). This is another version of the same figure as lay behind both Heathcliff and Lear/the fool. By giving Pan-ears to the representative of logic and virtue, Roddenberry was intervening directly in the semiosic chain leading from festival texts through Christianity. But his intervention does not recreate or reject the festival text, as Shakespeare did. Instead he reconstitutes a rationalist pre-text (implying that behind folk traditions of devils was only prejudice against a different race). The difference is important: reference to the same pre-text does not necessarily construct the same relationship to it, or the same semiosic meanings.

Given the importance of Spock, we can now see the significance of his represented death at the macro level, where communication occurs between a complex author (of the series) and a stratified mass audience. The death of Spock would be the end of the series. It would be the death of a universe for the community of Trekkies, an event whose impact HC will find hard to appreciate or regret. This 'death' would be interpreted by Trekkies in the light of a history which is part of the foundation myth of Trekkidom. In this history *Star Trek* has suffered a number of deaths. The first was NCB's rejection of the pilot programme, and the saviour was the Creator himself, Gene Roddenberry. The second was its cancellation after one season. This decision was reversed after more than a million signatures were collected to prove the popularity of the show. Even after the TV series ceased production, Trekky power proved formidable, mounting hugely successful conventions, sustaining hundreds of fanzines, constructing a large community whose reason for existence was *Star Trek*. This pressure finally led to the production of the series of films, of which *Star Trek II* was not in fact the last. After many anxious months, Trekkies heard with relief that a new film was in production whose plot, inevitably, was 'the search for Spock'.

The pattern in the semiosic plane – death and rebirth – has been frequently repeated in the mimetic plane in *Star Trek*. A recurring motif is an intimation of the death of Spock, who regularly seems to die or is thought to have died, always (till this film), recovering/being resurrected by the end, like the fool/new king in festival texts. *Star Trek II* repeated this pattern in both its mimetic and semiosic planes, foreshadowing death without resurrection in both planes and finally supplying resurrection in both planes with *Star Trek III*.

In box office terms this proved a great success, as it has with the ratings of many other TV series deaths, where a favourite character is written out (semiosically) and dies (mimetically). But the phenomenon is not of interest simply because of the money it generates. The box office/ratings figures indicate the presence of an important semiosic event. What series-deaths do is to give fans an experience of the death of the other, an experience that is more intense, of higher modality than the representation of death within a single text. *Star Trek II* was concerned in many ways to mediate death, representing a mourner (Kirk) achieving a successful resolution of his grief, funerary rituals (Spock is formally buried in space) and a final image of Spock's coffin landing like a seed in a green and paradisal planet. Like *Lear*, *Star Trek II* equivocates with the experience of death and with traditional forms of consolation. Like Elizabethan tragedy, media deaths are part of a general set of semiosic strategies for mediating death. As in Elizabethan and Victorian England, the modern death industry is large and diverse, though with its own distinctive tactics and authorities. It isn't the case that we can use a single text (*Lear*, *Star Trek*, *Wuthering Heights*) on its own as an index for a period or a culture. But we can judge the broad semiosic character and function of texts like these by putting them in the context of general semiosic processes, and in that framework they provide valuable insights into important social meanings and attitudes. In this context, the categories of 'author' and 'reader' become more complicated than in traditional forms of criticism, but they by no means entirely disappear. Concrete individual authors and readers remain as important kinds of semiosic agent, but we also need to understand the sets of often contradictory or conflicting meanings and relations that link them to each other and to their social and communication networks. The smallest unit, the semiosic exchange, is still inherently social, never the product of an autonomous individual, and at no level do we find the unity of a single homogeneous society speaking though a single representative individual. Faced with this irreducible multiplicity, analysts clearly need to know or know about an open-ended set of ancillary texts, which are as unlimited and uncontrollable as the New Critics feared. They also need to read with greater attentiveness to the bewildering array of semiosic syntagms than is usually deployed by either social historians or elitist critics of popular forms.

SOURCES AND CONTEXTS

There has been a large amount of work on the issue of reading and writing regimes, and the roles of readers and writers. New Criticism's attack on authorial intention has been complemented by a rather different attack on the concept of author, as a specific position valorized in a specific discursive formation, not a neutral description of any act of writing (see Foucault 1977: 'What Is an Author?'). This critique points out that not all writers are 'authors', that 'author' is an ideologically loaded way of classifying texts and kinds of writing.

Much work in semiotics in this area has been organized by the concept of the 'subject' as the grammatical subject of the verb in the mimetic plane and the semiosic plane (*énoncé* and *enunciation* respectively, to use the terms influentially proposed by the linguist Benveniste 1971). This theorization draws on the work of Lacan (1977) and Althusser (1971) to exploit the multiple ambiguities of the term 'subject' as both a linguistic and political category, to make important links between semiosic form and political action. For a useful introduction to this strand of theory see Silverman, *The Subject of Semiotics*, 1983. Now that these links have been made, the ambiguities of 'subject' lose their value, hence my own use of the less ambiguous linguistic term 'agent', which connects better with social theories of agency (see Giddens 1979).

Feminist theorists have broken new ground in their exploration of the construction of 'gendered subjects', drawing on the semiotic theory of the subject. See e.g. Irigaray, *Divine Women*, 1986. Film theory has seen a particularly substantial body of work along these lines. Prominent here has been the theory of 'the look' or 'the gaze', the use in film of a gendered semiosic positioning of the viewer, and filmic strategies for implicating the viewer in the semiosic plane, by the processes of 'suture' (literally, stitching in). See e.g. Mulvey 1975, Heath 1981, and for application to art history Berger, *Ways of Seeing*, 1973.

Film theory has also seen the development of *auteur* theory, a strategy for drawing on the prestigious category of 'author' to legitimate the study of this popular form, with its unmanageably large and complex structure of agencies: a strategy that is useful in so far as it has opened up the complex relations of agency in both literary and filmic practices, even though it runs the risk of simply endorsing the ideological meanings carried through the concept of 'author' in this differently organized genre. See Bordwell and Thompson, *Film Art: an Introduction*, 1979.

The shift in attention from authors to readers as semiosic agents has been a dominant feature of criticism of recent times (see e.g. the work of Fish, *Is There a Text in This Class?*, 1980, and the German phenomenological tradition, e.g. Iser, *The Act of Reading*, 1978, and Ruthrof, *The Reader's Construction of Narrative*, 1981). The Russian formalist Shlovsky's term 'making strange' 1965 was taken up in Brecht's concept of the 'alienation-effect', a strategy for disrupting the ideological effect of the reading regimes of traditional forms of theatre (Brecht 1964). Within theatre, the category of 'performance' has provoked a useful debate about the role of 'reading', as a complex act that can range between a faithful 'reading' of a text, and an originating act of meaning production whose agents may be actors or producers, within the determining framework of theatrical conventions.

The currently influential critical school of Deconstruction has militantly attacked the centring of meaning on the originating act of authors or writers. For a useful introduction see Norris, *Deconstruction: Theory and Practice*, 1982. This move, offered as a kind of radical intervention, shifts the balance of power to the reader as an active and unconstrained producer of meanings, and has usefully foregrounded the genres of writing in which 'readings' can be produced.

Research on material audiences and readers provides a necessary complement to the abstract readers of Deconstructionism, especially in regard to popular culture. Bennett (1983) uses the term 'reading formation' to theorize this set of practices. Radway in *Reading the Romance*, 1984, draws on what others would categorize as 'positivistic' methods of sociological inquiry to investigate gendered practices of readers of these gendered texts.

The key role of 'New Criticism' in providing the ideological underpinning of the dominant practice in the teaching of literature in America has been argued by Cain in *The Crisis in Criticism*, 1984. Belsey has argued that their critique of positivistic assumptions of 'expressive realism' was an important if incomplete break. In the teaching of writing, Britton (1975) has drawn attention to the artificial semiosic contexts of classroom writing as a crucial difficulty for the child writer, giving greater importance to genres which he sees as having more accessible and 'real' audiences. An influential tradition in America, the 'process' tradition, has taken over the category of 'author' in all its institutional specificity and mapped the activities of the child writer directly onto this production regime, as 'authoring' (see D. Graves 1983: and for a critique Gilbert 1988).

On funerary practices in the Elizabethan period, and the conspicuous consumption of the aristocracy, see Stone's *Crisis of the Aristocracy*, 1967. On the Puritan strategies for managing death, see Stannard, *The Puritan Way of Death*, 1977. For an important study of sixteenth-century carnival and its political potential, see the major study by Le Roy Ladurie, *Carnival in Romans*, 1979, examining a single occasion in a single French village in a work that is both exemplarily specific and suggestive. On the political meaning of festivals in England, particularly in the seventeenth century, see Underdown, *Revel, Riot and Rebellion*, 1985. Hill 1972 uses the phrase 'The World turned upside down' as the title of an important study of forms of popular radicalism which emerged into print during the Civil War period, though not specifically associated with traditional festivals. He also notes that the Brontës' Haworth was in the Grindletonian area, where a radical Puritan ideology was still strong in the nineteenth century (Hill 1972: 383). For a Marxist account of the Brontës see Eagleton 1975.

The concept of 'carnival' has become important in recent criticism owing to its use by Bakhtin (1968). Myth has been a perennially fascinating theme for literary criticism, used by T. S. Eliot as the resonant base for his *The Waste Land* of 1922, and a crucial category in Frye's *Anatomy of Criticism*, 1957. Powell, *The Celts*, 1980, describes what Celtic festivals were really like, as understood from archeology rather than from Graves.

4

Style as Meaning

The terms 'style' and 'form' play a crucial role in traditional literary criticism, yet in many ways they are puzzling and problematic. Literary students know that unless they can talk intelligently about 'style' and 'form' they aren't proper literary students, and 'style' and 'form' enter strongly into literary judgements (as they do into judgements about art). Yet although the categories are obviously important, they remain surprisingly obscure, not taught or discussed directly, shrouded in mystery. This mysteriousness is not a disadvantage to English as a discipline, however. If the ability to talk and discriminate about 'style' in an appropriate way remains elusive and difficult, it becomes a convenient marker of membership in the group of accredited literary critics. The mystification of 'style' serves an essential social function in the economy of criticism.

At the core of the mystery of the terms is a paradox. Instead of an opposition between form/style and content, literary criticism posits an equation: form *is* content. This proposition contains an important semiotic truth, but one that literary criticism is not able to explain, because of its logophilia, its valorizing of words over other semiotic systems. In terms of semiotics, what is called 'form' or 'style' is constituted by sets of signs most of which are not verbal. To illustrate, the phrase 'manners maketh man' has a very different content/meaning from 'man maketh manners', purely because of a difference of form. But that is because word order in English is a regular way of encoding meanings. Firstness signifies (among other things) the subject of a sentence, the agent of the verb ('manners' in the first case, 'man' in the second). This is 'content', i.e. it has a definite mimetic meaning. Other languages (such as Latin, Greek, Early English and Aboriginal Australian) add a marker of agency (usually a syllable added to the root of a noun) to indicate the subject of a verb, but the two methods (using word order, or using a suffix), precisely because they are so equivalent, show the unmysterious way in which 'form' can refer to signifiers of content. In practice, 'form' refers to a large set of semiotic systems, not a single one, all of which function in ordinary semiotic ways to produce their meanings.

Literary criticism adds another premise to its notions of 'style' and 'form' which is so ideological and restrictive that it has to be challenged directly. Within its domain, 'style' and 'form' have aesthetic values but no social meaning. Outside its domain, this premise is not easy to sustain. In more everyday usage, 'form' refers (among its other meanings) to things we fill in (in triplicate) at the behest of the bureaucracies that control our lives. 'Formal' as an adjective refers to behaviour that is strongly constrained by social rules. 'Style' in popular use has the same meaning as 'class'. The meaning of both is connected overtly to social class and class values. 'Style' is defined in dictionaries as a distinctive 'manner of doing' (speaking etc.). Manners, we remember, maketh man, as a set of social values that constrain social behaviour and construct social identity. The pressure of all these instances insists on a fundamental fact about style which becomes a basic premise for a social semiotic approach. The functions and meanings of 'form' and 'style' are inherently social in orientation and content.

'Grammar' is one aspect of 'form' that is usually distinguished sharply from 'style' within literary criticism. 'Style' is individual and variable but 'grammar' is seen as impersonal and fixed, establishing a standard of 'correct' and 'incorrect' which appeals to logic rather than aesthetics. But the yardstick of 'grammar' (or 'correct English') is typically used to rap the knuckles of aberrant individuals whose offence is more social (e.g. being 'vulgar') than logical. Errors of 'grammar' work as part of a system with 'accent', which is a style of speaking (especially pronunciation) associated with particular social groups. The notion of 'standard English', enshrined in rules of 'correct' grammar and 'standard' ('received') pronunciation, carries a valuation of non-standard forms as not simply different but also inferior. 'Grammar' then is functionally part of 'style', as is 'accent'. All of them have social meanings and fulfil the same broad set of social functions.

Within the vocabulary of traditional literary criticism there is one term, 'tone', which does imply a social meaning of style and has had to carry the complete weight of making that connection for the discipline, by analogy with the 'tone' of a speaking voice, which indicates the speaker's orientation to speech, topic and context. 'Tone' for literary critics refers to pervasive qualities in a literary text which foreground social meanings and semiosic processes.

What we have, then, is at least six terms (style, forms, manner(s), grammar, accent and tone) which are concerned with different but overlapping aspects of the same general semiotic phenomenon, each of them ambiguous in their scope and use, representing a common object in different ways to different users. To help us through this confusing situation I will use the single term *metasign* from social semiotics to describe a semiotic phenomenon that is a common component of all these terms. Metasigns typically pervade a text, signifying meanings in the semiosic plane (patterns of identity and allegiance). They are often in a different code from the dominant one in the text itself (most metasigns organizing verbal texts are non-verbal signs, such as word order, intonation patterns, gestures etc). Because of this and because their meanings are concerned with the semiosic rather than the mimetic plane they can seem 'meaningless', whereas in fact they carry considerable social meaning, often the most potent meanings of a text. They not only identify group allegiance, they also express it, signifying the ideology that constitutes the group. Although they are concerned with semiosic rather than mimetic meanings, they still work through and with the mimetic plane. since appeal to a common reality (mimetic content) serves semiosic functions. So as well as 'style' being 'content', 'content' itself can be 'style'.

By using this framework, we can not only see the common ground underlying these terms, we can also use them as part of a strategy to explore a crucial kind of social meaning in literary and other texts. In this chapter I will try to show the value of this usage by examining the social meanings of style in relation to individual writers, or the style of groups, classes and epochs within a language group and across differences of language, society and culture. 'Style' as used in literary criticism is cut off from its social orientation, and this serves to make the analysis of style seem irrelevant and incomprehensible to all other disciplines, and not even fully comprehensible to literary critics. But when its social meanings and connections are restored to it, it can become a powerful and accessible tool for all readers of texts, setting literary critics alongside historians and sociologists, anthropologists and critics of social and cultural forms, in an interdisciplinary form of analysis that can draw illuminatingly on 'literary' and other texts.

Conversely the social function of 'grammar' is acknowledged in the pivotal role it is assigned in the teaching of writing in traditional English classrooms, though the category of 'correctness' obscures the specific functions and interests that it serves. But in this traditional practice 'grammar' is assumed to be meaningless, expressing a pure logic which is also curiously language-specific, as though only the elite of one nation has attained this state of rationality. Paradoxically grammar, which looms so large in traditional pedagogies, is more difficult to teach when it is treated as meaningless. Grammar becomes much easier to teach and to justify when it is recognized as being meaningful in the same way as style is, carrying semiosic and mimetic meanings that are crucial enough and difficult enough to be incorporated into the core of every reading and writing programme that aims at literacy in its fullest sense.

Individual style and social meaning

At one extreme the 'style' of some writers is deliberately so unique that it defines the individual writer like a signature. But this individual identity is always constructed out of social meanings, as a social response in a broader social context. It projects an ideological meaning that is comprehensible to a social group, whose meanings and responses are in turn an intrinsic part of that meaning. The social meaning of style exists in the semiosic plane, linking qualities of texts to people and contexts, in specific kinds of semiosic syntagm. The meaning of the syntagms that make up style, then, is fixed by paradigmatic structures organizing aspects of the text (the markers of its 'style') and aspects of its context and situation. This double aspect determines how we must read the social meaning of style. It cannot be simply read off a text, in isolation from its semiosic contexts of use. Yet the reading of the stylistic markers within texts is an indispensable stage in the reading of a style when it is complemented by ways of assigning meaning to contexts.

I will illustrate this reading strategy by looking at the style of a particularly idiosyncratic modern poet, e.e. cummings. As a sample of his style, this is the start of a poem titled 'Impressions Number III'.

> i was considering how
> within night's loose
> sack a star's
> nibbling in-
>
> fin
> -i-
> tes-
> i
> -mal-
> ly devours
>
> darkness the
> hungry star

The first word is the point of anchorage of a dense set of social meanings. The lower case 'i' breaks two rules of grammar that are very well known from early in the English curriculum. Sentences should begin with a capital letter, and the first person singular pronoun should be capitalized. These two rules are both based on a transparent signifier, the meaning big = important. Most markers of style in practice are based on systems of transparent signifiers, organized by relatively simple paradigmatic structures, because in order to function as swiftly and simultaneously as they normally do, they need to be obvious. Yet their overall meaning is not simple or predictable beacause the syntagms of style are completed by the shifting, complex meanings assigned to users and use.

In this case, cummings refuses to refer to himself with the capital 'I'. In terms of the transparent signifier at the basis of this conventional rule, his usage repudiates the status conventionally assigned to the ego (unlike 'you', 'she' and 'it', with 'He' the only exception, when it refers to God in religious texts. cummings took this repudiation of the dominant construction of the individual ego so seriously that he changed the spelling of his name by deed poll to remove its capitals (a convention which I will follow in this chapter out of respect to his stand). But the meaning of anti-egoism signified by his new convention is overwhelmed by the meaning of its novelty, a meaning which comes from the full semiosic syntagm of its normal usage (in twentieth-century written English). Since this rule is taught early in the average individual's encounter with the written code, it projects a simple binary structure, in terms of which non-users of 'I' are either young or illiterate. cummings's usage challenges this simple structure by adding a further option: anti-literate. This difference is implied partly by the text (e.g. words like 'considering how' and 'devours', spelt impeccably, show that he is educated) and partly by knowledge from outside the text, including cummings's status as B.A. (Harvard) and avant-garde writer and artist. His challenge to the system of literacy acquires its meaning and status from its known position within the dominant logonomic system itself.

This has one important consequence for a reading of his style. As a transparent signifier his convention means the suppression of the importance of the individual ego, but in context as an idiosyncratic repudiation of the dominant system it signifies the opposite, becoming an affirmation of the individual over the oppressive system of rules. cummings's own recourse to the legal system to change his name is characteristic of American individualism, with its roots in the libertarian ethos of the Puritan colonists (he came from a well established New England family). His way of communicating this meaning, then, is idiosyncratic, yet in principle it is part of a widespread ideological position and practice within American culture. It repudiates egoism and individualism in a highly individual way, which has its own group precedents.

His practice of starting a sentence without a capital letter (and often not finishing with a full stop) is part of a general feature of his style that is also illustrated by the deformation of 'infinitesimally', spread out over seven lines and two stanzas. Again this is an idiosyncratic convention. Initially readers trained in the usual conventions of literacy and poetry will find this 'difficult', partly because they have to reconstruct the single word from its fragments in order to know its meaning (mimetic content). But the effect is built up out of transparent signifiers with a well recognized meaning, so that in many ways the 'style' itself has a clearer, more legible meaning than the text's verbal (mimetic) content, and this happens very commonly in writing which foregrounds style.

In the typographical conventions of English culture, poetry is distinguished from prose by its distinctive use of space to indicate boundaries of meaning. Prose use this transparent signifier too (e.g. space between individual words, after a full stop, and between paragraphs). Poetry has the additional signifier of variable space along the right-hand margin, creating the poetic line as a unit of meaning, whereas a line of print is not a unit of meaning. This unit of meaning can coincide with other boundary markers, as when the poetic line ends on a comma or full stop, or it can oppose it, as with 'run-on' lines. The length of the line can be fixed in advance, as in strictly metrical verse, or variable, as in 'free' verse. All these possibilities are transparent signifiers of attitudes to boundaries and to constraints, with 'free' verse signifying fluid boundaries and freedom from constraint and strict poetic form signifying the opposite.

The conventions of prose in print format present a rectangle of print surrounded by a blank margin. Print technology favoured a justified right-hand margin, and this condition of production became and continues to be part of the meaning of this feature of format. The uniformity of the block of print on page after page is a transparent signifier of mechanical uniformity imposed on the flow of sense. Hyphens developed as a transparent signifier of the connection within a single word that was cut in two by the necessities of print format. The density of words per page in a prose book signified a commitment to quantity over quality, to 'content' over 'form', with the converse, (i.e. fewer words per unit of space, more blank space shaped more intricately) a signifier of quality and form against quantity and content. The typographical conventions of prose and poetry are transparent signifiers of the social meanings of the two genres.

cummings's innovations deploy these meanings in a significant way. His first four lines use large amounts of blank space to break up the syntax of the line, in a way that is as arbitrary as prose though as deliberate as poetry. But where 'how' masks a syntactic boundary with the inserted phrase that follows ('within . . .'), in the next lines 'loose/sack' and 'star's/nibbling' break up a closer syntactic unit. This prepares for the radical assault on sense of 'infinitesimally', where the single word is fragmented and dispersed.

What this signifies is the use of poetic ways of making sense in order to destroy the integrity of the word as the primary unit of sense. The language is polarized between signifiers of poetry and prose. The shortness of the lines is at the furthest remove from prose, maximally poetic. But the hyphen is a signifier of continuity taken from prose conventions, without the technological necessities of prose and with a further idiosyncratic feature, a hyphen at the beginning of a new line (as in '-i-') as well as at the end.

cummings's attack on poetic and prose ways of making sense is, I've argued, initially more easy to decode as a meaning than the specific sense his words make. After we have restored them to a more familiar format, 'I was considering how, within night's loose sack, a star's nibbling infinitesimally devours darkness, the hungry star . . .' the sentence is not only comprehensible, it is easily classifiable as 'poetic' in style and content, in terms of genre norms that had been current for hundreds of years when cummings wrote. The markers of poetic style include the metaphors 'night's sack' and 'star's nibbling devours'. Metaphors do two kinds of thing. They make surprising connections (e.g. between a night sky containing stars and a sack) and they suppress the terms of the connection. The degree to which they surprise is relative, of course, but metaphors as a mark of style have one important quality in common with cummings's typographical tricks. Both features deform the basic mimetic sense of the text. Both erect a barrier against easy comprehension of 'prose' sense, and the two in combination increase the difficulty. Semiosically this has a common effect, to exclude readers who do not have the key to decode the text, and to constitute an elite group of readers who do. Poetry and all other forms whose production and reception signal difficulty construct an elite in this way. With modernist poetry such as cummings's, the elite is smaller and tighter, and the text's difficulty is a transparent signifier of exclusion to those who are excluded.

This quality of language is very common and occurs in many societies. The phenomenon has been labelled anti-language by the linguist Michael Halliday (1978), who studied forms and functions of the private languages of anti-groups on the margins of society – societies of criminals, prisoners, beggars, and other minority groups with their own subculture. Anti-languages coming from below express hostility to the dominant society by excluding it, and by mirroring and inverting its characteristic forms. They declare the identity and ideology of the group through its characteristic style, and their language use is concerned with style rather than content, with solidarity rather than clear communication. Anti-languages can come from above, too, as the language of an elite determined to exclude the majority, and poetry is often an anti-language of this kind. But cummings's style is created out of a double opposition, expressing a contradictory set of allegiances. He takes the typographical signifiers of poetry to an extreme which attacks poetry itself, by leaving his own 'poetic' images initially incomprehensible, and the signifiers themselves are emptied of their normal meaning by their own excess. These coexist with signifiers of prose (the hyphens and the irrational intrusion of breaks in meaning), but again they are used to attack the clarity of prose sense, not to maintain it. Similarly, his metaphors juxtapose 'poetic' and high-status words and vocabulary with prosaic low-status words and vocabulary (e.g. stars/sack: nibbling/devour).

cummings's position, then, is built up of a structure of negations and rejections. His critique of authoritarian structures and the canons of literacy allies him with the popular, the illiterate, but high literacy is still a condition of entry into his game, his world. His style constructs an enclave within the dominant culture which expresses opposition to that culture but does not connect with the meanings or aspirations of subordinate or oppositional groups outside it. The style expresses critique and contradiction from within the dominant, not opposition or revolution from outside. It masks and protects its hostility, it does not mobilize support. And though cummings's own style is unique, its forms mark him as belonging to a community that has proved a cohesive and effective force within twentieth-century European culture.

cummings's assault on grammar and its reclassification as a quality of style raises in an interesting way the problematic relation between literary studies as one major component of English, and the teaching of the skills of literacy as another. Mastery of grammar is unequivocally a central component of literacy, yet cummings's poetry seems to defy this whole system of rules, treating them as the raw materials of his subversive game. But that defiance is carefully bracketed by its place within the broader curriculum. It is labelled as 'literature' and reserved for the upper ends of the student population in terms of age and ability. It is regarded as not suitable for younger children, or low-ability groups, and the students who are admitted into the circle of those who are allowed to play such games must prove their credentials by writing critical essays on cummings in impeccable critical prose. In this way, the teaching of grammar, along with what this teaching implies about submission to the social rules and meanings that it encodes, becomes part of the hidden curriculum of 'progressive' English teachers, even in sites of apparent subversion. But such complicity is not inevitable. It only arises because the meanings of grammar and style are invisible in this practice, and that invisibility is something that I have argued can be addressed and overcome.

Style and the history of thought

If style and grammar carry major meanings for particular social groups, then histories of thought cannot do without strategies for reading these aspects of texts. To illustrate what is involved I will look at this kind of meaning in the poetry of Matthew Arnold. Arnold himself was an influential voice in nineteenth-century English life in a way that cummings wasn't in his own time and society. Arnold has been acclaimed as essayist, polemicist, poet and educator, and a major contributor to the establishment of the subject English. Conveniently for our purposes, Arnold himself was conscious of the nexus between poetic form and public meaning. 'My poems represent, on the whole, the main movement of mind of the last quarter of the century, and thus they will probably have their day as people become conscious to themselves of what that movement of mind is, and interested in the literary production which reflects it,' he wrote, without false modesty, to his mother in 1869.

As an instance of the style of this representative mind, I will look at 'Dover Beach', one of his most celebrated and central poems. It begins:

> The sea is calm tonight.
> The tide is full, the moon lies fair
> Upon the straits: – on the French coast the light
> Gleams and is gone; the cliffs of England stand,
> Glimmering and vast, out in the tranquil bay.
> Come to the window, sweet is the night-air!

Arnold's meditation goes on to touch on 'the eternal note of sadness', refers to classical Greece ('Sophocles long ago . . .') then comes to the spiritual crisis of his age, as he saw it:

> The Sea of Faith
> Was once, too, at the full, and round earth's shore
> Lay like the folds of a bright girdle furl'd.
> But now I only hear
> Its melancholy, long, withdrawing roar,
> Retreating, to the breath
> Of the night-wind, down the vast edges drear
> And naked shingles of the world.

He finishes with his positive: personal commitment ('Ah, love, let us be true / To one another!') in the midst of helpless resignation.

> And we are here as on a darkling plain
> Swept with confused alarms of struggle and flight,
> Where ignorant armies clash by night.

In contrast to cummings, Arnold's meaning (mimetic content) is clear, as clear as if this was prose. It seems a style without obvious style, the poetic form introducing very little distortion. But it does have a form whose meanings can be read. 'The sea is calm tonight' has a regular iambic pattern (unstressed – stressed – unstressed – stressed). Metre in poetry (like drumbeats in song and dance) is a transparent signifier of order. This line rhymes with the third line. The second line rhymes with the sixth, the fourth with the eighth. Rhyme is a constraint, so it is a signifier that constraint is accepted. But Arnold's pattern of rhymes seems without pattern and continues without pattern till the end. The same is true of line-length. The syllable count goes 6–8–10–10–10. Arnold has used both these transparent signifiers as the basis of a statement about their opposite; arbitrariness and the absence of a received external pattern. The meaning this projects reinforces the message of a 'crisis of faith': the grand organizing patterns of the past are no longer available, though fragments of them survive. Where cummings aggressively assaults traditional structures to express an anarchic defiance, Arnold's form signifies a passive enforced individualism which is as orderly as it can be in a world from which tradition has withdrawn.

Another 'poetic' quality of Arnold's poetry is the expressive use of sound. The regularity of the first line is a transparent signifier of the gentle rhythm of the sea, in effect adding to its mimetic content ('the sea is calm tonight – but still has waves'). The sound makes use of transparent signifiers in the sound system. It seems to flow because its stressed vowels are all long or diphthongs, and it avoids clusters of consonants. Long vowels, especially open vowels (as in 'calm'), signify unconstrained energy. Consonantal clusters signify constraint (as in 'and naked shingles'). Both instances seem to refer to mimetic not semiosic content, 'painting a picture with sound', or to use the technical term they are onomatopoeic. But they have a semiosic value as well. The 'expressiveness' they allow in the mimetic plane is achieved at the cost of semiosic expressiveness. The more the sound signifies the mimetic topic (sea waves) the less is it able to signify the individual tone of voice of a speaker interacting with others. The poet as an individual disappears as he becomes the sea.

If we turn to the syntax as a component of style we see the same meaning about the self. The word 'I' only appears once in the 37-line poem. Arnold spells it with a capital, but otherwise this poetic strategy attacks signifiers of ego as strongly as did cummings. We have perceptions without a perceiver, words (at great length) without a speaker, and even commands or exhortations ('come to the window', 'let us be true/To one another!') without an exhorter and an exhorted. The individual ego and his beloved are depersonalized and kept almost entirely out of the text, leaving empty positions ('I' and 'you') which can be filled by any melancholy literate Victorian male, and any Victorian woman willing to 'come' in these circumstances, in a relationship which is unspecific and without strong feelings. Where cummings places stringent and contradictory entry conditions into his text, Arnold does the opposite, removing human idiosyncrasies and individuality to allow the maximum scope for others to be incorporated into the structure of his pronouns and the semiosic situation. This is an appropriate style for a poet who wishes to 'reflect' the 'main movement of mind of [a] quarter of a century' as Arnold did, constructing a collective ego in which the relation of individual and society was unproblematic. cummings's style on the contrary constructs a desocialized ego whose relationship with other social individuals is difficult and contradictory.

Arnold's style is not only practically suited to his purpose, it expresses a

meaning that he also endorsed explicitly in words, in his role as a propa-
gandist. His most famous piece of polemical prose, *Culture and Anarchy*,
was published in 1869, two years after 'Dover Beach' (though the poem
may have been written at some earlier date). This work attacked the
middle-class Liberal movement in politics, especially its more radical non-
conformist wing. Arnold mocked what he called 'The Dissidence of Dis-
sent', and the 'Protestantism of the Protestant religion', with the slogan
he attributed to it of 'Doing as one likes'. This target is precisely the
individualism displayed by cummings fifty years later, as a product of the
same Puritan traditions Arnold associated with it. But Arnold's own 'free'
rhyme scheme and variable line length signifies a controlled form of it,
and the double meaning inherent in the notion of 'controlled freedom' or
rule-governed spontaneity is itself at the core of Arnold's ideological-
rhetorical programme.

Arnold's attack on individualism and Liberal ideology came from
within the broad Liberal movement. His father Dr Thomas Arnold,
famous as headmaster of Rugby, was a prominent Whig and social
reformer, who hoped to make the public school system safe for children of
the aspiring middle classes, allying them with the traditional ruling class.
Arnold's concern can be seen as a fear that the ideological forms appropriate to a challenger class were dangerous in those who were participating
in rule. He worried at the absence of a single unifying hegemonic structure
which would unite rulers and ruled as he believed the Anglican state
Church had once done. The 'crisis of faith' his work addressed focused on
the loss of hegemonic status of Christianity, especially in its official form, a
fear provoked in middle-class Victorian England by the religious census of
1851, which indicated massive working-class disenchantment with all religion, and the weak state of the Church of England compared to the other
denominations. Arnold's particular solution, 'culture', had more critics
than supporters, and despite its appeal for a new consensus it functioned
more as a critique than rallying point for his own class. So Arnold's
position was not so different after all from cummings's, though the difference in degree is still significant. And here again it is the pervasive style as
well as the particular views which explains the meaning and status Arnold
had in the Victorians' 'crisis of faith'.

If we turn to his grammar and syntactic forms, we can bring into
discourse an important set of meanings his work had. First, invisible
because so expected in writing of this period, is the remorselessly correct
grammar. The crisis of faith did not touch Arnold's belief in standard
English. He does not even use the option of an apostrophe 's' ('The sea's
calm' . . . .) as a signifier of informality, here or anywhere in his poetry.
Elsewhere he did use ' 'tis', and ' 'twould', but these are safely archaic
forms, as though only the past is allowed to relax.

The correctness of the grammar conceals the presence of style at this level, but even within this apparently homogeneous and obligatory system there are choices, and therefore paradigmatic meanings. There are two broad classes of clause type in English. One is concerned with actions or processes of various kinds, *actionals*. These are built around an agent (the source or cause of the action) and a verb (the action or process). These can either not specify what is the subject and object of the action (nontransitive, e.g. 'armies clash') or they can specify both (transitive, e.g. 'Sophocles heard it'). The other is concerned with relationships (*relationals*). These are built around a subject and what it is related to, in English pivoted around the verb *to be*, of which one common form is noun-adjective (e.g. 'the sea is calm'). Mimetically, these two basic forms are clearly different in content, since one refers to a world of actions, the other to a world of qualities. But an equally important distinction is semiosic. Actional clauses, as I will call them, reflect an external world of events presented to a receiver oriented to action and process. Relational clauses, as I call the other class, represent an act of judgement (description, classification, evaluation). They are oriented to reflection rather than action. So actional clauses are a transparent signifier of a group that is oriented to action and material work, and relational clauses signify orientation to intellectual or non-material work.

There are many distinct sub-classes of clause and combinations of features which allow clause types in a style to carry complex and contradictory messages. In the first six lines of 'Dover Beach' there are eight clauses, only three of them relational, which does not seem a strong bias. However, there are seven words functioning as adjectives ('calm', 'full', 'fair', 'glimmering', 'vast', 'tranquil', 'sweet'). As we inspect the clauses more closely, we can recognize the presence of a larger number of relationals in a disguised form. 'The moon lies fair' does not describe what the moon is doing (it isn't lying) but what it is like (fair). Similarly, 'stand' looks like a verb of action but the cliffs merely exist, 'glimmering and vast'. 'Is gone' could have been expressed as 'goes', to express an action (though strictly the light doesn't 'go', it just doesn't come). 'Gone' presents this action-that-isn't as a quality, not an action.

Arnold's style here we can say is strongly adjectival. Connecting this, as he did in his letter to his mother, to a 'movement of the mind', we can see one thing this mind seems to do consistently. It analyses the material world into a set of objects: it lists them in an order which seems random: and it attaches at least one descriptor to each, giving either a subjective value (e.g. 'fair') or an objective value (e.g. 'calm', 'full'). This mind turns actions and processes into seeming qualities (e.g. 'gone', 'glimmering'), and conversely turns relations into seeming actions (e.g. 'lies', 'stands'). Very rarely are material actions or processes represented and these mostly have as agent the sea or, in the conclusion, 'ignorant armies' who appear from nowhere in an explosion of confused activity.

This pattern is part of the mimetic content of the poem. It constructs a physical world that is a collection of objects neatly and reassuringly described, or a field of low-energy events. The social world of alliances it constructs are relationships without energy or action, ('Ah, love, let us be true/To one another' not 'Ah, let us love one another') or violent, dangerous activities. Since this meaning is represented through style and grammar, it allows us to say a number of things about it. First, it is pervasive and repeated, and therefore is assigned high significance. Second, as a feature of style it has semiosic value, defining a class of speaker. It allows us to recreate a sense of identity as well as a set of meanings – or more precisely it gives a set of meanings that defines an identity.

Analysed in this way the text becomes a more revealing document of intellectual history. The words of the poem seem to state very little that illuminates the mid-century Victorian 'crisis of faith', At the purely verbal level, Arnold simply seems to contradict himself: the actual sea is at the full, but makes him feel sad, while the sea of faith is not at the full, but that makes him feel sad too. How could such a gloomy *non sequitur* be counted as thought, or an example of Mind? But if we add to its explicit verbal meanings the further meanings carried by its style the poem becomes a more complex and interesting document. The 'crisis of faith' that defines Arnold is constructed out of signifiers of the intellectual class to which he belonged, immediately recognizable to that class. These signifiers are not concerned with presence or absence of religious beliefs. They construct a fragmented, unordered and de-energized physical world, with a passive disconnected ego at its centre, incapable of acting directly on either its physical or social environment. And outside this inert world is another world, of violent, hostile and incomprehensible others. The poem does not label the ego and these others in class terms, but the middle-class affiliations of the ego are strongly established, and the defining feature of the armies is their 'ignorance'. The 'crisis of faith' is a crippling sense of alienation and impotence which afflicts and disables the class itself, yet is inseparable from its characteristic and identifying qualities.

The status of the meanings of style needs to be clearly understood. In a sense these are unconscious meanings, but not in a Freudian sense. They are so taken for granted that they do not need to be focused on consciously, but they are obligatory not forbidden meanings, belonging to the social group not to a private 'id'. Yet the fact that they are encoded in the non-verbal systems of style and form does serve to protect them from exposure to dispute in the verbal code. In general, the more meaning that is coded in style the more defensive a group is about these meanings. Because of this we can suggest the following generalizations which are important for the social and historical study of literary texts. The more distinctive (different, marked) the style of a text or genre, the more strongly the existence of an anti-group is signalled, conscious of its opposition to other groups in society, so that high stylization is a transparent signifier of high polarization and conflict. And secondly, the meanings coded in form and style will be core meanings in dispute that organize group against group, so that this class of meanings is indispensable to a comprehensive analysis of intellectual movements in a social history of thought.

Stylistics and the spirit of an epoch

The term 'style' is important in many brands of literary studies, but in none more so than an enterprise which calls itself 'stylistics'. Stylistics, born around 1945, was always at best a marginalized practice, insecurely attached to mainstream literary criticism, and over the last decade it has moved closer to the periphery. There are a number of good reasons for this status and fate which I will look at. But even so, the scope of what stylistics attempted was not without interest, and the methods of analysis developed have potential strengths within a social semiotic framework. The handicap stylistics never overcame was its origin in linguistic theory. Linguistic theory at the time was narrow and formalistic, without an adequate theory of meaning or of society, unable therefore to be of any interest to historians and sociologists. Stylistics applied this sterile theory of language to literary texts, and hence was unable to impress literary critics that it had any useful expertise, so the hybrid discipline won few converts from literature, while seeming dangerously 'soft' (i.e. possibly becoming slightly interested in the meanings and effects of texts) to the hard-core linguistics of the time.

But if we look at the aims of the enterprise as formulated in 1948 by Leo Spitzer, one of its founding fathers, there is much to commend it. All it needs is a theory of social meaning such as social semiotics provides. Spitzer's aim was to go from qualities of style to what he called the 'soul' of a writer and the 'soul' of a nation and an age, its *Weltanschauung* ('world view'). Because he was a linguist, the markers of style he looked at were grammatical features, thus making the important link between grammar and style which literary critics typically are unable to make in a consistent way, though one cost of this for Spitzer and stylistics was a narrow conception of style, restricted to its grammatical exponents. The theory of history and society behind terms like 'soul' (from the German *Geist*, soul or spirit) or *Weltanschauung* is in even greater need of criticism and development, but it is still a theory on the appropriate scale, investigating connections between style and individual and group meanings over a historical span.

The theory is so obviously defective and problematic, for anyone seriously interested in social meaning and process, that it may seem pointless to try to rescue this discipline from oblivion. My reason for doing so is that I believe the method of stylistics was much better than the theories of language and society and history which determined its specific forms. At the core of this method was a meticulous and quantifiable description of whichever aspects of language (grammar, style, form) seemed strange or unique enough to mark an individual or group, as the first step in a dialectical movement between these features of texts and a cluster of meanings or signifiers (the 'etymon' as Spitzer called it). This was followed by a further movement outwards, from individual to group and from moment of production to historical framework, then back again to features of language and text. Far from depending on its earlier theoretical framework, the method functions more elegantly and powerfully if it incorporates the very different assumptions of social semiotics.

To establish the terms of a comprehensive social stylistics we also need to set in place the kind of theories of economic and social history that can connect with theories of style. As a starting point I will take the classic study by Max Weber, *The Protestant Ethic and the Spirit of Capitalism*. This book, which has been a seminal text for history and sociology, also contains, I will argue, a suggestive contribution to social stylistics. Weber's central aim was to trace causal links between a religious phenomenon (Protestantism) and a set of attitudes at the base of the economic practices of capitalism. The most obvious point of contact with Spitzer is the term *Geist*, from their common German philosophical heritage. For Weber as for Spitzer, this refers to a complex of meanings associated with a group consciousness that can be exemplified in a concrete instance. Weber connects this *Geist* with an 'ethic', i.e. the assumptions underpinning a social practice, something Spitzer was not concerned with. Weber's analysis reaches as far as individual texts produced by 'typical' individuals, but he does not have much to say about the forms or functions of style.

Weber was not the first to notice the historical association between Protestantism and capitalism (Matthew Arnold for instance had taken for granted the link between middle-class Liberals and 'Dissenters', the Protestant nonconformists of his day). But his analysis of the connection between forms of thought and social and economic practices was powerful and subtle. He located a peculiar and contradictory set of values and beliefs that he saw as indispensable to capitalist economic activity. The 'rationality' that distinguished capitalist thought, he argued, was based on a central irrationality whose contradictions he enshrined in the phrase *innerweltliche Askese* ('worldly asceticism'). This term described an 'ethic' of unscrupulous acquisition, where sensuous pleasure was repudiated in the interests of material acquisition, and unlimited profit and inexhaustible work were valued for their own sake, as ends instead of means. So strange and irrational a set of beliefs seemed to Weber to demand an historical explanation, which he found in the doctrine of

Protestant theologians several hundred years earlier, pre-eminently Calvin (though how these irrationalities emerged there he chooses not to worry about – irrationality in religion it seems was unsurprising to Weber, and not in need of explanation).

In articulating the historical object of his inquiry (the 'spirit of capitalism') he adopts a double method. One is to painstakingly construct elements of it from a variety of sources. The other, which he deploys in the second chapter of his work, is to fix a single example, a 'document of that spirit' which contains its qualities 'in almost classical purity' (Weber 1930: 48). We will defer any discussion of the problems this step leaps over, and follow Weber's discussion of his chosen documents: two works written by the American Benjamin Franklin, *Necessary Hints for Those That Would Be Rich* of 1739, and *Advice to a Young Tradesman* of 1748.

> Remember, that *time* is money. He that can earn ten shillings a day by his labour, and goes abroad, or sits idle, one half of that day, though he spends but sixpence during his diversion or idleness, ought not to reckon *that* the only expense. He has really spent, or rather thrown away, five shillings besides. *(Necessary Hints)*

> The most trifling actions that affect a man's credit are to be regarded. The sound of your hammer at five in the morning, or eight at night, heard by a creditor, makes him easy six months longer; but if he sees you at a billiard-table, or hears your voice at a tavern, when you should be at work, he sends for his money the next day; demands it, before he can receive it, in a lump. *(Advice)*

Weber mainly attends to the mimetic content of this text, the behaviour and values it describes, but equally important to his argument is its semiosic character, its 'tone' as literary critics would describe it. Weber has no such technical terms but is still able to indicate the quality in impressionistic terms. 'What is here *preached*' he puts it, the word implying the crucial semiosic and stylistic point he wants to make, that this pragmatic advice is set in the framework of a self-confident exhortation, offered as morality not 'mere business astuteness'.

I will begin my discussion with the mimetic content of this text, because it too is concerned with style. As Weber notes, Franklin in this text is very much concerned with virtues as part of a system of signs. This opens the way to the charge of hypocrisy, which was directed at Puritanism from its earliest stages, but Weber insists that Franklin is not recommending hypocrisy (they are real hammer blows that a creditor is to hear, not an ingenious machine that simulates the sounds). Franklin is focusing on the semiosic use of actions to signify qualities of character, as metasigns of identity. He is explicit about the social role of this set of signs (which includes clothing and other codes that express the same meaning, identi-

fying Puritans to themselves and others). These signs do nothing less than
enable the social relations that are indispensable to capitalism, the cash
nexus that binds capitalist (owner of capital) and entrepreneur (user of
capital) in an effective and cohesive community. Instead of a closed set of
relationships held together by a long history (the history of relations
within a specific group, as in feudal relationships), this sign system allows
a more open set of relationships to be sustained with a shorter history,
supplemented by the metasigns of behavioural style. It is not of course
that Puritans invented this way of creating and sustaining a community. It
is a basic proposition of social semiotics that all groups do this. The English
aristocrats of the Elizabethan and Jacobean periods who clashed so fiercely
with the Pilgrim Fathers created their own kind of credit, and constructed
their own community simply with a different set of signs in a different
style, one which signified consumption not accumulation. In Franklin's
New England, Puritans formed a dominant group in the community, not
an oppressed minority organized as an anti-group in opposition to the
ruling elite as in England. But the group constructed by the signifiers of
Puritanism even in eighteenth-century Massachusetts was still conscious of
its oppositional status, its independent identity separate from those who
'waste their time' in idleness and diversion, many of whom still lived in
large numbers in the new community.

    Franklin's verbal style functions as part of this system of metasigns, so
we will now look at its characteristic features. The Spitzerian method (like
Weber's) relies on an 'intuitive' identification of what is odd,
idiosyncratic and significant in a text – a procedure which is less problematic than a term like 'intuition' suggests if what is at issue is a public sign
system whose purpose is precisely to express a public identity through a
publicly recognized set of markers of difference. One feature of this style is
contained in the first sentence, which clearly struck Weber forcibly and
which has entered into the language as a compressed signifier of the
capitalist mind: '*Time* is money.' This is a startling and dramatic phrase
because of its form. It links an abstract, metaphysical concept ('time') and
a concrete term ('money') with the strongest, most emphatic linkage in
English, 'is'. The effect of this is to attack those key paradigmatic categories enshrined in English, concrete/material and abstract/immaterial.
The result is a double transformation: the abstract 'time' is treated as
though it is as concrete as money, and the concrete 'money' (not moneys,
or shillings) is treated as though it were an abstract noun like 'time'. This
double transformation leads to exactly the same contradictory status in
these terms as Weber saw was characteristic of the 'spirit' itself: a metaphysical materialism or a materialist metaphysics.

    'Style' is a pervasive quality, so we need to specify what exactly is
pervasive. One feature of this style is its use of *nominalization*, that is, a
process by which nouns are formed from actional clauses built around

adjectives. Here the two most significant nominalizations are 'labour' and 'credit'; others are 'diversion', 'idleness', 'expense' and 'actions'. The principle at issue here is analogous to the previous one we looked at. Here a quality or process is represented as though it were a thing, but this thing has a double status, as abstract (in relation to the process or quality) yet treated as a concrete material thing (e.g. 'labour' earns money, and 'credit' is affected by 'actions').

Another related feature of this style which seems 'odd' or 'distinctive' is the use of numbers. The figures ten (shillings), half (a day), and six (pence) are meticulously recorded, as part of a process of quantification extended to become a kind of pseudo-precision (they stand for 'early', 'late' and 'long' respectively). This feature of style has negligible mimetic content, but serves to signify an ideology and mark an identity. It is like a mannerism, but precisely for that reason it serves its semiosic functions.

These are significant presences. There are also significant absences – significant because of the allegiances they repudiate as components of the identity at issue. One such absence is the world of sense impressions, signified by the grammatical category of adjective. Matthew Arnold's poem was full of relationals and adjectives. This text is almost without adjectives. This absence expresses at the level of style the repudiation of sensuality Weber saw as a key characteristic of the Protestant ethic. Apparent exceptions, such as 'idle' (and 'idleness') in fact serve to illustrate the rule, since this term is a classification of persons or actions, not a sensuous apprehension of them. This absence is itself significant semiosically, since it signifies a repudiation of an identifiable class of social others – not Matthew Arnold of course, who was not yet born, but those contemporaries who indulged in 'diversions' or tavern talk.

Scanning the sentence structures themselves (a central activity in Spitzerian stylistics), I am struck by a quality that impressionistically I would term 'jerkiness'. The sentences read awkwardly, like a series of pellets strung together. Stylistics encourages a more precise description of the qualities of text that give rise to such impressions. In this instance, one contributing signifier is excessively heavy punctuation (e.g. the commas after 'Remember' or 'idle'). This is a transparent signifier of boundary maintenance. A related feature is the frequency of 'or' as a conjunction. This conjunction signifies a world divided into two distinct parts, even though in most cases Franklin's either/or pairs are equivalent (e.g. 'goes abroad' and 'sits idle' are both equally a waste of time and/or money).

This kind of conjunction is an instance of the kind of conjunction Franklin employs generally. There are two broad ways of linking clauses together, known as *parataxis* (linking in parallel, side by side) and *hypotaxis* (linking with subordination of one element to another). Parataxis is a transparent signifier of an egalitarian, loose order. Hypotaxis is a transparent signifier of hierarchy and complex order. Franklin's 'jerky' style is extended but paratactic. This signifies a complex message, repudiating hierarchy, affirming boundaries and opposition, while incorporating more into this loose frame than it can easily bear. The resulting 'difficulty' both expresses an ideological message and also unobtrusively serves to exclude those who are not orientated to the style. It is a mild form of anti-language, even though it constructs this opacity out of seemingly simple and commonplace elements of English.

Finally we will look at the semiosic syntagms that the text projects, as an intrinsic component of its style. Weber compared it to a sermon, but this is not an exact comparison. It contains an element of exhortation, carried by imperatives ('remember') and modal auxiliaries attached to verbs ('ought to', 'should'). The semiosic effect of this is to construct a relationship of confident authority of writer over readers. But this semiosic syntagm is completed by the social meaning of the participants. This is constructed by Franklin in his titles *Necessary Hints to Those That Would Be Rich* and *Advice to a Young Tradesman*. These titles signify a relative equality between writer and reader, a bond constructed by the needs of readers rather than by the authority of the writer, but this bond must be sustained by continuous demonstrations of authority by the author, through style as well as content, and freely accepted by readers who purchase this commodity.

Franklin's text is one among many in the 'Advice' genre which was a dominant form in Puritan culture. The genre served a crucial function in selectively disseminating a common pattern of behaviours and a common style throughout a dispersed community. It is ideally adapted to print technology, to a social form organized by the print medium reinforcing other systems of signifiers. The cohesion it allows is paratactic not hypotactic, diffused intermittently through an egalitarian society not disseminated from a centre. Members of this community have freedom to buy the book or not, and thus to choose to belong or not.

We have not looked at other codes (e.g. speech and clothing style) which helped to organize exchanges at the interpersonal level. Two macro codes in particular performed a crucial role in organizing this open-ended paratactic anti-community: money and print. (By a nice coincidence, Franklin was a printer as well as author, and his firm won the first contract to print money for the state of Philadelphia.) These two codes had the scope necessary to give cohesion to a community dispersed in physical and social space, so that it could act as a class-for-itself. The metasigns in the various codes formed part of a single system, each code referring to meanings in other codes. Together the full set of codes performed a decisive role in constructing the social relations that enabled economic activity in Franklin's society.

Weber believed that he had challenged the Marxist theory of causality as he understood it, by showing that a 'superstructural' phenomenon (religion) could pre-exist and influence the base (capitalist modes of pro-duction). Franklin was part of the proof, since he showed such a pure form of the capitalist spirit in a Puritan but economically primitive community. But if we examine the role played by 'style' and the systems of metasigns in Franklin's New England community we do not need to go back in time to understand the rationale of the Puritan-capitalist 'style' as part of a current social and economic system. This 'style' actively constructed a cohesive group within and opposed to the rest of the community, estab-lishing class identity and class difference. The system of metasigns was anchored through the behavioural code (e.g. acts of conspicuous thrift and ostentatious work). As material activity this contributed to the accumula-tion of capital and as semiosic activity it established both personal and group identity. So it makes equally good sense to include style as part of the economic base, to use the classic Marxist term, although it also acts as an effective site of ideological formation. The interrelation of style and the economic and social order undoubtedly had a history, and religious affilia-tions played a significant role in that history, but this is a different matter to claiming that sixteenth-century doctrines constructed that eighteenth- and nineteenth-century economic order. When Weber's thesis is reco-gnized as a contribution to social semiotics and a study of style, it becomes possible to use social stylistics as part of a strategy for exemplifying and explaining, extending and criticizing his specific influential but contro-versial proposals.

Refractions of style

Style functions within specific semiosic contexts, and the versions of society that it constructs have their meanings by reference to the relation-ships of semiosic participants. Since a marked style is normally formed in a situation of opposition, serving to exclude some people while it incorpo-rates others, it will normally have a double value and double function for these opposing groups, surrounding its common core. A description of the social meaning of style must incorporate its meanings for those it excludes as well as for those whose style it is. To illustrate, I will quote from a popular contemporary text, Patricia Marx and Charlotte Stuart's *How to Regain Your Virginity . . . and 99 Other Recent Discoveries About Sex*, published in 1983.

> *Two out of three cases of lost virginity are never reported.*
> According to the latest Police Index on Crime:
>
> * More people lose their virginity than their wallet.
> * More people lose their virginity per month in New York city than died in the Korean War.

*   2 percent of the people who lose their virginity have it returned in the mail.
      (p. 35)

Contemporary readers of this text will have no problems in judging that it
is a humorous parody. It parodies the 'How to' genre which stems from
the form that Franklin's *Necessary Hints* belonged to. It embodies the
stylistic markers of the 'capitalist spirit' (paratactic structures,
quantification, turning process into abstract entity, abstract into concrete), in a form that is even clearer than in Franklin's text or Weber's
analysis. In so far as it is read as parody its style signifies a critique of the
'spirit of capitalism'. Since it is a popular text it shows that this critique is
now easily recognizable and accessible knowledge. But this double meaning must incorporate not only the stylistic markers of capitalist thought
but also a criticism or rejection of them. The stylistic markers of capitalism
are part of the mimetic content of the text, but the authors use this style as
a form of quotation that reconstructs the ideology of its typical users. They
then incorporate subject matter (sex, crime, and war) which comes from
domains where mercantilist thought is seen as inappropriate or dangerous, in terms of dominant noetic regimes: domains of pleasure and
irrationality.

Stylistic parody and quotation are widespread phenomena, deployed
by children who mimic the accents of others in the playground and by
adults in many contexts. Parody and quotation do not signify a single
semiosic stance. They always signify an element of opposition since they
juxtapose markers of two groups, but that opposition can range from
emulation to contempt, from complicit mockery to savage criticism. And
the difference can't be determined from the text alone, because it is a
function of both textual form and semiosic relations.

The same problem arises with literary texts and the meaning of their
style. As documents in the history of the 'capitalist spirit', the novels of
Daniel Defoe have been much examined. Between 1719 and 1730, he
published six novels which many literary critics have claimed are key texts
in the 'rise of the novel' as the dominant bourgeois literary form (Watt
1957). But these works have also been seen as exemplifying the spirit of
capitalism in a pure form. Karl Marx described *Robinson Crusoe* as the
classic study of *homo economicus*, the individualist ethic of capitalism.
The 'New Critic' Mark Schorer summed up *Moll Flanders*, Defoe's major
novel, in similar terms: 'without in the least intending it, *Moll Flanders* is
our classic revelation of the mercantile mind: the morality of measure-
ment which Defoe has apparently neglected to measure,' (Defoe 1965).

Against this there is an alternative line of literary criticism, as articulated
by Dorothy Van Ghent (1953:43): '*Moll Flanders* is a great novel, coherent
in structure, unified and given its shape and significance by a complex
system of ironies.' Literary critics oscillate between these two judgements,

which hinge on the key stylistic feature of 'irony'. The uncertainty not only serves to polarize literary critics, but also seems to split literary critics from social and economic historians. The closer the text is to 'a classic revelation of the mercantile mind' the more comparable it is to Franklin, but the less interesting, apparently, to literary criticism. Conversely, it might seem, the presence of a 'complex system of irony' may make the text unusable as evidence for a historian.

To explore these issues in more detail, I will start with an analysis of the title page:

> The fortunes and misfortunes of the famous Moll Flanders who was born in Newgate, and during a life of continued vanity, for three score years, besides her childhood, was twelve years a Whore, five times a Wife (whereof once to her own brother), twelve years a Thief, eight years a transported Felon in Virginia, at last grew rich, lived honest, and died a Penitent. (Defoe 1965)

This text exemplifies the style of the 'spirit of capitalism'. A life (Moll's) is offered for sale as a commodity, itemized with numbers attached. The title rolls on like a list, a paratactic structure without an obvious oervall ordering principle till the end. But the semiosic framework of the text remains ambiguous, at least to a twentieth-century reader, unlike the Marx–Stuart text, which unmistakably (given our confidence that we know the relevant noetic regimes) went over the top in its mimetic content. Is 'five times a wife' over the top? Or is it just a bait to the naïvely salacious? Or does it mark the historical coexistence of two competing noetic regimes, so that what is absurd to one is commonplace and acceptable to the other?

The text signals the most elementary form of paratactic structure, nouns or phrases linked by commas or 'and'. But the opening words invoke a simple binary opposition (fortune–misfortune), and then unmarked binaries continue in the text, 'whore–wife' and 'thief–felon', and in the conclusion 'lived (honest) died (a Penitent)'. 'Rich' is one half of a binary pair with 'poor', which itself has links with 'honest'. But in this text, conventional opposites are not simply unmarked, they tend to merge. A woman who is Wife five times is not much different from a Whore; or perhaps a whore is not much different from a wife.

The conjunction of 'rich' and 'honest' suggests another equivalence – that the rich are normally honest, or that only the rich can afford to be honest. This is a judgement that Moll herself implies during her story. Even 'lived honest: died a Penitent' has a curious muffled opposition to it, since 'lived' is undoubtedly the opposite to 'died', and suggests therefore that penitence may be the opposite of honesty – a suspicion that many modern critics of Moll feel strongly about her.

These structures have an elusive relationship to the text, because they are aspects of paradigmatic structures, which at the moment of production or reception only exist inside the minds of semiosic participants. This text both triggers and subverts these binary forms: invoking them yet treating them as irrelevant. Presence or absence of these structures is semiosically very significant, marking two opposite orientations to the text. The strong binarist will read contradictions at every level in this discourse, and adopt a critical perspective. The non-binarist will identify with the text in its lack of signals of contradiction.

The novel itself is written in the persona of the 'famous' Moll Flanders. Here is a sample of the text, describing an erotic scene early in the book:

> However, though he took these freedoms with me it did not go to that which they call the last favour, which, to do him justice, he did not attempt; and he made that self-denial of his a plea for all his freedom with me upon other occasions after this. When this was over he stayed but a little while, but he put almost a handful of gold in my hand, and left me a thousand protestations of his passion for me, and of his loving me above all the women in the world. (p. 38)

Literary critics have noted the 'mercantile mind' at work in the style of this passage, which is typical of the book. The small number of adjectives signifies a desensualized world, especially marked because as with 'How to regain your virginity' the mimetic content would seem to require the opposite quality. The lack of erotic detail contrasts with the calculating precision of 'almost a handful', signifying her precise estimate of his equally finely calculated generosity. The passage also signifies another set of qualities through words like 'freedoms' and 'that which they call the last favour'. The euphemisms are typically nominalizations. The gentleman quickly moves into a trade-off of 'freedoms', as though these are each assigned a cash value as commodities. This style of language signifies the mind or ideology of mercantilism, but the moral values it transforms into this style are those of religion: piety not profit. It is Moll who uses the terms, but she selfconsciously attributes 'favours' to others ('that which they call the last favour') as though distancing herself at this point from this kind of language, while tacitly accepting the other instances as her own.

The text is constructed around a set of fissures; initially between mimetic content (illicit sexuality) and style (mercantilism and piety). There are fissures in the semiosic context also. The contructed speaker is Moll Flanders, female, low-class, criminal and socially mobile. The writer is Daniel Defoe, male and middle-class, an undischarged bankrupt and equally mobile; 'thirteen times both rich and poor' he wrote of himself in one poem, ostentatiously counting, in the bourgeois style, how many times he'd counted wrong. But the exact relationship between author and narrator, and hence its social meaning, was rendered obscure and ambiguous by Defoe, so that his contemporaries as well as modern critics could not easily decode it. His preface claimed that Defoe simply transcribed the text, and cleaned up the style. Modern critics normally assume that the text is a fiction constructed by Defoe, but this assumption is not entirely justified either. Defoe's story was probably based on the narrative of Moll King, which Defoe had taken down earlier and published in his role as journalist. So Moll King was co-author of the novel, to a degree that is now impossible to determine. Defoe was giving a voice to a group who have been largely silenced from history, at the same time as he was appropriating that voice. In the process he was constructing a new voice, male/female, middle-class/low-class, respectable/criminal, as fragmented, marginal and discohesive as Franklin's was coherent, central and persuasive. So in spite of the gratifying (to some critics) crudity and inappropriateness of the mercantilist style in Defoe's text, it cannot be analysed for its 'purity' (the identity between author and narrator) as Franklin's can; though even Franklin's purity is only relative. But 'impurity' can be just as widespread and no less interesting to a social stylistics, if its positioning within a social context can be established. Defoe's text is a refraction of the style, but the refractions of a style are an indispensable part of its social meaning.

We are now able to reconsider the category of 'irony' and the debate within traditional literary criticism about the status of *Moll Flanders*. Investigations into irony cannot remain a purely textualist strategy, as in both traditional stylistics and literary criticism. We also have to use some of the methods of literary history, looking at other texts by the author and other contemporaries, and at texts about the reception of these texts, scanning both kinds of document for clues about semiosic relations and reception regimes. In a case like Defoe's the indications are that we have a case of aberrant reading, which will require us to search particularly carefully for relevant metatexts.

From this point of view, two texts provide suggestive evidence. One is an earlier work by Defoe, entitled *The Shortest Way With Dissenters*. This pamphlet, published in 1702, seemed to argue strongly for the persecution of Dissenters (of whom Defoe was one). It was greeted with outrage by Dissenters and with delight by High Church Tories, as a straight contribution to the debate. Defoe then revealed that he was the author and claimed that it was meant to be a parody. Further outrage followed this revelation, and he was sentenced to the pillory for what he claimed to have meant. The text itself, however, contains no clues that it is ironic, no discrepancies with the style or beliefs of prejudiced High Tories. It is entirely understandable that they accepted it at its face value. It would only seem ridiculous to those to whom the position was ridiculous. Defoe clearly miscalculated the effect of his text, entering so totally into the style and thought of the enemy that all difference disappeared. There is no simple judgement we can make on all this. Defoe's later history as an agent for both Whigs and Tories suggests an amphibious politics and style, rather than a clear partisan position. But the episode demonstrates the existence of conflicts within Defoe's semiosic context, and a resulting instability in reading regimes.

In his preface to *Moll Flanders*, Defoe writes what are ostensibly instructions how to read the text. 'But as this work is chiefly recommended to those who know how to read it, and how to make the good uses of it which the story all along recommends to them, so it is to be hoped that such readers will be much more pleased with the moral than the fable'. The style of this, with its explicit oppositions and careful symmetries, signifies quite different social allegiances to Defoe's more casual style (and to Moll's). This is the style of bourgeois constraint and conformity, assuring this community that their meaning will be a dominant subtext in the novel itself. Since such a reading is difficult to sustain for modern readers, it is natural to suppose that Defoe is being cynical or hypocritical or ironic.

But the instruction also shows another quality in Defoe, his consciousness of a stratified readership with different reading regimes which constructed different and irreconcilable meanings from a common text. The resulting quality is not irony, because irony presumes a secret but single right reading, controlled by a socially recognized reading regime which vindicates the elite in their sense of superiority. Defoe's text was produced outside a stable semiosic system. It incorporated opposing styles in a state of unresolved antagonisms and strained alliances. Where Franklin's style gave cohesion and purpose to a self-confident elite class, Defoe's style expressed discohesion and ambivalence. The position of Puritanism in mid eighteenth-century New England was very different from the position of Dissidents in early eighteenth-century England. A recognition of this difference helps us to recognize and make sense of differences in the social meaning of even those features of style they seem to have in common.

Texts like the Marx–Stuart and the Defoe make it easier to see one basic premise of social stylistics. Style as meaning is like every other social meaning. It is communicated by specific agents in specific contexts for specific purposes. So people can use styles deliberately or habitually to oppress or impress others, to incorporate or exclude, to amuse or deceive. Naïve stylistics would fail to see that Marx–Stuart have more in common with Weber than with Franklin. The meanings that social stylistics recovers and articulates are as important as they are invisible in most reading strategies. The similarities and differences it can demonstrate between Defoe and Franklin and Arnold and cummings and Marx–Stuart pose important questions, even though neither stylistics nor literary criticism could ask or answer them on their own, without recourse to other and fuller versions of history.

Comparative stylistics

I will conclude this chapter by addressing a paradox affecting the scope of 'English' and the limits of literary analysis. If so much content is encoded in style and grammatical/linguistic form, how can the average student understand another literature in another language? Every translation will seem too inadequate to be worth studying (unless the translator is important in his/her own right), and the original will be inaccessibly shrouded in its alien language and form. The paradox is that this kind of respect for the otherness of other languages and cultures leads to their elimination from English, and the centre of the curriculum. This is a serious loss, if one of the values of studying literature is to increase understanding across national and cultural boundaries. For this purpose we need a method of analysis that respects difference but isn't paralysed by it. Otherwise, literary studies for most people in monolingual English speaking countries will be confined to a single self-contained national literature, with only a privileged few able to engage in a still fragmentary form of comparative literature.

Related to this curriculum problem is a problem for Weberian stylistics as a comparative enterprise. Weber set his analysis of capitalism and Protestantism in a broad comparative context that included Asian religions and social types. He argued that capitalism and Protestantism were both unique forms, appearing only in Europe and America, emerging in their exemplary form in Puritan America. He was at pains to distinguish this development from others which seemed to have something in common with it. This assumption seemed plausible to Weber writing in the early twentieth-century, when the industrialized West seemed to have a permanent monopoly on capitalist forms of economy. If Weber had been right, other countries would have had to develop a Protestant type of ethic, a Protestant 'style', as the precondition for competing in this way. Forty years after the Second World War the world economy looks rather different. First Japan emerged as a major capitalist producer, followed by other Asian economies that economists quaintly label NICs (Newly Industrializing Countries). The 'economic miracles' of these countries make a specifically Protestant basis to capitalism look rather less necessary. One major difference has been their corporatist form of capitalism, with high levels of state intervention, as opposed to the individualistic freemarket economies of classic Western capitalism. Yet Weber's more basic contention still makes good sense. The success of the NICs clearly depends on attitudes to work and discipline which are as irrational in their way as the Protestant ethic, with roots in traditional patterns of behaviour and belief. A comparative stylistics can usefully explore this crucial issue by looking at earlier stages of these Asian cultures, using a kind of Weberian framework to discover where Weber's analysis went wrong.

As a focus for the discussion, I will look at a Japanese haiku from the seventeenth-century by Matsuo Basho. Japan was the first of the Asian NICs and still has the most advanced and sophisticated economy, with highly developed electronics and computer industries, yet Japanese insist that this success is built firmly on the 'Japanese way', on attitudes laid down during the period of Japan's withdrawal from the world economy, initiated by the Tokugawa Shogunate in 1639. Basho was born in 1644, only sixteen years earlier than Daniel Defoe, and became the most famous master of haiku, itself the most prized and distinctive poetic form of the period. Born to a Samurai family, Basho's poetic career was subsidized by a rich merchant, one of the *chonin* class who at this period were politically marginal but economically vigorous, and major patrons of poetry and art. Basho's haiku were thus produced for the class in seventeenth-century Japan that corresponded to the Puritan mercantile classes whom Weber saw as so important in the rise of capitalism, though the position of merchants in Basho's Japan was different in many respects from that of their Anglo-American cousins.

Information like this can be gleaned from any standard history of Japan. Our primary concern, however, is to link these considerations with the analysis of form, style and language in particular texts and genres. Here then is a famous haiku by Basho, first in Japanese, with a word-for-word translation and also a twentieth-century translation by the American imagist poet, John Gould Fletcher:

Kare eda ni	Withered / branch / on
Karasu no tomari keri	crow / of / perch / ed
Aki no kure	autumn / of / evening

> A crow is perched
> Upon a leafless, withered bough –
> The autumn dusk.

It is convenient to start with Gould Fletcher's translation, since that is the most accessible text for non-Japanese speakers. How far can it be trusted? Brooks and Warren in their influential guide to the analysis of poetry make this comment on his text:

> Most readers will find that the solitary crow perched in the dusk of autumn on a withered bough suggests loneliness, the pathos of the end of the season, or some related mood. (1976: 69–70)

'Most readers' here tacitly assumes contemporary English-speaking under-graduates, but the writers also warn that these images are 'rich in special associations', which will give them a different set of suggestions and a different meaning for Japanese readers – an anxious recognition on their part of problems of translation and linguistic and cultural difference. To gauge how justified these anxieties are, I asked a Japanese friend of mine to give a general response to the poem. Her comment was: 'The poem is a little bit sad, but it makes me feel quiet, and serene, after the stress and tensions of the day.' This response is reassuringly similar to the Brooks and Warren summary. I will look at some significant differences in a moment, but we can accept that the Anglo-American reader is not after all reading a totally different poem.

To anchor the reading, a useful place to begin is with the transparent signifiers of style and with its mimetic content. Both versions of the poem are strikingly short: (seventeen syllables for the Japanese, sixteen for the English). But this short form itself has structure ($5 + 7 + 5$ for the Japanese, $4 + 8 + 4$ for the English). This combination of smallness and structure is a transparent signifier of miniaturization – smallness which has its own coherence and completeness, the smallness of a microcosm not a fragment.

But the semiosic meaning of this same signifier is very different in Japanese. All haiku have seventeen syllables, in a $5 + 7 + 5$ form. Its semiosic meaning in Japanese is its unremarkable acceptance of this precise con-straint. In English we don't count syllables, so beyond an impression of compression and symmetry this signifier would hardly be noticed. If it was, its semiosic meaning would be the free decision of Gould Fletcher to take a constraint of this kind on himself – if he even counted the syllables. And this count added up to sixteen not seventeen, in a different, more sharply differentiated pattern, so that his form is highly individual if not unique, whereas Basho's haiku is formally identical to all other haiku, by himself and others, over a period of 500 years of Japanese history.

Translation and original have a similar mimetic content: a crow perching, a bare branch, and a time (autumn, dusk). Both include a similar portion of the world and exclude everything else, and their inclu-sions and exclusions have similar meanings in terms of what seem at the moment to be comparable noetic regimes. The poem contains a spectacu-larly small proportion of the world: nature not man; a branch not a tree nor a landscape; an arrangement of objects, not an action or event; an image, not an observer nor a comment.

All this is fairly comparable for both the seventeenth-century Japanese and the twentieth-century Anglo-American poet, but it has different semiosic meanings. For instance the inclusion of the *kigo* or 'season word' (autumn dusk) is required and expected in a Japanese haiku at this time, thus signifying Basho's conformity to the rule system and constituting a bond between him and the community of haiku readers and writers. For

Gould Fletcher there is no such expectation, and no sense of solidarity is constructed by it. Japanese readers are thus reassured in their Japanese identity; Anglo-American readers are displaced from their own cultural identity without being incorporated into Japanese. This sense of dislocation might be experienced as alienation, isolation, reinforcing the 'suggestion' of loneliness which Brooks and Warren saw as the dominant mood of the poem (for Anglo-American readers). Loneliness and alienation should not be semiosic meanings of this form for Japanese readers, but the opposite. Yet the solidarity of Japanese readers is something that can be understood by Anglo-American readers, not least at the moment of their exclusion from it; and vice versa for Japanese readers, for whom the solidarity is a constructed meaning, not an inevitable or unchanging social fact. Or to put the difference more practically; both Japanese and Anglo-American readers could understand and talk about these differences very fruitfully, as a common problem not an unspeakable gulf, within an average literature classroom context.

In analysing style we have isolated a number of transparent signifiers, and then tackled the more difficult task of interpreting their semiosic meanings by reference to literary history of an elementary kind. In analysing the language itself we run into apparently much greater problems. How do we proceed if we do not know Japanese (as I do not)? This is a crucial question, for if there's nothing to be done short of a complete course in Japanese (or whatever is the language of a text) then comparative stylistics labours under heavy difficulties. But there are a number of sources of assistance to draw on. Some specialists do describe the general features of languages for non-speakers, in enough detail so that some of these meanings can be seen acting in specific texts. Of course, there will be many more meanings of this kind available to the native speaker, but that fact should not detract from the meanings that we can understand in this way. There is in practice no single comprehensive reading of texts even within the one language. The claim that there is carries a questionable ideological message, about the essential unity of the community that transcends all differences of class, age and subgroup. Those who emphasize the uniqueness and untranslatability of languages are reinforcing the ideological meanings carried by 'grammar' as against 'style'. So finally the same pedagogy that stresses grammar as obedience not meaning in English also protests an exaggerated respect for the otherness of other languages. This deference to the 'discipline' that is required for full conformity to these alien rules paradoxically leads to less communication across the barriers of language and culture, in the name of cross-cultural understanding.

It is often possible to find ways around this impasse. In this case, for instance, I was able to discuss the language of the poem with my Japanese friend, and my understanding of it owes a lot to her comments. She is a contemporary Japanese speaker, not a contemporary of Basho's, but those are rather rare nowadays. Nor is she a literary scholar, Anglo-American or Japanese. That simply gives her comments a different value, from a different perspective; and one that has its own importance if one function of comparative analysis is to improve cross-cultural understanding.

The first linguistic feature I will isolate is the fact that Japanese does not mark nouns as singular or plural, definite or indefinite. *Karasu* is either 'the crow' or 'a crow' or 'crow' or '(the) (some) crows'. A translation into English has to choose among these alternatives, because in English we have to be clear about the matter. Gould Fletcher opted for 'A crow', singular and indefinite. Brooks and Warren's commentary accepts and embellishes this grammatical choice: 'the solitary crow'. This decision isn't arbitrary or even necessarily un-Japanese: my friend on this point said that she imagined only one crow, because that would be more in keeping with the sadness of the scene. But there is still an important difference. Solitariness becomes an inescapable meaning of the scene in this translation – one crow, one branch, one autumn. But for the Japanese reader this is an optional meaning, not an enforced one. Illustrations of the poem exist which show several crows, and several branches. The Japanese language establishes a systematic ambiguity about the status of an entity, whether it is an isolated individual, a typical individual (connected therefore to others by typicality) or a group. The distinction that exists in English between individual and group, and concrete and abstract, does not obtrude in the same way in Japanese.

So an ideology of individualism, which Weber regarded as a constituent of the Protestant/capitalist spirit, is directly opposed by this feature of Japanese. However, the quality does enshrine an ideology which is highly compatible with corporatism (in which the individual is not distinguished from the group or the mass) and with mass production (in which the individual unit-commodity is replicated indefinitely). This feature is signified not only by the grammatical form but also by the semiosic feature we looked at earlier. Basho in spite of his eminence as a master of the form and the leader of a haiku 'school' is still a collective-individual, occupying a space not a point, a social role not an autonomous individual. His position as haiku-poet, with its considerable constraints, is not unlike a place in an assembly line. Basho produced about 650 carefully crafted haiku in his last eight years. Saikaku, another haiku master, was less inhibited. He is said to have set the formidable record of 23,500 haiku in a day and a night, one haiku every four seconds. The Guinness book of records, that quintessentially Protestant/capitalist phenomenon, would have found Saikaku's attitude eminently comprehensible.

We can begin to understand another characteristic of the language of this poem by looking at its prepositions, (or post-positions as they are in Japanese). Each line has one: *ni – no – no* (on/at, of, of). Gould

Fletcher's poem has only one: 'upon', translating the first *ni*. My Japanese friend sharply distinguished between the two instances of *no*. The second *no* (literally 'autumn's dusk') she said was essential ('it wouldn't make sense without it'). In English, we could say 'the dusk of autumn' but 'autumn dusk' sounds more normal: in Japanese the opposite is closer to the truth. But the first *no* puzzled her. It was not necessary (without it, the words made good sense, as 'the crow was perched') and she couldn't quite see or say what its exact function was, though she was sure that it did have some force.

Japanese grammar can help us articulate what is going on here. Japanese doesn't distinguish the main parts of speech (noun, verb, adjective) in the same way as English does. *Tomari keri* has the meaning of a verb, referring to the crow's action (of perching). But with a *no* in front of it, it functions like a noun, which we could translate as 'the crow's perchedness'. That is, the action is transformed into an entity or thing, an abstract-concrete which is then linked, by *no*, to the crow as its possessor. This is structurally similar to the Protestant/capitalist syntactic transformation that we saw in an exemplary form in Benjamin Franklin's text. This is not an isolated instance in haiku or Japanese, either. The obligatory *no* in *aki no kure* ('autumn's dusk') expresses a relationship of classification (this evening is not a spring or summer evening but an autumn one) as though it were a spatial-possessive one. The word *no* appears very frequently in Basho's haiku, in the two broad kinds of usage. So does *ni*. They often serve as primary structural nodes linking the constituents of the haiku world, as here. Conversely, verbs as signifiers of activity are often absent, leaving a world of things related in space and located in time. From this comes a quality that was more prominent for my friend ('quiet and tranquil') than for Brooks and Warren. In the translation, the action-which-is-not-an-action ('perched') suggests this, but not as strongly as the Japanese, which has transformed the only action into a quasi-permanent possession of the crow.

In some respects, the meanings we have seen in the style and form of this text and genre are highly compatible with the values appropriate to contemporary Japanese corporate capitalism: meticulous precision, careful quantification, transformation of activities into things, absorption of individual into group. Like 'worldly asceticism' as described by Weber, it fuses concrete–sensuous and abstract–general. But there is one aspect of my friend's response we need to recognize. She liked the poem not because of its similarity to her everyday experience (she works in an office at a job so stressful and repetitive that she was recently off work for many months with Repetitive Strain Injury) but the opposite. It suggested 'quiet' and 'serenity' precisely as the antidotes to her stressful conditions of work, and she associated it with 'evening', her own evenings after work. Basho's haiku split the world of poetic contemplation from the world of work, constructing an anti-world of abstract sensuality opposed to and excluding the concrete, routinized world of labour and commerce. This seems the opposite to Weberian 'worldly asceticism', but in practice the tendency to construct a spiritual anti-world alongside the world of material activity coexisted in Protestant-capitalist practice as well, institutionalized in Protestant respect for the Sabbath as a 'day of rest'. From my friend's reaction we can see how functional this contradiction is, even today. The style and form of the haiku are constructed in many respects out of the ideological values of the world of work, yet its mimetic content is a repudiation of that world. The contradiction allows it to affirm the work ethic at the very moment of denying it, creating an escape that is never allowed to get away.

An analysis as brief as this runs the risk of simplifying a complex set of relationships. I have tried to stress that Basho's haiku is sufficiently comprehensible to us, even if we don't understand Japanese, so long as we are prepared to work hard and listen well. However, that is not to say that it is really much the same as English Protestant poetry and thought. If it were, there would be less value in attempting to read and understand it. Nor do I claim that Basho's haiku is the modern Japanese work ethic writ small – any more than that nothing essentially has happened in Anglo-American culture since Benjamin Franklin's day. Yet in both instances the affinities are as real and as important as the differences, and the connections at issue – between past and present, poetry and economics, East and West – are as vital as they are difficult to trace. It is relations as complex yet obscure as these that give comparative stylistics so fruitful a role to play.

SOURCES AND CONTEXTS

Stylistics has been a marginalized enterprise within the practices of literary criticism, seen primarily as an application of current linguistic theory to literary texts, drawing on a discipline which was potentially a threat to English itself. Spitzer, *Linguistics and Literary History*, 1967, and Auerbach, *Mimesis*, 1953, were influential and acceptable, partly because the linguistic theory they drew on was not current within the linguistics of their time, partly because they situated their analyses in a broad framework of concerns. Halliday (1978) and Jakobson (1971) were the only major linguists who also did work in 'stylistics', work which was outstanding in comparison with most other examples of this practice. A useful introductory text in this tradition is Carter, *Language and Literature*, 1982. For a critical survey, see Birch 1988.

Social stylistics has had a different trajectory. Here the most significant work (on which the present chapter draws extensively) is the 'Critical Linguistics' tradition, as formulated in Kress and Hodge, *Language as Ideology*, 1979, Fowler et al., *Language and Control*, 1979, R. Fowler, *Literature as Social Discourse*,

1981, and *Linguistic Criticism*, 1986, and a recent collection edited by P. Chilton, *Language and the Nuclear Arms Debate*, 1985.

Some Marxists have used a fairly traditional form of stylistics to good effect, to read the ideological meanings of specific forms of grammar and language. See e.g. Goldmann, *The Hidden God*, 1964, Jameson, *Marxism and Form*, 1971, and Pecheux, *Language, Semantics and Ideology*, 1982. Whorf's social reading of forms of grammar (*Language, Thought and Reality*, 1956) left itself open to criticism for its hyperbolic claims, but still made a major contribution to social stylistics.

Social stylistics has more to learn from sociolinguistic theories of language than from traditional formalistic linguistics. Labov, *Sociolinguistic Patterns*, 1972, treats 'style' as a social marker, with social meaning. Style in this sense includes markers such as pronunciation and grammar, and this theory is a useful basis for looking at attitudes to the markers of 'literacy' and 'correctness' that underlie the conservative attack on the teaching of English. Social stylistics could also play a decisive role in the long-standing debate over the role of grammar in the teaching of English, since it makes sense of an object of teaching normally associated with 'Back to Basics' ideologues, but with a very different orientation.

Labovian sociolinguistics also provides an appropriate framework for looking at linguistic prejudice and language policies directed at minorities within English or across different languages. Hebdige's *Subculture: the Meaning of Style*, 1979, analyses the oppositional meanings constructed through style, in a way that is entirely compatible with the kinds of social stylistics I have been describing in this chapter.

Style is a major category within art history, but not usually understood as having a social meaning: but see Berger's *Ways of Seeing*, 1973. Within 'History' the use of art is, like literature, seen as a difficult interdisciplinary enterprise, not a central activity (see e.g. the earnest discussion in a special edition of the *Journal of Interdisciplinary History* edited by Rabb and Brown (1986) and their editorial 'The Evidence of Art: Images and Meaning in History'). The centrality of this enterprise for historians is argued forcefully by Porter, 'Seeing the Past', 1988, drawing explicitly on semiotic theory.

The nexus of style, ideology and medium in the semiosic regimes of 'literacy' and 'oralcy' are also important to historians and to the debate within English pedagogy about the forms of literacy (see e.g. Spencer, 'Emergent Literacies: a Site for Analysis', 1986). Here the provocative generalizations of McLuhan (*The Gutenberg Galaxy*, 1962; *Understanding Media*, 1964), and the more specific propositions of Goody and Watt ('The Consequences of Literacy', 1968) warrant further research and more precise formulation. See also Ong's useful overview *Orality and Literacy*, 1982.

Many of the central issues of feminism and feminist history concern aspects of social stylistics: the issues of women's and men's distinct 'voice' and language and culture, and their mediation through a dominant language and social order that sustain a patriarchal order. For the case that women's language and women's writing have distinctive features, see Cixous, 'The Laugh of the Medusa', 1980. A recent book that shows the value of a subtle analysis of language, style and ideology for feminism is Poovey, *The Proper Land and the Woman Writer: Ideology as Style in the Works of Mary Wollstonecraft, Mary Shelley and Jane Austen*, 1984.

On Arnold's style as an ideological achievement, see the influential work by

Trilling, *The Liberal Imagination*, 1951. On the Victorian 'crisis of faith' an authoritative work is Chadwick's *The Secularisation of the European Mind in the Nineteenth Century*, 1975. On American Puritanism, an important influence has been Miller, *The New England Mind*, 1961. On Franklin, see Esmond Wright, *Franklin of Philadelphia*, 1986. On Defoe a recent introduction is Bell, *Defoe's Fiction*, 1985.

On the relation between religion and the development of capitalism in NICs in Asia, see Perkins. 'The East Asian Development Experience', 1985. For a helpful introduction to classic haiku, see Henderson, *An Introduction to Haiku*, 1958, which gives literal plus free translations with commentary on some famous examples of the form. On the Japanese language see Young and Nakajuma–Okano, *Learn Japanese*, 1984. On Japanese history see Storry, *A Short History of Modern Japan*, 1975. On the problem of translation, for the case that translation is impossible, see Steiner, *After Babel*, 1975.

5

Transformations

Theories of literature and art have always been concerned with the complex and problematic relations between texts and their objects, between 'art' and 'life' or 'nature'. The relations involve both identity, because works of art are typically 'about' something, their 'object', and difference, since objects of works of art are always transformed in various ways. A theory of literary transformations, explicit or unacknowledged, is therefore at the base of almost every theory of literature. By 'transformation' I mean simply a constructed difference. A transformational theory, then, is one that attempts to account for relations of difference and identity in terms of agency and process. It looks at what is changed to what, and who is doing it and why. Transformational theory within the framework of social semiotics will also presume that these acts of transformation refer to material social events, so that transformational analysis will be concerned with social agencies and conditions as part of its account of transformational phenomena.

A theory of this kind offers a powerful and comprehensive account of reading and writing and the processes of the literary construction of meaning. At various times, literary theories have privileged the role of the author/producer or the reader/audience, but both roles become significant only in so far as they are theorized as the site of major transformational activity; for instance the author as creator of a 'world' or 'vision', the reader as the necessary (re) constructor of the meanings of the text if it is to exist as a literary event.

Any study of the transformational work that has constituted literary texts at all times will soon recognize that the relation between a text and what it is about is never more than one part of a broader transformational phenomenon. Texts always refer to, incorporate or displace other texts, in a continuous process of intertextuality. The act of reading situates one text among others related in terms of genre, context or purpose. The word 'reading' itself ambiguously refers, in literary criticism, to two semiosic acts, one an act of interpretation that attempts to reconstruct the original act of production, the other a piece of writing which incorporates the text-as-read into a new text. Different kinds of reading texts, such as commentaries, paraphrases, translations, exist as distinct genres themselves, organized by rules of intertextuality which specify what transformational relations can be expected. Kinds of intertextuality have been important in the institution of literature at all times, regulated by a set of transformations which are prescribed or forbidden to specific classes of agent, under specific conditions. The forms and conditions of intertextuality have been so multifarious and variable in different periods that literary criticism needs an appropriately powerful and coherent theory of transformations.

Other disciplines have been productively concerned with aspects of transformational theory, and have much to contribute to social semiotics and the analysis of literary texts. Freud's work, formulated within the context of psychoanalysis, remains an important and influential contribution to a general theory of transformations. He enlarged the scope of such a theory by tracing the same fundamental set of transformational processes in dreams, jokes and symptoms as in literature and art. Some of Freud's particular analytic moves have been rightly criticized for lapsing into unverifiable speculation, but a great strength of Freud's basic theory of transformations from the point of view of social semiotics is the rigorous materialism which determines its premises. Freud usefully called transformations a kind of *work*, insisting that it is a form of action which involves identifiable individuals with discoverable reasons or motives working on texts and meanings which exist in some form in the present or the past.

Unfortunately, most of the relevant pre-texts in most media quickly cease to exist, and they have to be reconstructed from texts that survive. Written texts survive better than texts in other media, but even with literary texts the task of tracing transformational processes involves speculative reconstructions and irrecoverable moments of transformation. This fact can make transformational analysis seem irredeemably speculative, especially when it is deployed on texts from the past. But it is one thing for a materialist theory to recognize the intrinsic difficulty of a strictly materialist transformational form of analysis, and quite another to use this difficulty to justify abandoning the search for prior texts. Freud's own analyses involved speculative leaps that others have found unconvincing, but these were stages in a process that included the careful, meticulous collection and reconstruction of a multiplicity of texts. Transformational analysis necessarily rests on guesses, but some guesses are better than others. It is in search of the basis for better guesses that I would commend a materialist theory of transformations, such as underpins both good Freudian analysis and also conventional notions of 'sound scholarship' in literary or historical studies, even though traditional scholars might be surprised to have Freud as bedfellow.

A transformational theory and strategy is at the base of every reading and writing practice in the disciplines of the humanities and social sciences. Historians of all kinds, for instance, deploy specific transformational operations on the texts that constitute their primary data, and every text that they produce is itself positioned against countless other texts and structures of meaning by those who read and use it. So a general transformational theory is a powerful form of critique of these specific disciplinary practices. The documents that historians typically read as static, self-contained pieces of information originally functioned as part of a transformational network, and it is this network that has the explanatory power that is the real target of all historians.

A concept of transformations also plays a crucial though invisible role in debates about the purposes of English in the classroom, and the goals of literacy. This debate takes a number of forms, opposing such categories as reading and writing, process and product, criticism and competence, creativity and control, but underlying differences on particular issues is a more fundamental dispute about the proper role and value of transformational capacities. For instance in a programmatic statement about the role of English in the 1980s, David Horner wrote:

> Our aim in the 1980s will be to help students understand how and why a variety of forms of text are created. Our aim will be to help them to see how and why their culture is constantly being created and recreated. Our expectation is to help students to perceive their place in culture, interpret their experience of it and acquire the means to change it . . . To achieve these ends we will have to treat literature in ways radically different from those of common practice. (1982: 75)

Horner here sets transformational power at the centre of the English curriculum, as the primary objective of English teaching, because he assumes that culture itself is constantly undergoing transformation, so that children can only fully enter into their culture if they become active agents of change, prepared for this role by their grasp of prior changes and the process of change itself. 'Radicals' and 'conservatives' alike agree on this basic diagnosis, though not of course on what should be done about it. Conservatives for instance typically accept that change is endemic, but that is precisely why it should be stopped or controlled. Prophets of doom from left and right condemn the one-dimensional mind of mass consumers in a frenetic post-modern society, the mass inability to see behind surfaces to the underlying constitutive processes. So a transformational capacity is desired as an urgent educational priority, even by those who despair of achieving it. The role of texts from the past in conservative pedagogies is in fact to enable reverse transformations, establishing a route back from the depressing and shallow present to a golden past, golden because it is the past. The issue in practice is not after all over the existence or importance of transformations, but over which transformations of which objects should be enabled, for which people under whose control.

Formalism and its uses

The transformational processes constituting literary texts are so continuous and operate at so many levels that any formal method of analysis is liable to drastically limit a sense of the fluidity and complexity of the meanings at issue. Transformational analysis is itself an intervention which transforms its object at the very moment it is claiming to represent its essential nature. But this is true of every strategy of interpretation, and with formal analysis as with other genres of interpretative discourse, we can use this awareness as the basis for informed wariness, rather than be reduced to silence or deafness.

In this spirit I want to introduce an elementary set of terms and conventions towards a formal method of transformational analysis. The first convention is a double arrow, ⇒, indicating a proposed transformation and its direction. The second convention is the use of brackets to indicate a hypothetical or reconstructed element, since the difference between an existing and a reconstructed element is so crucial. The third convention is the naming of the agent of the transformation (in brackets, where this is offered as a guess). This is necessary in order to clarify claims about agency, which are crucial to social semiotic analysis and the relations between semiosic and mimetic meanings and transformations.

To indicate something of how these conventions can be used in a formal analysis I will take the 'manuscript' of early drafts of Keats's famous poem 'Ode to a Nightingale', as reproduced by Monty Python.

~~Batman~~
'Ode to a ~~Gynaecologist~~
Night~~watchman~~
ingale

aches
~~pong~~
My heart ~~goes ping~~
drowsy
And a ~~lousy~~ numbness pains my sense
Hemlock
As though of ~~Watney's I had drunk~~
emptied some dull opiate to the drains
Or ~~thrown up all over your carpet~~
~~Alright, officer I'll come quietly~~

The Keatsian scholar may possibly query the authenticity of this text, but for the moment we will accept the claim that this is a draft of a poem by 'Keats' and that the transformations are his. The title has been considerably rewritten: 'Ode to a barman/gynaecologist/night(watchman)/ingale', listing the alternatives in the order that they appear from top to bottom. But the crucial order for interpretation is the reconstructed order in which they were composed in real time. The text contains clues (mainly from positioning) which allow us to hypothesize a different order: 'Keats': gynaecologist ⇒ barman ⇒ nightwatchman ⇒ nightingale. This is the order I will analyze, though different orders could be hypothesized, with different meanings resulting from each. This sequence has two kinds of meaning in the normal semiotic way. One is a mimetic meaning, the product of the syntagms and paradigms that make up each sequence. The other is a semiosic meaning, the meaning of the semiosic syntagms assuming a particular kind of agent ('Keats' in this case) and a specific context.

The transformation of 'gynaecologist' to 'barman' is the first move in this chain. Strictly speaking this may seem merely an alternative selection from a paradigmatic set which contains these two terms (among others). Here as always, the meaning of choosing each term is derived from the features which distinguish them. In this instance, as is usually the case, there are a number of features that different readers could invoke to distinguish between the two terms, thus producing different meanings. 'Gynaecologist' is opposed to 'barman' by features including professional/specialist/high-status versus commercial/non-specialist/low-status, and by gender assumptions (gynaecologists serve women, barmen serve men). But establishing the terms of difference is also the crucial first step in establishing the meaning of the transformation, since the meaning of a transformation is precisely the movement across difference. In this case, the meaning of 'barman' includes both the choice of the features that determine it and also the repudiation of the opposing features that determined 'gynaecologist'.

The text we have in front of us gives evidence of something stronger than choice, since 'Keats' has not just chosen one word ('barman') from the set, he has transformationally deleted one specific word ('gynaecologist') and replaced it with another. Yet the meanings of a paradigmatic choice are similar to those of a paradigmatic transformation. Both are the meanings attributed to an action (choice or transformation) by features that constitute its terms.

The same kind of analysis can be applied to each successive transformation, or to clusters of them. With gynaecologist ⇒ barman ⇒ nightwatchman, these first three units can be treated as a single semiotic chunk, opposed to nightingale by the features common to them all (i.e. human/non-poetic), as against the nightingale's classification as non-human/

poetic. It's important to insist that even if there's an agreed series of textual elements, there is still not a single meaning to the transformational process. Even the chosen starting point is arbitrary, since before 'gynaecologist' there may have been other terms.

Our analysis is not complete, however, without an attempt to specify the agent of these transformations in the semiosic plane: in this case 'Keats'. The semiosic syntagm at issue here is constituted by the meaning of this agent and the meaning of his action. 'Keats' here has the conventional value of 'poet' – a major poet engaged in his poetic craft, at the height of his powers writing what is currently labelled as one of his major works. The semiosic syntagm that links agent, text and transformation here is constituted by an unmediated opposition between the poetic/aesthetic/spiritual/high status of the poet and the non-poetic/pragmatic/materialist/low status of his original topic and most of his transformations.

All the other corrections in the 'draft' signify this structure of oppositions or contradictions. So do the oppositions within the syntagms as originally written by 'Keats'. For instance, 'Ode' in the title is a traditional poetic term, whereas 'barman/gynaecologist' is not. The same is true of the syntagm 'my heart' plus 'goes ping/pong'. The meaning and effect of the aberrant syntagms in the text, all of them except for the final version, could be read as part of a parody whose effect is clearly equivalent to the meanings of the semiosic syntagms constituted by the transformations. The resemblance is not fortuitous. Transformations are a kind of syntagm, to be read like any other syntagm. They are simultaneously an event and a meaning, an event that signifies a meaning. What survives in text is a set of products, no longer the process, but if the products carry traces of the process then they have that meaning.

My reading thus far may seem like naïve pedantry carried to absurd extremes, since in its context this text is not meant to be taken as an authentic lost manuscript by Keats, but as an irreverent parody by Monty Python. But the transformations I have reconstructed are crucial to the meaning of this text in any interpretation. They are at the base of its parodic function, sufficiently implied by various cues carefully planted by Monty Python. Reading this as parody requires us to recognize that their agent is Monty Python not Keats. With this different agent, we have to propose a second transformational sequence, with 'nightingale' in the title the first term not the last. This new order is the trace of a kind of reading whose aim was not to recover any buried original but to project a counter-text. This counter-text implicitly demands to be read as the intersection of two very different transformational choices: the pseudo-history (reconstructing the creative agonies of 'Keats') and the alternative projected history, which recognizes Monty Python's assault on a masterpiece of English poetry as significant action.

The Monty Python transformational work involves semiosic transformations as well as mimetic transformations. First, we have the transformation of the author of the Ode from Keats to 'Keats'. Again, the meaning of the transformation is given by a movement across the terms of difference: from a consumptive aesthete, lover and poet to an embarrassing and violent drunk. We also have another semiosic transformation, occurring in the semiosic frame itself. The convention of publishing first drafts is a recognized genre, and it is this genre not Keats's Ode which is being parodied here. The author in this genre is labelled 'scholar', the kind of scholar who attempts to record minutiae associated with the works of great writers. The author of the parody, then, is an 'anti-scholar', as indifferent to historical accuracy as the scholar is obsessed with it. Monty Python is the agent of this transformation, rather than the anti-scholar, who is a fiction constructed by Monty Python.

The Monty Python parody clearly has a subversive intention and meaning, and these are carried primarily by the transformational work it is understood to be doing. The mimetic transformations, 'discovering' a real-world prior text for Keats's poem, open a space for questions about Keats's own real-world prior text, and the transformational processes by which it was constructed. These concern the 'how and why' a text like this was created, and beyond this the 'how and why' the culture that it derives from was constituted and maintained. The transformation of Keats to 'Keats' and the scholar to the anti-scholar imply acts of protest against the English literary canon and its official guardians that raise further questions about cultural transformations and systems of control.

However, it's necessary to point out that this text on its own cannot shake the pillars of the establishment. That is because the transformational work does not have a single or irresistible ideological value in isolation from specific contexts, purposes and domains. As published it functioned in a popular domain where educational regimes do not hold sway and therefore are not effectively challenged. The same text produced or studied within a school setting would have a different semiosic meaning and effect. Parody, irreverence, or any hostility to great poems, great poets and serious scholars are not encouraged within English, at any level. Yet if transformational capacity is a primary component of powerful and flexible semiosic strategies, then even so crude a tactic as parody should be a more valued and common activity than it currently is in English, along with a whole range of other strategies for tracking and generating transformations.

Transformations and the buried text

The Monty Python 'ode' is a good text to illustrate transformational excavation of buried texts precisely because this one is not buried but carefully planted and designed to be seen. Usually the search for buried texts is more difficult and always in some sense labelled as inappropriate, since the act of burial declares the intention of the burier to conceal this level of meaning. Exhumation is always an assault on the property of another. Reading and interpretation are always political acts, whose social meanings are given by the semiosic dimension.

Freud's seductive example reveals dangers as well as attractions in the process of exhumation. The psychoanalytic encounter consisted of clients employing another, an expert other, to recover a text that they had irrecoverably buried. The psychiatrist was a detective paid to expose the criminal concealed within the patient, and to bring the criminal (unconscious) text to the sanitizing light of day. But such a semiosic context and set of semiosic rules are very specific. We need a broader framework that recognizes that different kinds of texts are more or less deeply and irrecoverably buried by different kinds of agent, and that acts of burying and exhuming can have widely different kinds of meaning.

Freud was concerned with highly private texts which were buried by the individuals but which erupted through the surface to trouble their personal lives. Some theories of culture suggest that culture itself functions as a kind of buried text. Theories of cultural reproduction (see e.g. Bourdieu 1977) see culture as an instrument to reproduce difference, through a set of knowledges that are unequally distributed in a society by means of the unequal distribution of capacities to read the primary cultural texts. Anyone can go into a museum or library or a great cathedral, the argument runs; but only the cultured can read these texts in a powerful way to produce the authoritative tokens of culture that mark them as members of the elite. The argument applies with special force to the written culture that is transmitted in the subject English. 'Cultural literacy' in this sense includes transformational abilities at its core. However, the 'buried texts' controlled by these transformational processes are highly desirable but restricted commodities, not ubiquitous but forbidden, as is the case with the objects of Freudian analysis.

I want now to show how a transformational framework can enable these issues to be usefully examined in specific instances, by focusing on a single literary text, 'Philomela', a poem by Matthew Arnold. In the previous chapter we examined Arnold as a 'representative mind' for his age and class in mid-nineteenth-century England. Arnold was also a consummate ideologue who argued on behalf of what he called 'culture' as an instrument of salvation for his embattled class and nation, as he saw it. His major work along these lines was titled *Culture and Anarchy*. In it he opposed those two categories as the alternatives the English nation must choose between. 'Culture' in his argument had a double form, oriented to a double audience. Arnold himself was a product of the public school system, whose curriculum was firmly based on Latin and Greek classics, but he was employed as an inspector in Her Majesty's schools, where he recognized that quite different priorities had to apply for the lower classes. So 'Culture' in his polemics incorporated both religion and literature, and within the category of literature it blurred the boundary between vernacular literature (mainly in English) and the classics of Latin and Greek.

Arnold's programmatic claims on behalf of literature proved a very powerful basis for the legitimation of English in the curriculum, and he has become one of the acknowledged founding fathers of the discipline. However, for Arnold himself, the position of Latin and Greek was both more ambiguous but more important as components of the 'culture' that he proposed, with Greek (less well developed even in the public schools) the more crucial. Arnold praised the spirit of 'Hellenism' as characterized by 'sweetness and light', in which 'the idea of beauty, harmony and complete human perfection [were] so present and paramount'. He acknowledged that this tendency needed to be complemented by what he called 'Hebraism' or the Judeo-Christian moral sense, the 'moral fibre' which needed to be considerably more braced than the Greeks ever managed, and gave an all-important consciousness of sin. In Arnold's history of Western culture Hellenism appeared first and was found wanting, and had to be replaced by Hebraism. In his analysis, the time had come for a return of Hellenism, in a suitably modified form.

The text we will look at, 'Philomela', declares its relevance to this debate through its title, a word of Greek origin referring to myths about the nightingale from ancient Greece and Rome. I will quote three sections of the poem.

> Hark! – ah, the nightingale –
> The tawny-throated!
> Hark, from that moonlit cedar what a burst!
> What triumph! hark! – what pain!   (1–4)

> Dost thou tonight behold,
> Here, through the moonlight on this English grass,
> The unfriendly palace in the Thracian wild?
> Dost thou again peruse
> With hot cheeks and seared eyes
> The too-clear web, and thy dumb sister's shame?   (16–21)

> Listen, Eugenia –
> How thick the bursts come crowding through the leaves!
> Again – thou hearest?
> Eternal passion!
> Eternal pain!   (28–32)

In order to interpret this text at even the most basic level we need to project a fuller absent text. One entirely normal strategy for doing this is to use a knowledge of English and common-sense versions of reality assumed to be shared by English-speakers as the basis for reversing some transformations which are signalled by the text. For instance we know that people and not buildings are friendly, so 'the unfriendly palace' invites us to project a fuller form: '(x is) unfriendly (to y) (in a) palace'. It is then obvious to ask who is/are this person (or persons) and why are they being unfriendly to y, who we can guess from the text is Philomela, the nightingale. This explanation is so unsatisfactory that we're likely to either invent a fuller narrative or look up the myth. It turns out as we shall see that there are a number of versions of the myth, but for the moment we can use standard works on Greek mythology to enrich the hidden text with a few actors and a basic narrative. Tereus, ancient king of Thrace, first married Procne, daughter of Pandion king of Athens, and then lusted after her younger sister Philomela. He abducted and raped Philomela, and then cut out her tongue so that she could not tell her sister. The dumb Philomela wove the story into a cloth for her sister and Procne the lawful wife killed her son Itys in revenge and sent him to Tereus, who ate him unawares. When Tereus found out, he attempted to kill the two sisters, but all three were changed by the gods into birds.

The myth not only gives us the fuller cast of characters whose existence we suspected, it also makes 'unfriendly' seem a remarkably weak word, to describe the complex narratives of rape, murder and cannibalism in the myth. The difference between the two buried texts – the grammatical projection by the non-classical reader and the fuller version available to the classically educated – is striking. For the non-classical, the buried text is a lost world where vague unfriendliness existed. For the classical, however, the sequence is, in broad outline, as follows: 'A: (rape, murder, cannibalism) ⇒ unfriendliness'. Arnold is the agent of this transformation, which offers the ignorant a sanitized version of the classics, but to the well informed (classically trained) it might arouse a respect for the sanitizing work Arnold has done. In a stark form we see the double face of culture created before our eyes: one a feeble version for the uncultured, the other a much more gutsy version for the cultured.

The language of this text is marked by many other regular transformational processes which could be included in a basic grammar of English. For instance the phrase 'dost thou behold?' is an archaic form for 'do you behold?', and the question derives from the indicative 'you (do) behold'. We can take this a step backward, seeing 'behold' as an archaic version of 'see' (though this step might have occurred earlier in the transformation chain). In this poem, the question 'do you see?' seems to imply a prior 'I see': and behind this is a statement of the existence of the object of perception, 'is'. As with all such transformational reconstructions, this one is a hypothesis not a fact, and others may dispute particular details. With this caveat I will set out the sequence as I have reconstructed it:

A: (it is) ⇒ (I see it is) ⇒ (I) behold ⇒ (you) behold ⇒ do (you) behold ⇒ dost thou behold.

In the previous instance, the transformations were primarily mimetic, and affected the meaning directly. Most of these transformations are primarily semiosic, and do not so obviously affect the meaning. But the semiosic meaning of these semiosic transformations is more or less as follows. The starting point is a consciousness of an object ('it is'): then a consciousness of that act of consciousness: then a displacement of that selfconsciousness from everyday discourse of the present to aestheticized discourse of the past: then a transformation of the self to the other in the discourse ('I' to 'you'): then a shift of authority in the semiosic frame (from 'I' to 'you'), with a weakening of the authority of the utterance, since it isn't certain that the other does 'behold' the scene; and finally the use of the archaic form ('dost thou') which distances this from the present, as did the use of 'behold'. The cumulative effect of all this semiosic work is not to obscure the mimetic content of the text greatly, but to render obscure the text of Arnold's relationship to his own perception, so that it all seems fanciful, 'poetic' and easy to disregard.

What Arnold/the nightingale beholds is a contrasting set of scenes, whose terms are located in space ('here' = 'this English grass' *v.* (there) = 'the Thracian wild') and time ('tonight' *v.* classical or pre-classical times). 'Behold' relates these categories through the narrative of a hypothetical journey which the bird might have taken. This equivalence between a journey (within a narrative) and a transformation (by a narrator or author) is a very common phenomenon in narrative, which provides a powerful aid to a transformational analysis of texts of many kinds. Again an attempt to be meticulous about the order of these processes and their individual meaning is essential. I will begin, then, with a first transformation that leads to the present text:

1   Philomela: Journey (past ⇒ present: Thrace ⇒ England)
    ⇓
2   (Arnold): transformation: (present ⇒ past, England ⇒ Thrace)

This is a complex operation. Arnold has transformed his own cognitive act (his double transformation of the scene before him) into a physical act, a journey by a different agent, the bird. Thus there is a transformation of himself into the bird (i.e. he becomes a buried but recoverable agent of the journey). The bird's journey, however, follows his 'journey' in reverse, since it has (in the poem's fiction) come from the past and Thrace. The two forms, then, have common terms but opposite directions, and also they are classified in different ways: as cognitive versus physical act, as journey versus transformation.

But Philomela's journey in this poem is a substitute for the journey she and her sister took in the original myth. This act of substitution can be regarded as another tranformation whose agent again is Arnold, and the original journey itself as a transformation (by an unknown agent) of primary cultural categories for the society of the time. This original journey was between Athens (representing culture, to the ancient Greek authors of the story) and Thrace (a wild outlier of the Greek hegemony). In the myth there is another division of places along similar lines, between a place in the woods where one of the sisters is kept after she has had her tongue removed, and Tereus' 'palace', where he lives with his son and wife. The action moves from the place of crime in the woods back to the palace, where the act of revenge occurs. The two sisters then flee to the woods, and change to a nightingale, a bird of the woods, and a swallow, whose habitat is with civilization, nesting under the eaves of houses. The full narrative, then, contains a number of journeys between nature and culture, moving in both directions. The journey between Athens and Thrace also involves a major change of status for the two sisters: from a comfortable pre-sexual existence with their father Pandion to a dangerous adult existence, where the choice for the women is married neglect and / or violence, or extramarital rape: i.e. from youth, innocence and joy to maturity, danger and suffering.

All these narratives and the meanings they carry exist as possible buried texts behind Arnold's own narrative. For purposes of interpretation the doubt arises whether Arnold is the agent who buried these narratives, or whether they were interred somehow before he became aware of them. Such doubts are endemic in transformational analysis. They are not, however, good reasons not to attempt it: only reasons for proceeding warily at every stage.

We can be reasonably sure, however, that the main terms of the journey did exist as part of Arnold's buried text, since these terms are redundantly present in so many component narratives or episodes in the original, and are also present in Arnold's own final text. That is, Philomela/Procne's journey from youth to maturity, civilization to wild nature, has been transformed to Philomela's journey from past to present, and from Thrace to an England which is specified as civilized and tame ('English grass'). This journey, which is the narrative in the actual text, is the end-point or fusion of at least two earlier partly buried texts: the mythic narrative, and the narrative of Arnold's own transformational work.

The 'sweetness and light' of the Hellenic mind is already hopelessly compromised by now, and replaced for Arnold by a primitive, dark and brutal world in which civilization is at risk. We have no option now but to follow his nightingale back in time to hear the worst, as a classical scholar like Arnold would report it if he were being honest (a virtue which he would of course normally try to avoid). Classical sources give us two versions of myth, one of which can be labelled Greek, since most extant Greek sources give it, while the other, usually later, is Latin. In the Greek version, Philomela, who has her tongue cut out, is transformed to a swallow, while Procne the murderous mother becomes a nightingale. In the Latin version, Philomela is the captive in the wood, is raped and loses her tongue but becomes the nightingale, and Procne the mother becomes the swallow.

Arnold would certainly have known both these versions. His text implies which version he endorsed: the nightingale peruses the 'too clear web' (which was woven by Philomela, the violated sister). So like a good Hellenist it seems that he followed the Greek version, and his nightingale is Procne, the murderous mother. In an early version that has survived, this becomes unmistakable: after line 21 he had added:

> Dost thou still reach
> Thy husband, weak avenger, through thyself?

But the title of the poem as published is 'Philomela', aligning the poem with the Latin versions which had Philomela turning into a nightingale. The original version was untitled. So he seems to have composed a Hellenist poem, then half transformed it to the Latin version by giving it a Latinist title.

The analysis seems to have taken us into a confused and trivial debate, of the kind that might delight the sort of scholar parodied by Monty Python but no one else. But what is at issue is a complex set of transformational relationships of the kind anthropologists like Lévi-Strauss try to understand in their analysis of different versions of a myth. In order to make sense of the complex process, once again we need to be clear about structures and changes, order and agency. The Greek version as the earlier is a proper place to start, so we will set out the structural core of this version as follows:

1 Tereus marries Procne (legitimate sexuality) and rapes Philomela (illegitimate sexuality).
2 He deceives Procne but she discovers his secret: he silences Philomela but she communicates.
3 Procne kills her son and feeds him to his father: Tereus eats his own son.
4 Procne is changed to a nightingale (a wild, eloquent and private bird): Philomela is changed to a swallow (a tame, non-eloquent and domestic bird): Tereus is changed to a hoopoe.

This order follows the narrative. The first three describe actions with a common set of participants: the first in the sphere of sexuality, the second in the sphere of knowledge or communication, the third in the sphere of nurture (production and consumption of food). This order, like the order in a journey, encodes transformational relations. Tereus' rape of Philomela is an inverse transformation of his formal sexual relations with Procne, and that split is replicated as it is transformed into the sphere of knowledge, where Tereus attempts to cancel communication in the two halves of his split mate, so that his licit unbeloved will hear nothing, and his illicit beloved will say nothing. But each reverses the prohibition, one hearing / learning the forbidden act, the other communicating it. Because of this inversion, Procne becomes an anti-mother, killing instead of creating life, and Tereus becomes an ignorant anti-father, consuming instead of providing for his son.

Thus far the narrative is common to Greek and Latin versions. The crucial difference is at step 4, where the gods intervene with a literal transformation. We will treat this as we have treated other transformations, analyzing the meaning of the work it does, and assigning it to an agent, in this case 'the gods'. But there are considerable difficulties with the Greek version of the transformation of the two sisters. Procne was the sister associated with the domestic sphere, with procreation and motherhood, and her problems with communication concerned listening, not speech. All these are properties of the swallow. Philomela was associated with wildness, nature, sexuality and triumphant communication, properties of the nightingale. The Greek gods, it seemed, got the transformations wrong. The Latin versions, then, were simply correcting a 'mistake' in originals which they otherwise deferred to. They were under strong pressure to do so, since in both Latin and later Greek the word 'philomela' came to mean 'nightingale'. The pressure that was too much for Arnold to resist had already been too much for Latin and later Greek authors.

But a 'mistake' repeated by so many writers becomes an interesting phenomenon. Precisely because it is so illogical, transferring the qualities of each sister to the opposite bird, it serves to cut the meaning of the bird off from the meaning of the narrative. It then becomes difficult to associate the wild beautiful song of the nightingale with Procne the murderous mother, and the darting domestic swallow with Philomela. The effect of that transformation is to help to bury the grisly narrative, not to recall it: overlaying its message with the inoffensive beauty of a nightingale's song. It is a clear example of what Arnold saw as the Hellenist transformation of irrationality into harmony and beauty – though the grisly narrative is also there in the Greek tale. But Arnold's ambiguous reference to both sets of myth does further transformational work. His nightingale is both Procne and Philomela, the two halves of womanhood (wife and mistress, illicit lover and excessively licit wife) fused in a single person / bird. Part of the work he has done is to eliminate the swallow, unnecessary now because the ambiguous nightingale carries both sets of meaning.

His own narrative has no mention of the Tereus-bird, the hoopoe. But no version of the myth, Arnold's included, has any mention of a bird equivalent for one person in the myth: Itys the murdered son. If switching birds helps to bury the narrative of the sisters, Itys's non-transformation into a bird is an even stronger deletion from the text. Itys' role is puzzling in another way. Why is his mother's act in killing him, and his father's in eating him, treated as a matter of indifference by the gods? Why was the mother not punished, somewhat more than the innocent sister/aunt? This curious feature of the myth points to the suppression of another text, the Itys text, which is both present and absent in the full myth.

The Itys text is the text of a son who is killed by an anti-mother, and eaten by an anti-father. If we were interested in Greek mythography rather than Arnold's text we might investigate other versions of this motif (e.g. Kronos, who swallowed his sons, including Zeus; Medea, who killed her sons in revenge against her husband Jason). But there is one Greek legend which has assumed a key place in modern views of Greek myth: the Oedipal myth, subject of some famous plays by Sophocles, who was Arnold's favourite dramatist and the inspiration for Freud's theory of the Oedipal complex. The central event of the Oedipal myth is the son who marries his mother and kills his father. But in the full Oedipal narrative this is linked causally (and therefore transformationally) to the events of Oedipus' birth, where his mother left him to starve (anti-nurture) for the sake of his father, who was therefore the 'innocent' agent of his son's death. This is a version of the Itys myth; and the Oedipal narrative established clear links between the Itys myth and the Oedipal myth (in its classic form) – links which can be attributed to Sophocles and Greek narrators as their own meanings, not to Freud or to Arnold as nineteenth-century readers.

This excursion into Greek myth is liable to encourage one kind of misinterpretation of Arnold's text, not least because his poem encourages it by pointing backwards for the resolution of the difficulties. Arnold's text, in fact, is formed by the interaction of two texts, which we can call the Philomela text and the Eugenia text. In terms of quantity the Philomela text is dominant by twenty-seven lines to five, and the wealth of texts from Greek mythology tempts us into increasing this dominance. 'Eugenia' appears (an assumed name) at line 28, and she is given only one action: to listen/hear/hark. We are told so little about her that we can suppose we are being instructed by the poet to ask nothing. 'Eugenia' represents a text carefully buried by the poet, and if we respected his wishes we would ask no further.

However, while we have a transformational spade in our hands, let us continue to dig. 'Eugenia' declares a meaning rather than an identity. It comes from the Greek, meaning 'well bred' or 'aristocratic by birth'. Since this poem was published in 1853, and probably not finished in final form for the 1852 edition of Arnold's poetry, we can provisionally date it, in its final form, between 1851 and 1852, though its prior version could be earlier. Arnold had two significant romantic attachments that have reached the records. One was to a French girl, 'Marguerite', subject of many poems, whom he seems to have had an affair with between 1848 and 1849, but she for some reason was not good enough for young Matthew. The second was Frances Wightman, daughter of Justice Sir William Wightman, who felt that Matthew and his prospects were not good enough for his beloved Frances. But Wightman's consent was finally obtained, and the wedding took place in June 1851. Arnold's father-in-law had a house at Hampton, by the Thames, where Arnold often stayed after his marriage. Since this poem mentions 'the sweet, tranquil Thames', it seems likely that it was composed at the Wightman house (or 'palace') and that 'Eugenia' referred to the cool and superior Frances, who finally honoured Matthew with her hand.

These identifications are not meant to imply that the events in this text 'really' happened. They are simply meant to give specific points of contact between meanings of the text and the structures and meanings organizing Arnold's social world. In these terms, the meaning of Eugenia (irrespective of whether Frances watched nightingales with him that moonlit night) comes from the opposition between Frances and Marguerite, replicating the opposition between Procne (the virtuous wife) and Philomela (the object of illicit love). Eugenia's task is to 'listen': to the poet and to the nightingale, with their common message of strong, painful and illicit emotions. But the text of her response is buried by Arnold, so it is not clear whether she could decode secret messages (like Procne) or speak in spite of being dumb (like Philomela). So 'Eugenia' is transformed, to become potentially both sisters or neither; just as the nightingale in the final version becomes both sisters, though she (like Eugenia) is primarily one of them, the good respectable one. This is an attempt, at the level of meanings, to fuse the qualities of 'Marguerite', whom he had loved and abandoned, with those of Frances, whom he had wooed and won.

The myth itself had points of contact with Arnold's own familial text. For most of his life he lived in the shadow of his famous father, Dr Thomas Arnold, headmaster of Rugby, who died in 1842, when Matthew was twenty. Poems like 'Rugby Chapel' state the son's sense of inadequacy before his father. Poems like 'Sohrab and Rustum' explore the situation of famous fathers who (accidentally) kill their aspiring sons. Arnold's life was like an Itys text in which the father died, not the son, condemning the son to live the endless death of fulfilling one's duty.

These observations are not 'facts' beyond dispute, but they still form part of a public text, one that is not buried. What is buried, however, is Arnold's reading of this text, and its relationship to texts such as 'Philomela'. The reconstruction of this relationship is therefore speculative: which requires us to proceed meticulously in our transformational analysis, so that errors and lapses will be more easily detected, if not always avoided. For Arnold as reader, his familial texts could have three points of contact with the Philomela text.

1   A: Matthew ⇒ Itys (living ⇒ dead son)
                        (virtuous mother ⇒ murdress)
                        (virtuous father ⇒ rapist)
2   A: Matthew ⇒ Tereus (respectable husband ⇒ adulterer)
                          (respectable husband ⇒ seducer)
3   A: Matthew ⇒ Philomela (m ⇒ f)
                        (son ⇒ mother/wife)

This transformational work follows a highly redundant pattern, splitting himself and significant others along the same line of cleavage: analogous to the split between Procne and Philomela in the myth or between 'Frances' and 'Marguerite' in his poems, or between Hellenism and Hebraism in his essays, but more stark and irreconcilable. But as with the Monty Python text, we presume a different order in reconstructing the transformational work that constitutes his final text. We can represent this schematically as follows:

$$\underbrace{\text{A's familial texts} \Rightarrow \text{mythic texts}}$$

⇓

Final text ('Philomela')

It remains for me to situate this reading and the kind of analysis I have employed. The 'buried texts', with their violent and subversive sexuality, sound like the typical results of a Freudian reading, but the texts that it draws on are not private dreams or symptoms, but well known and highly valued public texts. In fact, these texts occupied a privileged place in the educational programme that Arnold so influentially advocated, so these meanings do not remain a private matter between Arnold and ourselves as his unpaid analysts. The ambiguities of the 'buried text' connect with concepts he espoused as an earnest, respectable Victorian sage. His concepts of 'culture' (and poetry) contain an acute contradiction between licentious subversion and public duty, and between a universal audience (who need 'culture' as a central component in a mass education system) and an elite (who alone have access to its dangerous meanings). Arnold's position was not in favour of either licence or repression: instead it affirmed the unpleasant necessity and high cost of repression. As he wrote to his favourite sister on 25 January 1851 (at the same period of his life as he wrote 'Philomela'):

How strong the tendency is, though, as characters take their bent, and lives
their separate course, to submit oneself gradually to the silent influence
that attaches us more and more to those whose characters are like ours, and
whose lives are running the same way with our own, and that detaches us
from everything besides, as if we could only acquire any solidity of shape
and power of acting by narrowing and narrowing our sphere, and diminish-
ing the number of affections and interests which continually distract us
while young, and hold us unfixed and without energy to mark our place in
the world; which we thus succeed in marking only by making it a very
confined and joyless one.

This is a clear and direct account, by a not yet eminent Victorian, of the
transformational processes he was conscious of, shaping him for his class
position and function: the growing identity of interests along class lines;
the repudiation of both people and feelings that are inconvenient; the
sense of inevitability of the process; and finally the feeling of joylessness
and confinement as the process nears completion. It is an elegant and
explicit account of the ideological constitution of a social identity and a
transformational process. This socialization process, and Arnold's experience of it, are part of a social history of Victorian England. A study that
attempts to reconstruct the buried texts and specific transformation of
even a single text like 'Philomela' can contribute to that social history.

The crucial point to recognize, in this representative performance, is
that in some respects the two kinds of 'buried text' that we initially
opposed, the Freudian forbidden text and the privileged cultural text,
turn out to have a surprising degree of overlap. Arnold's reading of the
classics formed the basis of a kind of writing which also incorporated an
analogous capacity to read (and conceal his reading of) his own
pathologies. Self-analysis it seems was a component of the hidden curriculum of Arnoldian culture. The discipline of English has inherited this
component, in a form which however repudiates the name and control of
psychoanalysis, in favour of an ideology of 'personal growth' and 'self-
exploration' (see Mares 1988). But naturally there are limits put on the
'self' that is to be allowed to grow and be explored within the subject
English. An effective and productive understanding of the kinds of transformation that Freud was concerned with remains too powerful to be
available to all.

Ideology and competence

The category of ideology as originally formulated by Marx and Engels
privileged one major class of transformations, the inversion of representations of the social world, produced by ideologues on behalf of themselves
and their masters. Later reworkings of the category have tacitly recognized

that there is a greater variety of transformations at work in the construction of ideological versions, so that ideology does not always and equally refer to a false consciousness of an inverted world. The functions of ideology as described by Althusser in some respects parallel the functions of culture as described by Bourdieu. Althusser's theory marked an advance in theories of ideology in so far as it incorporated semiosic as well as mimetic meanings. Referring specifically to the Ideological State Apparatus (ISA) of education, he made a distinction between the reproduction of useful skills ('know-how') and the reproduction of sets of attitudes that are required to maintain the existing class society, differentiated like Bourdieu's 'culture' along class lines:

> i.e. reproduction of submission to the ruling ideology for the workers, and a reproduction of the ability to manipulate the ruling ideology correctly for the agents of exploitation and repression, so that they too will provide for the domination of the ruling class 'in words'. (Althusser 1971: 132)

What Althusser here calls 'manipulation' is clearly both a reception (reading) strategy and a production (writing) strategy, two aspects of a transformational capacity that is indispensable to a member of the ruling class, if they are not to be neutralized by their own ideological productions. As a reading strategy it enables (controlled) access to a powerful level of the meaning of texts: i.e. demystification. As a writing strategy it empowers the generation of new ideological texts: remystification. The maintenance of this difference will clearly need to be built into logonomic systems, which will specify and control who is to be allowed to use or know about the set of transformations at issue, and the knowledges that are their precondition. Where culture as described by Bourdieu seems merely an instrument to construct difference through unequal access to markers of prestige, Althusser is talking about a transformational capacity that seems to be a genuine competence, which justifies the dominance of the dominant. But in practice Bourdieu's 'culture' is not always easy to distinguish from Althusserian ideological competence, and in terms of a transformational framework there is no need to insist on an absolute difference.

One illuminating instance of the intersection of culture and ideological competence is the set of practices commonly referred to as 'etiquette'. Etiquette is normally seen as a rigid set of rules of good behaviour that mark cultivated persons on formal occasions. These rules of politeness or etiquette exclude or displace many things that otherwise those concerned think and say and do. That is, they are obligatory transformations, not a taken-for-granted set of behaviours. Much of what is excluded is not unconscious. On the contrary, polite people know exactly what isn't said or done in polite society, and they continue to say and think such things in other more private domains. Training in these rules is an explicit and conscious part of the socialization process, in many ways acting as an exemplary instance of the social control of behaviour.

In terms of a transformational framework, polite behaviour is a transformed text whose meaning is derived partly from its own mimetic content, and partly from the prior text from which it is transformationally derived. Politeness as a text encodes an ideological prescription, i.e. a version of society which is foregrounded on occasions of politeness. For instance the politeness code in Matthew Arnold's circles required men to stand in the presence of women. The ideological content of this rule is a world in which men defer to women like servants to their masters, an ideology of female superiority. However, polite males who knew that they should express exaggerated respect to women in these circumstance also knew that women in Victorian England had no vote, no entry into political life and great restrictions on their entry into economic life. This second version of gender relations is no less ideological than the first, but it also corresponded far more closely to the 'reality' of everyday life among the Victorian middle-classes. But the ideology inscribed into the politeness code (and there are many other instances) was not exactly a lie, since it was meant to deceive nobody. Its full meaning was a contradiction, the contradiction between its required meanings and the opposite equally required meanings that prevailed outside the domain of politeness. This full meaning, then, consisted of both polite behaviour and the transformational processes which constructed it. Social competence included both, and also the ability to move between the two, and to recognize which version had the overriding value.

In this respect, 'culture' in Arnold's scheme is like politeness, and the two contribute to a single social function. Both express social identity and mark membership of a class. Both function as a transformational capacity which confers power and status on those who can read through / deconstruct the privileged texts and recognize the presence and necessity of contradictory anchoring texts, containing an opposing ideological scheme. Those without this transformational power are bewildered and seduced by culture and politeness, equally excluded from the inner group by exaggerated respect or by angry rejection. And such exclusions are part of the function of these forms.

There is one important aspect of etiquette that connects directly with language and the practices of English: that is speech etiquette, pivoting around the concept of accent. Accent in the narrow sense, as a different way of pronouncing the 'same' sound, seems a trivial signifier of social difference to carry such weight. But a general theory of accent (cf. Voloshinov 1973) connects accent as a form of pronunciation with a complex set of signifiers of identity and difference which work like and alongside accents in speech as part of single functional whole: e.g. different choice of words or phrases to say 'the same thing', different topics or ideas

or experiences, different clothes, foods or habits which mark group identity and membership. The ensemble of these markers of difference make
up a culture, of the kind Arnold or Bourdieu was concerned with. They
also have an ideological meaning, since they imply a social world and a set
of social relationships.

Like other forms of etiquette, accents are usually described as though
they were rigid and absolute systems of difference, whereas in practice they
always refer to a repertoire of differences linked by known and available
transformations. All speakers move across part of the range in their own
production, and they are able to 'read' a much wider range than they
produce. So upper-class speakers immediately recognize and interpret a
lower-class accent, as a well understood deformation of a common norm,
which is not in fact their own class dialect. Lower-class speakers use the
same general model to interpret their own and others production. This
model, which incorporates the transformations that link the different
accents in a speech community, is an essential component of full social and
linguistic competence. As with systems of etiquette generally, the upper
extremes of accent are only properly used on formal occasions, and the
competent upper-class speaker must also be able to shift register into more
informal modes which are in some respects closer to low-class forms.
Similarly, 'lower-class' speakers also operate within a range, not from a
single stereotype.

In general accents signify class identity, whereas languages signify
national identity. But in practice different languages are only created
when the process of accent formation is carried beyond the point where it
still organizes a sufficiently unitary community. Accents on their own are
sufficient to signify national identity, and the national identities constructed within the English-speaking world (e.g. American, Australian,
Irish, West Indian) are all signified by distinctive accents. For each such
community there is an accent, which describes a continuum of styles of
speaking, and a stereotype, a single foregrounded position on the accent
continuum which is taken, however, to have a peculiar signifying power in
marking national identity. Educated speakers of English do not only speak
with a recognizable accent in this sense, they are also expected to possess a
repertoire of accents-plus-stereotypes (including those of many communities other than their own).

But if this knowledge remains in the form of a set of stereotypes, it is not
enabling but the reverse. Only as linked tacitly to a transformational
framework does it become powerful and enabling knowledge. The same is
true of another manifestation of accent that is of particular importance in
the teaching of English: the role of spelling as the signifier of literacy
within the traditional teaching of English, and for traditionalists in the
community. Spelling is the specific accent of the written code. So mis-
spellings (typically too close a correspondence to the spoken code) indicate

an inability to construct the difference of the written code, while mispronunciations show the inability to manage transformations from the written to the spoken code. In both cases, what is at issue is the demonstration of difference and its mastery.

National character is the signified which makes accent as signifier so important and complex a social phenomenon. My illustrations will concern the stereotype of the Australian National Character and the accent system which encodes it, but the same form of analysis applies to all other stereotypes within the English-speaking community. As constructed by actors like Paul Hogan and Barry Humphreys the 'Australian National Character' is a recognizable and saleable commodity in Britain and America as well as in Australia. At the core of the image is a set of qualities which together constitute an ideology. The stereotype Australian is easygoing, informal, hard-drinking, loyal to his mates, afraid of intimacy but fiercely egalitarian, refusing to acknowledge any differences of rank or class.

Australian critics either praise the legend as a radical ideal (e.g. Ward 1958) or condemn it as obnoxiously racist, sexist and inauthentic (e.g. McQueen 1970). But the greatest problem with the stereotype is that most Australians most of the time don't look or sound or behave in this way and never have done, any more than actual Irish people are typically Irish, or Frenchmen (and women) are typically French. Yet Australians laugh at Paul Hogan and Barry Humphreys as though recognizing an essential truth at the very moment that they are repudiating it. The social function and meaning of the phenomenon, then, clearly repays more careful attention.

In order to show how transformational analysis reveals the complex processes at work in accents and the construction of 'national characters' I will take the print in plate 4, from a popular satire of the 1960s, *Let Stalk Strine* by 'Afferbeck Lauder' ('Alphabetical Order', the alias of John Morison, a Sydney journalist). In a transformational analysis of this text and its ideological meanings we need first to be as clear as we can about the main stages and the structures of agency. The text itself, the essential starting point, is a written text. This one is incomprehensible until translated into a recognizable spoken text, so we will begin with the transformations that mediate between speech and writing. The next stage draws on the transformations that constitute the Australian accent itself. Where the primary agent at the first stage may be supposed to be Lauder, the transformations of the second stage are attributed to the Typical Australian (Oz). Finally the text constructs two women, whom I'll call Carmen and Saula for convenience, who are the immediate agents of a number of further transformations.

Lauder's form of spelling is clearly a frontal assault on the written form of the English language. For illustrative purposes I'll concentrate on just

Carmen F. T. Withers.	Theng Saula Syme
We revving	butter monner
ching liffis.	diet.
Jellike ching liffis?	I fed a bitifer
We F.N.B. Neffen	gairstrick
roe smeal slightly	stummick lightly.
wither tellion	Spin plier
the kitser nawl.	nuppagenner bit.
Yeckered	Arlga mauve rafter.
calm strife rom	Oliver
work	bye tweet first

Plate 3   Culture as Deformation. *Let's Stalk Strine* by Afferbeck Lauder-Ure Smith, Sydney.

one moment of this assault: the different versions of the single word spelt 'come' in standard English. In more formal terms we can set this out as follows:

$$(\text{Lauder}/\text{Oz}): (\text{'come'}) \Rightarrow \begin{cases} \text{Carm(en)} \\ \text{calm} \\ \text{gam (auve)} \end{cases}$$

But in order to interpret what 'Lauder' is doing we need to take the sequence back to the next stage, because Lauder is not simply misspelling 'come', he is also representing the distinctive forms of the Australian accent. We can set out the hypothetical rules at this level as follows:

(a)   Pronunciation (Oz): English 'u' ⇒ Oz 'ar'

(b)   Spelling (i)   (Standard English): Sound 'um' ⇒ $\begin{cases} \text{ome (come)} \\ \text{umb (dumb)} \\ \text{um (gum)} \end{cases}$

        (ii) Rule: Every word has a single correct spelling

One meaning of Lauder's spelling system comes from his focus on the contradiction between the two kinds of rule listed above. The first spelling rule represents the arbitrariness and irrationality of the English spelling system, even for English as the English (whoever they are) speak it. The second controls this irrationality by declaring the authority of a single correct spelling for every word in English. A large amount of time in schools, in Australia as in England, is devoted to acquiring 'correct spelling' and achieving effortless submission to these rules. Lauder's pattern of transformation, then, is 'typically Australian' in that its anarchic system attacks received authority. In so far as the written code is a signifier of an elite intellectual class, it is anti-intellectual, mocking the irrationality at the very core of the dominant code of rationality.

However, Lauder's transformational work also invites a contradictory reading, because the final text he produces would not be classified as Australian or comprehensible, by either Australian or English readers. He has deployed Australian values and Australian speech patterns on an English system of rationality to construct an alien and incomprehensible language which excludes all potential 'mates', except those willing to become cryptologists: not a quintessentially Oz occupation. If we consider the question of agency we realize the ambiguity of 'Lauder' as the agent who helps to constitute this semiosic syntagm. Lauder is both typical Australian and anti-Australian, an intellectual anti-intellectual producing an inaccessible popular text. This kind of ambivalence towards the Australian National Myth by satirists and those who laugh at them is very widespread. It is far more 'typical' than is the typical Australian (or the typical Englishman or Irishman or Scotsman for that matter).

Lauder's text also implies a theory of the Australian accent, which we will now look at. The single word 'Carmen', as transformationally derived from 'come and', incorporates enough of this theory for our purposes:

(Lauder/Oz): (come and) ⇒ Carmen

The meaning of the differences here affects vowels (*u* to *ar*, *a* to *e*) consonants (dropping *d*) and word boundaries (the two words fuse). All these lead to the conventional judgement on Australian speech as 'lazy'. But the work done on vowels isn't exactly laziness or lack of energy. The vowel 'ar', compared to 'u', in some ways releases more energy, not less. The shorter, more clipped vowel 'u' expresses control rather than energy, or more exactly, energy locked up in a system of control. Similarly, precise articulation of consonants blocks the flow of sound in complex ways, and thus expresses control rather than energy, and lack of consonants (in Australian and in most informal forms of speech, including upper-class English) signifies not so much laziness as an indifference to formal systems of power. This is one meaning of the Australian accent, then, which is entirely compatible with the national image as an ideological construct.

Lauder's version of the accent however is a transformation not a truth. The Australian accent does have tendencies along the lines of this parody, according to scholarly studies of it. But there are two differences between the scholarly account of the accent and Lauder's. Their version of the accent is a continuum which ranges between 'broad' Australian and 'standard' Australian, and Australian speakers move along this range, depending on context and audience. Lauder's Oz accent is cut off from this continuum, presented as a distinct language, with a separate sound system. And his speakers are locked into this closed system, unable to speak in any other way. So the accent, which is a live transformation for actual Australian speakers and for readers of this text, is not accessible to Oz speakers as these are constructed by Lauder. That is, the transformational meanings of the Australian accent are (in Lauder's satire) not meanings that Oz speakers themselves can understand or be conscious of. Only educated English-speakers or middle-class Australians (like Lauder/ Morison) who know both terms in the transformational process can understand the meaning of 'strine' (Australianness, and the Australian accent). Lauder's strategy here is a mirror image of Arnoldian 'culture'. Where the uneducated are excluded from Arnoldian high culture because they do not know the actual classic texts which constitute the base-line of culture's transformations, uneducated Australians are supposedly excluded from Morison/Lauder's popular culture because they do not know the high code that makes their own code both significant and ridiculous.

Lauder has constructed a dialogue which illustrates the 'accent' in the narrow sense and also extends its range. The Australian stereotype is (among other things) exclusively male, but Lauder dramatizes two women using this accent. Accent expresses difference of gender and class and race as well as national or regional identity. Lauder does not modify the sounds of 'Strine' to express gender identity, but the drawings and the content of the discourse together show how accent can also signify ideologies of gender and class.

Carmen is contrasted to Saula in a number of ways. Her clothes and hairstyle are more constrained and more ordinary than Saula's. Saula wears eye make-up, a patterned dress, a (slightly) plunging neckline, and an artfully simple hairstyle. In terms of dress codes of Sydney in the 1960s, Saula has been assigned the markers of an upwardly aspiring lower-middle-class woman, whereas Carmen is assigned the markers of a conservative upper-lower-class woman. Systems of accents, in clothes as in speech, can express subtle but important social differences within a nation or region simultaneously with the cruder meanings of national identity. As with all accents, the meaning is derived from a displacement from a normative standard (e.g. high-low necklines, more or less make-up) where this normative standard – what constitutes the standard height of a neckline or amount of make-up – is not absolute or universal but often highly specific to a particular social group at a particular time.

The speech styles of the two women are also opposed. Carmen's mouth is wide open and she looks directly at Saula. Saula looks away and her mouth is pursed. Carmen's postural text is the closer to the norm, since it confirms the solidarity that the words of both express: i.e. it is less transformed. Saula's posture, then, can be read as a transformational deletion of intimacy. If this picture represents the female equivalent of male 'mateship', then each woman expresses contradictory aspects of it: Carmen more conservative and repressed but direct, Saula more daring but uptight and evasive.

Even the topic of conversation is subject to a system of accents, expressing social meanings. In this exchange the topic is food. Kinds of food are always organized by paradigmatic systems within a particular culture, and these paradigmatic systems give meaning to the choice of one kind of food over another. But the meanings of choice correspond closely to the meanings of an equivalent transformation. The same paradigmatic system gives the meaning of a food-accent, (that is, a recognizable and distinctive set of choices of preferred foods) viewed as the product of transformations that define social identity. Australia doesn't have a national food which signifies Australianness. On the contrary, kangaroo, one of the best candidates, is virtually a forbidden food by law. Instead, the system of food choice is normally deployed to express social class. The Carmen text illustrates the way meanings can be constructed out of transformations of food syntagms. Her invitation is to a meal of *ching liffis* (chicken livers), but she also describes the meal that is not being offered, *roe s meal s* (roast meals). The meaning of chicken livers then is partly derived from this process:

(Carmen) : roast meal ⇒ chicken livers

The categories at issue here include formality, status and expense. Carmen's invitation codes a lack of generosity or a partial negation of her offer. Saula's refusal then completes the process of negation, even though the excess of her two excuses is weakened by Carmen's ungenerosity

(Saula's diet and gastric stomach would be hardly affected by the micro-scopic quantities of chicken liver she could expect at Carmen's).

The object of Lauder's satire is now no longer Australianness as such, but the sort of politeness conventions that determine the form of inter-action of these two suburban Australian women. The conventions, like most such conventions, foreground meanings of generosity and friend-ship, while providing mechanisms for the covert expression of their oppo-site. We can see clearly how systems of speech style (accent) function as part of an overall system of etiquette, controlling all major semiotic codes, at all levels of society. We can also see how national stereotypes must be read, by those who are socially competent in the society concerned, as transformed texts, to be produced or trusted only on certain occasions, not as unvarying guides to social behaviour.

Lauder's text was published in the 1960s, part of a significant wave of critiques of the 'Australian myth' of that period. To see a different kind of text written at a different period in the construction of Australian identity we will look briefly at a short story, 'Steelman', by Henry Lawson. Lawson, writing in the 1890s, was a key figure in a nationalistic artistic movement of the period, that was presided over by the magazine *The Bulletin*. Lawson is often said to express the radical egalitarian ethos and cult of mateship of the Australian bushworker which was the ideological core of the national image. But in the stories like 'Steelman' he scrutinized the functions and practices that gave meaning to that ethos.

Steelman, the central character in this story, is a 'hard case'. Steelman's little trick is to exploit the ethic of mateship to get free board with former mates who have married and 'settled down'. The story deals with one incident involving a 'victim' named Brown whom Steelman has attached himself to as a 'guest'. Brown tries many polite ways of ejecting Steelman, but Steelman ignores all such hints. Finally Brown is so exasperated that he goes out, gets drunk, then returns to kick Steelman out. But Steelman gives him a hiding instead. And next morning Steelman sits beside Brown's bed and more in sorrow than anger he assures Brown that as an old mate, he Steely will overlook the embarrassing incident and kindly continue to stay on as permanent guest. The basic structure of the story, then, is simple. It juxtaposes the discourse of mateship with the reality of aggressive, exploitative relations between men and men. The narrative establishes both a prior text which is transformed by discourse, and the two kinds of agents who operate through the discourse.

Here is one attempt by Brown to eject Steelman, as represented by Lawson:

'Look here, Steely, old man, I'm very sorry, but I'm afraid we won't be able to accommodate you any longer – make you comfortable, I mean. You see, a sister of the missus is coming down on a visit for a month or two, and we ain't got anywhere to put her, except in your room. I wish the missus's relations to blazes! I didn't marry the whole blessed family; but it seems I've got to keep them!'

Pause – very awkward and painful for Brown. Discouraging silence from Steelman. (Lawson 1948: 55)

Lawson here hasn't tried to represent a broad Australian accent, except marginally in the use of 'ain't'. On the contrary, he's even included a semi-colon, which signifies a high literary mode of organization. But he has incorporated a number of fragments from the discourse of mateship, and provided them with a transformational context.

First there is the term of address: 'Steely, old man'. The name is a transform from a surname – Steelman's public name (we never hear his first name). This is then shortened, to signify informality, then '-ie' an affectionate diminutive is added. The series of transformations encodes the nature of the relationship: the transformation of a public relationship, not real intimacy. The 'old man' is added, a key term in the discourse of mateship in Lawson's stories. It functions as a transform of 'old friend', referring to the length of the relationship not the age of the friend (just as 'the old woman' refers to a wife, not a mother or other old woman). Yet the term deletes the term for friendship ('mate' is only used of casual acquaintances). So this key term signifies the unspeakability of intimacy and equality even in the relationships where intimacy and equality are allowed. At its best, the mateship relationship is tenuous and difficult: and 'Steely' doesn't represent it at its best.

This short text shows a number of transformational operations by Brown. There's his slip of the tongue ('accommodate' ⇒ 'make you comfortable', declaring then cancelling his real construction of the nature of Steely's residency). There are polite lies ('I'd be very glad if only', 'I'm very sorry, but') and outright lies (the sister's visit is a fiction, we learn without surprise). But these operations only highlight the power of what is unspeakable for Brown in the discourse of mateship: i.e. loyalty, liking or intimacy to a woman, even (especially) his wife; and resentment towards a male 'mate'. So powerful are these prohibitions that he is paralysed before Steely's manipulations. The code allows him only one transformational option: to get very drunk and have a fight. But the code also brackets out fighting and drunknness, allowing meanings expressed in these conditions to be ignored, by a 'good mate' or by a parasite like Steely. In spite of its working-class origin, this code is as repressive and misleading as middle-class codes of politeness, and the archetypal Oz is the same kind of figure with the same kind of truth as the archetypal middle-class gentleman. Lawson's narrative strategy is the same kind of enterprise as Henry James's study of Bostonian façades and transformations, which was written at the same time though from such a different place.

Lawson and Lauder offer a useful contrast for the deployment of transformational analysis. Both provide materials for a transformational analysis. Both provide materials for a transformational reconstruction, and their primary literary meaning is the meaning of those processes. With both, the transformations they are concerned with are those that constitute a national character; the same national character at a different period. Both are critical of the Australian myth, in their different ways. But what is crucial is the difference that comes from their different point of insertion into the transformational processes that construct such myths. For Lauder, the myth is the end point of the transformational chain he sets up, it is the goal of interpretation. For all his parodic contempt, his text is dependent on the solidity of the myth, for without the myth to rest on his text would not exist. Since he draws power from the myth, he has no wish to provide powerful ways of reading it. Lawson, in contrast, starts with the myth as a surface text and provides other texts in his narrative that reveal the transformational processes that constitute it. Lauder represents the extremes that constitute the Australian accent, and provides a provocation to mobilize the transformations that link them, so his text can serve an enabling function, contributing to the ideological competence of those who already have it. But Lawson's narrative provides ways out of and around the myth, not ways into it. His central character is unable to find those ways himself, but his readers are equipped and motivated to do so for themselves. But in spite of these contrasts, the two authors illustrate a common characteristic of texts. Texts do not simply represent versions of reality, they also represent and provoke transformational processes which can constitute their primary meaning and major social function. Interpreting texts always draws on kinds of transformational anaylsis: though not always the same ones, or to the same effect.

SOURCES AND CONTEXTS

The theory of transformations developed in this chapter is more fully described in Kress and Hodge, *Language as Ideology*, 1979, and in later articles: Hodge, 'Transformational Analysis and the Visual Media', 1981, Hodge and Kress, 'Functional Semiotics', 1982.

Important theories of transformations were developed within linguistics by Harris, 'Discourse Analysis', 1952, and by Chomsky in *Syntactic Structures*, 1957. The notion of transformation was subsequently trivialized out of effective existence within mainstream linguistic theory in so far as it formed around the Chomskyan paradigm, and this tradition is no longer of interest to a theory of transformations (or even to anyone seriously interested in language as a social fact: for a critique see Hodge, 'Discourse in Time', 1989)

F. Smith's 1978 application of Chomskyan theories to reading has been influential, though transformations do not play a major role here. Psycholinguistics and studies of child language acquisition before 1970 made interesting use of transformational ideas (see e.g. Greene, *Psycholinguistics*, 1972). Piaget emphasized transformations as central in his theory of children's development (1959 and 1971). See Hodge and Tripp 1986 for a discussion of Piagetian ideas in a transformational framework, and their application to a developmental account of children's entrance into full literacy in visual and verbal media.

Freud's theory of transformations is still the most powerful model available. See his *Introductory Lectures in Psychoanalysis, The Interpretation of Dreams* and *Jokes and their Relation to the Unconscious*. Commentaries on Freud are too many and too well-known to need listing here. An influential application of Freud's ideas to literary texts has been Empson's covert Freudianism in *Seven Types of Ambiguity*, (1936). A useful recent introduction is Elizabeth Wright, *Psychoanalytic Criticism*, 1984.

The application of Freud's ideas to history is viewed with as much suspicion as their application to literature. For a recent discussion of the issues see Ashplant, 'Psychoanalysis in Historical Writing', 1988. A controversial but significant recent work that deploys a sophisticated semiotic range within a Left-psychoanalytic framework is Theweleit, *Male Fantasies*, 1977, a study of the roots of Nazism. For an indication of how valuable a non-Freudian transformational analysis of texts can be for the enterprise of 'people's history', drawing on oral sources, see Passerini's 'Work Ideology and Consensus under Italian Fascism', 1979. See also Figlio, 'Oral History and the Unconscious,' 1988.

For Lévi-Strauss's understanding of various kinds of transformation, see especially 'The Scope of Anthropology' and 'The Story of Asdiwal', 1973, and the concept of *bricolage* in *The Savage Mind* 1966.

On the category of 'play' in a transformational enterprise, see Derrida's complex game in 'Structure, Sign and Play in the Discourse of the Human Sciences', 1970. On Derrida and Freud, see Smith, *Taking Chances: Derrida, Psychoanalysis and Literature*, 1984. The movement that is labelled 'Deconstructionism', which is heavily influenced by Derrida's ideas and manner, can be seen as characterized by a commitment to a specific form of transformational activity, not necessarily as negative in its intent as the name implies. On 'Deconstruction' see Norris 1982, and for some implications for the teaching of English, see Atkins and Johnson, *Writing and Reading Differently: Deconstruction and the Teaching of Literature and Composition*, 1985.

Other traditions valorize play, understood as a form of transformational activity. Hudson, *Contrary Imaginations*, 1967, distinguished between 'divergent' and 'convergent' thinking to explain a kind of creative ability (divergent thinking) that he believed was disvalued by the education system, though 'convergent' thinking is also transformational activity, working in the opposite direction. De Bono has shown that creativity pays with a successful series of books that teach or exercise 'lateral thinking' (e.g. de Bono, *The Uses of Lateral Thinking*, 1967). 'Creativity' itself is an overworked word, especially within a particular ideology of English teaching, but in spite of critiques of this tradition (see e.g. Gilbert, 'Authorship and Creativity in the Classroom: Rereading the Traditional Frames', 1988) a radical pedagogy could hardly justify an uncompromising assault on the transformational capacities gestured at by the term, only on its programmatic uses.

On the importance of Arnold's concept of 'culture' in the tradition of 'English', see Williams 1977, and Eagleton 1976. Bourdieu's account of culture as in effect transformational (reading) power is contained in Bourdieu and Passeron, *Reproduction in Education, Society and Culture*, 1977. The critique of contemporary culture influentially argued by Baudrillard in *For a Critique of the Political Economy of the Sign*, 1981, in effect diagnoses an absence of transformational capacity as the key disability in the contemporary (mass) mind. It is a similar diagnosis as Marcuse came to, in *One Dimensional Man*, 1964: and both positions need to be confronted with a systematic account of the transformational capacities that in practice constitute the 'culture' of ordinary people. For a critique of the passivity that theories of reproduction imply, see Giroux, *Theory and Resistance in Education*, 1983. On everyday strategies of making sense see de Certeau, *The Practice of Everyday Life*, 1986.

6
The Reality Factor

If literature and art have always really been understood as transforms of 'reality' or 'life' as I have argued, then we can see why the issue of 'reality' has always been a major obsession in literary theory. Transformations are a kind of bias, a distortion, a lie. In the first classic of literary theory in the West, Plato argued that all literature was a lie. For 2,500 years critics and philosophers have wrestled with the problem that Plato was clearly right yet somehow also equally clearly wrong. The theory of literature remains part of the theory of legitimate lies, lies which for some extraordinary reason are not only legitimate but highly prized, and not even safely or consistently false.

The problem does not remain abstract or philosophical either. Reality is at issue in every reading strategy, every reading regime deployed on every literary text. Literature itself is always distinguished from other kinds of discourse by the kind of reality that can be expected of it. Within the category of literature (as this has been defined at different times) the reality-values of different genres are normally distinguished. Literary devices like metaphor, irony and wit are reality-games that readers and writers love to play. Literature has never been positioned unambiguously or at a single point along the continuum between 'reality' and unreality. 'Reality' and 'truth' of some kind have always been markers of value of works of literature and art, even with traditions that have announced themselves as opposed to dominant norms of reality. Yet even the most militantly realist traditions have rested on the mastery of illusion, in the craft of fiction.

This is not simply a problem for literary theory or theories of art. It bears on a central phenomenon in social semiotics itself. All messages are constructed. Every representation distorts, and everyone who uses representations can manipulate or be manipulated, and we learn to guard against deception by any means available. It is not only within literary texts that truth and reality are decisive. They are the most important stake in every semiosic struggle, every semiosic exchange. Belief (in the reality of the representation) is the key to semiosic power, the power of a text to persuade or move to feeling and action. Yet disbelief has its functions too. If high reality-value is the key to semiotic power, then low reality-value is a source of freedom, the freedom to speak the unspeakable in safety, the safety of impotence. So complex combinations of high and low reality-value can have their own function, and the more contradictory the combination, the more effective it can be.

So crucial a set of functions affects the form of every semiotic code in every context, not simply the specifically literary use of verbal language. It is the key to all writing which attempts to persuade, whether polemical genres or 'factual' genres whose effectiveness relies on their skill in concealing their contructedness. It is therefore an essential component in all reading regimes, which unite a community of readers around a common sense of 'truth' and 'reality', and which defend them against the illicit claims of other truths. The discipline of History is as concerned with these issues as every other discipline. The discourse of historians constructs belief by a variety of means, appealing to a taken-for-granted reality of the past as an outline that needs only to be filled in here and there, drawing on a set of documents whose reliability must be essentially accepted for the discipline itself to be viable. So great is this need in History that it has developed strategies for removing markers of truth from texts which construct the historical record. One of the clearest instances of this is the endemic practice in academic history of paraphrasing 'content', and the use of fragmentary quotations which remove most of the markers of truth from the original context. Because this set of practices is so widespread, the 'truth' of texts is a potentially explosive issue in historiography.

One particularly good place to start an investigation of the general form of the systems at issue is with what are called in linguistics the *modality systems* of language, i.e. the systems for assigning relative truth or certainty to a message. We have mentioned modality as a category earlier, because it is hardly possible to discuss literary effects without this category, but now is the time for us to look at it in greater detail.

I will begin by illustrating some important general points about modality by reference to some simple verbal examples. Take for instance the series of sentences in English: 'You are on holidays', 'You went on holidays', 'Did you go on holidays?' and 'You may have gone on holidays.' In traditional grammars of English, the word 'may' is termed a modal auxiliary, because as attached to the main verb of a clause it functions to affect its modality (certainty, truth value), making it less certain, indicating the attitude of the speaker to the statement. But in this series, it is clear that the question-form has the same function, a modality function. So, in a less obvious way, does the choice of tense, because the definite statement about the past is still less certain than the statement in the present, since the fact is there before the very eyes of the speaker. This choice itself is, as with transformations, a significant act, a kind of intervention by the speaker, expressing particular motives and meanings. Finally we can consider the modality of the statement 'You are on holidays!' said when the person is actually present and evidently not on holidays ('You call this a holiday?'), where the context gives the statement an ironic modality, which is in effect the same as a negative.

From this simple example, we can say a number of important things about modality in general.

1 There are many markers of modality in any code. It is so important a dimension of any message that it is signified with massive redundancy by multiple forms; a point that will be illustrated at greater length in what follows. Some of these (like 'may') are relatively opaque signifiers of modality, but many others (like question forms, use of the past) are relatively transparent signifiers of modality.

2 Modality is a form of negation acting on the bond between mimetic content and the world of referents. So 'may' for instance indicates that the link between content and reality is relatively weak.

3 Modality is an action in the semiosic plane, and modality operations are semiosic transformations affecting the key relationships of semiosis, the relation of message to referents and to social relations in the production of meaning.

4 Judgements about modality and the meaning of modality markers depend also on assumptions about what is obviously true or false, inscribed into neotic regimes that determine what is to count as truth.

5 Modality therefore typically has to be understood by reference to both referential world and social relations.

These propositions apply to every level of every kind of text, thus allowing us to see the interconnections of reality-operations from the smallest level (words, sentences, sounds, gestures) to the largest (genres and kinds of discourse). And in this broader framework we can understand the curious nature of literature's licence to lie, in all its social ramifications and possible uses.

Problematizing modality

Precisely because claims to reality are so potent they need to be scrutinized with very great care. In literature, realism is a seductive mode, and in the nineteenth century the dominant forms in prose and drama were strongly realist. Such works were often regarded as influential in the world of public affairs: novelists like Dickens or Zola or Harriet Beecher Stowe, dramatists like Ibsen had immense impact through their works, helped by the credibility constructed through realist conventions. This credibility has made them seem more usable by social historians, seduced by their seeming transparency and truth.

Outside literary criticism, the issue has been usefully theorized through the category of 'common sense,' a set of assumptions about how the world is that is not in dispute within a particular society or group, which therefore establishes the baseline for a shared version of reality. The Italian theorist Gramsci (1971) gave a criticism of the category of 'common sense' which pointed out its particular position and role in ideological processes, as a version of reality which was genuinely shared by all groups in society and therefore taken for granted, yet still ultimately a partial view which served the interests of the dominant. In Gramsci's account, 'common sense' naturalizes its version of reality so that it seems indistinguishable from reality itself. It conceals the constructedness of its 'reality', the contradictions it masks and the interests it serves. This 'common sense' is like a cognitive loaded dice which gives the battle for minds to the establishment again and again. So to even the odds, 'common sense' must be deconstructed, exposed in its constructedness.

When realism and common sense combine, they construct a kind of discourse that seems beyond criticism in its self-evident truth. So powerful is this combination that the claims of 'realism' have been attacked by a radical tradition of criticism this century, on the grounds that the power is achieved at the price of an unacceptable level of complicity. Certainly it is the case that realist modes must affirm the common sense of their time, and thus they affirm the taken-for-granted world of the dominant order, even when the particular messages contain fierce criticism of the establishment (as was the case with Dickens, Zola, Stowe and Ibsen). So the assaults on realism associated with various forms of modernism carry a message about the politics of modality which in this respect is more radical than any programme of political revolution, since it attacks the ideological substratum of the dominant order. Whether that makes post-modernist techniques inherently more 'revolutionary' or not is another issue, which we will look at in a moment.

One influential moment of anti-realism this century was the so-called 'Theatre of the Absurd', based mainly in Paris in the 1950s, with Samuel Beckett and Eugene Ionesco among its most important figures. The effect of 'the Absurd' associated with this movement came from the foregrounding of semiosic over mimetic meanings, a quality which makes these works especially useful sites for the study of literary and theatrical semiosis, and a source of interesting insights into general forms of modality.

I will begin by looking at a short exchange from Ionesco's play *Amédée*, first performed in Paris in 1954, and in English at the Arts Theatre, Cambridge, on 3 June 1957. It occurs towards the beginning, as voices off-stage:

The voice of the Concierge: So you're back from your holidays, Monsieur
   Victor!
The Neighbour's voice: Yes, Madame Coucou. Just back from the North
   Pole.
The voice of the Concierge: I don't suppose you had it very warm
   there.   (Ionesco 1965: 28)

The Concierge here begins with a high-modality statement, a statement
that declares her high confidence and certainty. 'You're back' (*vous
revenez*) is in the present tense, its self-evidence reinforced by M. Victor's
actual presence. But the self-evidence is in fact illusory, because what is
evident is only that M. Victor is there, not that he is back, nor that what he
is back from is his holiday. Or even that this is indeed M. Victor. These
statements are implicit in her speech, transformed into innocuous shortened forms:

   Coucou: (You are) M. Victor ⇒ M. Victor
          You (went on holidays and now have come) back ⇒ back

What has most significantly been transformed and deleted here, along
with the verbs, is the modality markers that normally cluster around verbs
in French as in English. These statements have had all modality markers
removed. But paradoxically this gives them the highest modality value of
all, since like 'common sense' nothing can be more certain than what is
taken for granted, and therefore without need for indicators of certainty.
   Madame Coucou's certainty expresses more than her knowledge of M.
Victor's movements. It declares her right to know, and the kind of relationship that as concierge she has with M. Victor. The certainty communicates solidarity and a kind of power, though there are unstated limits to
both (she does not call him by his first name, using the formal *vous* form in
the French, and she does not presume to know intimate details of his life).
The modality operations imply and therefore express a particular social
relationship (concierge – occupant in middle-class apartments in Paris in
the 1950s). We can see in miniature from this how particular social relations are underwritten by the common and unexamined assumptions that
structure modality in everyday discourse.
   Madame Coucou's second utterance illustrates another set of modality
characteristics of everyday discourse, in its English translation. 'I don't
suppose you had it very warm there' bristles with modality markers. At the
core of the utterance we can hypothesize a high-modality statement 'It's
cold there.' Since this is the North Pole she's talking about this is likely
enough to be true – at least as likely as M. Victor's supposed holiday
there.
   But this statement has undergone a large number of modality transfor-

mations: It's cold ⇒ It was cold ⇒ It wasn't warm ⇒ It wasn't very warm ⇒ you didn't have it very warm ⇒ I suppose you didn't have it very warm ⇒ I don't suppose you had it very warm. As with all transformational analysis these are only hypotheses, but the utterance leaves traces that signify some such sequence. Each operation progressively weakens the modality of the utterance very slightly, negating the right of the speaker to make strong claims about its truth. Each modification also signifies the diffidence of the speaker in relation to this portion of reality, in relation to this hearer. Uncertainty declares deference, a solidarity based now on the power imputed to the other, a weaker solidarity than that of the previous utterance.

But this different attitude is just as conventional as the previous one, and the modality markers still underpin a social relationship, even if it shows a contradictory face. In her first utterance she claimed certainty about matters she could only guess at, in her second she professes doubt about what she believes she knows, but either way she speaks as concierge to occupant, expressing the curious mixture of power and dependence that Ionesco represents as typical of that relationship.

So far we have only considered the modality markers in the verbal text. This speech can be spoken in many ways. She could say her first statement in a hearty tone, with every non-verbal signifier declaring her confidence in the relationship, and carry these over into the second exchange, where they would be contradicting the tentativeness of the words but maintaining her cohesion as a social person. Or she could emphasize the fissure in her persona, by adopting a tone of whining deference in the second speech. There are very many performance options, ranging between kinds of realist interpretation (opting for a single consistent social persona, eliding or naturalizing contradictions) and anti-realist interpretations which would foreground inconsistencies and contradictions.

The effect of 'translation' from text to different performances is very great. Its scale gives a useful perspective on the well known problem of translation from one language to another. This too has very great effects on the modality of specific texts, so great as to give rise at times to the sense that different texts are constructed by the act of translation. In this instance, Mme Coucou's words in French are *'Vous n'avez pas eu chaud!'* This is much less heavily modalized than the English translation, as well as using a different set of modality markers. She employs the perfect tense, the normal form of the past in colloquial speech, and does not attach the complex markers of modality of 'I don't suppose'. Ionesco punctuates this with an exclamation mark, a direction to the actress to signify high solidarity, high modality, though here as elsewhere she uses the formal *vous* not the intimate *tu*. The process that we reconstruct is so different that almost nothing of our analysis of the sentence in English applies to the French text. But the differences are not greater than those that can be constructed by different performance styles, and they have similar kinds of meaning and effect. The problems about the two kinds of 'translation' underline the same crucial point about modality, that it is not an absolute quality that inheres in a text, but is always a function of semiosic conditions and textual properties.

Whatever their precise modality value, these two lines are the realist wrapping around an Absurdist speech: M. Victor's reference to the joys of the North Pole as a holiday resort, which is treated as entirely reasonable by Mme Coucou. This would have been easily identified by audiences in both Paris and Cambridge as 'absurd', that is, as mobilizing and breaking with a shared 'common-sense' categorization of places as suitable or not for 'holidays'. This in turn is implicated in a shared understanding of what 'holidays' are, how they relate to the everyday world of work and life, and therefore where they are properly to be located. Again we see that the innocuous assumptions of 'common sense' carry considerable social meaning, no less potent because they are compressed and masked by their status as common sense.

The theatre audience does not share the common sense that binds Victor and Coucou, and they are positioned precisely by this exclusion, repudiating the couple and their relationship. The exchange is mildly comic, and audiences usually laugh. In so far as they do, they construct a reassuring solidarity with each other, united in their sense that people just do not go to the North Pole for holidays, and that any one who thinks they do is a fool. They may also recognize that this is a satire on the whole edifice of holidays and places for holidays prescribed within their own noetic regime, that their own choice of Bognor or the South of France is no less constrained and no less absurd. But their laughter brackets the modality of the realization (laughter is a major indicator of modality) and weakens its force. 'Common sense' is not easy to displace after all, since it establishes the base-line for all other modality judgements. It is too important to be lightly abandoned, and too deep-seated to be easily removed.

Similar strategies and problems are to be found in other aspects of the Theatre of the Absurd. Audiences come to texts with their expectations about modality and their 'common sense' already pre-formed. *Amédée* opens, according to the stage directions, as follows:

Scene: An unpretentious dining-room, drawing-room, and office combined.
On the right, a door.
On the left, another door.
Backstage centre, a large window with closed shutters; the space between the slats is, however, wide enough to let in sufficient light.
Left centre, a small table strewn with notebooks and pencils. On the right, against the wall, between the window and the right-hand door, a small table, with a telephone switchboard on it, and a chair. Another chair also

*close to the centre table. An old armchair well down stage. There should be
no other furniture in the first act, except a clearly visible clock, with hands
that move.*

(p. 27)

Although this text is describing the staging of an Absurdist play we note in
its language all the modalities of certainty. There are no 'mays' or
'mights', not even many 'ises' or 'ares'. The shorthand takes for granted
the reality of a specific community, knowledgeable about stages and
theatricality and not needing to question its taken-for-grantedness. This
taken-for-granted world has a rectangular set divided geometrically into
left, right and centre, front and back stage. The invisible geometry
stretches outside the set, constructing an enclosed and specialized acting
space complete with proscenium arch separating the dramatic action from
the space occupied by the audience, who themselves are encased in the
conventional geometries of rows of seats, in a neatly rectangular purpose-
built theatre, such as the Théâtre de Babylon in Paris where it was first
performed, or the Arts Theatre, Cambridge, where it was first performed
in English.

An audience coming to the play does not read stage directions. Instead
they read a stage with scenery authored by a producer or members of a
production team, who could decide to resist the prescriptions of these
directions if they wanted to. But whatever they decide, they cannot construct meanings in a void, without reference to pre-existing background
knowledge and expectations of the audience, meanings sedimented into
the movable and immovable conditions of staging, connecting in
innumerable ways with the norms of 'common sense' about both theatre
and reality, and the complex systems of modality that have been developed in countless encounters in social life.

The kind of theatre that this play was first performed in incorporates
conventions that encode precise modality instructions, and these control
how the 'reality' of the text is to be read. The time and space of the
theatrical action are marked off from the time and space of the audience,
in their roles as audience and as members of a wider community. The
audience sits in darkness while the stage is in light. The time of the
audience is night-time, outside the rhythms of the day. The darkness
conceals their regimented situation and their status as replicated social
individuals, as 'bums on seats'. These conventions, then, bracket the time
and space of the theatrical action both from the everyday world and from
the semiosic act. Whatever happens on stage, then, is pre-assigned a
weakened modality and therefore a weakened effect. If the stage action is
not bracketed (e.g. in street theatre or other conditions that deconstruct
the conventions of the proscenium arch theatre) then the semiosic situation is assigned a higher modality, and so the transaction seems more

connected with everyday normative realities. But part of the price of this strategy is to raise the modality-stakes for the performance itself. The function of the modality-bracketing is to legitimate the illusionism of the performance. Without it, street theatre runs the risk of asking to be judged by more exacting standards of modality, and being found wanting.

The type of theatre is one set of framing conventions. The set and its style is another. The scene as described here includes three kinds of architectural space, a dining-room, a drawing-room and an office. The modality of this depends partly on a particular 'common-sense' understanding of what is normal, partly on markers of modality. The walls of this room might be anything from indeterminately painted backcloth to solid stage architecture, each a transparent signifier of a kind of modality, the more solid the more real. But solid, well made sets are also signifiers of wealth, too, since the construction of realistic illusions is understood to have its price. Again we have a subtle nexus between 'realism' and an affirmation of the status quo and the dominant economic and social order.

The normality of a space which does not mark off the three functions of formal eating, formal entertaining and work is dependent on the same kind of very specific social rules as was the case with holidays. Bourgeois lifestyles in France and Britain of the 1950s insisted on a marked boundary between home and work, and within the home between eating and entertaining. The conflation of the three in this set, however, would not inevitably be marked as 'absurd', or not so obviously as holidaying at the North Pole is absurd. Paradoxically, the absurdity would be stronger the greater the realism that is claimed by the other modality markers.

If the furniture and the rest of the setting are maximally solid and realistic, for instance, then the disparity between the categories of space would become more apparent and foregrounded, just as the absurdity of the exchange between Victor and Coucou is intensified by clear indicators of high modality in their discourse. This comes from the mathematics of modality, in whose terms two negatives make a positive. So realistic rooms and furniture (positive modality) plus non-normal linkage (negative modality) gives an overall negative modality, where non-realistic set (negative modality) plus non-realistic linkage (negative modality) gives a positive modality. In the same way in speech, to say that something is not unreal is to say that it is quite real. Note that the mathematics only works out approximately. 'Not unreal' is not as positive as 'real', because the phrase leaves traces of modality operations, even though they cancel each other out. In the same way the double negation of unreal set plus unreal linkage has its modality effect. In fact the effect of the absurd, if it is to challenge common-sense constructions of reality, must incorporate elements with a high modality: fragments of speech or situation or character or action which are marked as recognizably authentic.

Amédée inserts an unreal plot into the fissured reality of its world. In another room, never seen during the course of play, we are told that there is a corpse that continues to grow, which is now embarrassingly gigantic. In terms of 'common sense' there are no corpses in bourgeois bedrooms, and if there were they would not continue to grow. The plot premise, then, clearly has a very low modality. Yet from some points of view it is not so ridiculous. The corpse is the object of embarrassment and guilt felt by the members of the household, feelings which are assigned a real modality by the speech and actions of the characters. Even in everyday speech, a corpse could be used as a metaphor for the object of generalized feelings of anxiety and guilt. In dreams a corpse could function similarly, with less clearly marked modality. And in literature, especially in poetry, metaphors abound, and there the metaphor of a dead and growing corpse would not be felt as at all surprising or ridiculous. The reading regimes that form the core of the literature curriculum in France as in Britain prepare the modality-grounds for this seemingly radical and iconoclastic text.

A basic principle of modality is that texts can only have importance and impact if in some respect they have a high modality-value for a significant group. This is the case even with a text like *Amédée*, which seems to attack the very basis of common-sense modality. These plays were praised by their admirers as being more true, more realistic than realism, not less. Martin Esslin, an influential advocate, contrasted them with the preceding convention of the realist 'well-made play':

> The basis of the well-made play is the implicit assumption that the world does make sense, that reality is solid and secure, all outlines clear, all ends apparent. The plays that we have classed under the label of the Theatre of the Absurd, on the other hand, express a sense of shock at the absence, the loss of any such clear and well-defined systems of belief.
>
> There can be little doubt that such a sense of disillusionment, such a collapse of all previously held firm beliefs is a characteristic feature of our own times. The social and spiritual reasons for such a loss of meaning are manifold and complex. (Esslin 1965: 13)

Esslin here challenges the reality of 'reality', the seamless, solid and unquestioned basis of the previous order of 'common sense'. But he challenges it on behalf of a new community which is given its own identity and cohesion by its common experience of disillusion, its shared loss of clear and well defined systems of belief. This belief in the absence of belief has its own solid reasons which he proceeds to list, using the modal indicators of unquestioned certainty ('is', 'are'). This kind of nihilism is after all part of the current 'common sense' (along with its opposite), and Esslin writing in 1965 evidently did not feel the need to argue too strenuously on its behalf.

But Absurdist theatre (and other forms of modernism and the avant-garde) do not simply present an alternative version of 'reality'. Ionesco's primary concern is with the plane of semiosis, with meanings about the conditions of production of meaning. Since semiosis is a material social reality, writers can be as intensely realistic about it as about any other aspect of the world that they represent in the mimetic plane. In this way we see that Esslin is right to claim that this kind of writing is equally concerned with reality, and hence has its own modal force, even if it deliberately avoids any plausible or 'sensible' mimetic content. He is also right to see this kind of writing as a radical challenge to the dominant tradition of realism. This challenge is itself a meaning, not an unmediated fact about literary and social history, but as a meaning its appearance and currency is a social fact that a historian should attend to. It does not demonstrate that there was a crisis of modality or a major shift in the conditions of literary semiosis at this time, but it does show that significant sections of post-war European society thought that there was.

The modality of realism

Realism undoubtedly has been used as means of legitimating the status quo, but writing with this aim typically has a less than total commitment to a depiction of reality-as-it-is. One of the most successful instances of a 'realist' strategy of legitimation is Jane Austen. Her novels about a narrow stratum of English middle-class existence were published during the trau-matic period of the Napoleonic wars and their repressive aftermath, but barely mentioned any of these disturbing issues or events. Yet discriminating readers then and later have admired the accuracy of social observation and the pervading irony which together give her work an authority and sense of 'truth' that have continued to hold sway up to the present. A novel by Jane Austen is still felt to be a good choice in any literary curriculum.

The opening of *Emma*, her second to last novel, published less than a year before her death at the age of forty-two, allows us to see some of the modality strategies that proved so successful in her work:

> Emma Woodhouse, handsome, clever, and rich, with a comfortable home and happy disposition, seemed to unite some of the best blessings of existence; and had lived nearly twenty-one years in the world with very little to distress or vex her. (1946: 19)

This opening paragraph in the novel has as its mimetic content a descrip-tion of Emma, its central character, about whom the reader as yet knows nothing. At the end of it, the reader knows very little more, at least as far as material facts are concerned: what colour are her eyes, how tall she is, and so on. Nor are we given a precise description, here or later, of the physical environment that she inhabited. Yet for this very reason the credibility of both is more strongly assured, because each is left to be underwritten by the experience of the readers, constructed out of a consensus 'common sense'.

We can be specific about the vacuity of the world that is presented here, the absences that characterize it. Physical action is almost entirely absent, with only two actional verbs, 'distress' and 'vex' (both almost negated), with 'lived' functioning almost like the verb 'to be'. Verbs are the primary site where modality is marked in English, but since these parts of speech are minimized, the text as a whole is left with very few markers of modality. That is to say, events in this world are represented as being so few and so unremarkable as to be beyond doubt.

Attention is focused instead on the activity of judgement, carried by adjectives and adverbs, clustering around the relatively few nouns that represent things in this world. This quality of judgement begins to define the source of that judgement, the persona of the narrator, as every act of judgement constructs a perspective and social context from which the judgement is made. One characteristic here is the sheer ubiquity of acts of judgement: most nouns have at least one adjective. Another is precision or scrupulosity: 'seemed to' allows for the possibility of error, 'some of' acknowledges that there are other 'blessings of existence', and 'nearly' and 'very' register the effort to be exact. Finally, the three opening adjectives, 'handsome, clever, and rich' indicate another kind of subtlety of judgement. Each invokes a paradigmatic set of judgements, and each paradigm contains at least one item that is more highly valued. 'Handsome' is opposed to 'beautiful', 'clever' to a set of terms indicating judgement ('sensible', 'intelligent', 'well-judging', 'rational'), and 'rich' is opposed to 'well connected', 'important' or 'of consequence'. Emma's imperfections are implied by this choice of words, as is the narrator's own precision of judgement.

Only the three words are in the text, of course; the paradigms exist outside it (though all these words will occur in the novel that follows). The effect of the strategy here is to imply an invisible critique of Emma, a critique only visible to those who know the (or a) relevant paradigm. It constructs a social world divided into aberrant members (Emma), aberrant judges (those who do not recognize the implied negative judgement) and the community of correct judges, the narrator and those who already know the distinctions she is making. This community, of course, is still open to incorporate readers who come to recognize over the course of the novel what distinctions are to be made about Emma, and what authority is to be attributed to the narrator/Jane Austen.

The novel that follows traces the 'education' of Emma, her transition from a woman who is, in spite of her assets, unsuitable for the one career a woman should pursue, to become the dutiful wife of a man who is 'sensible', well connected, and eighteen years her senior. She makes a series of judgements which subsequent events demonstrate were unequivocally misguided, before she realizes that she should marry appropriately into her class, to her brother-in-law, and that others likewise will be happier marrying into their own class. The last paragraph of the novel describes her wedding:

> The wedding was very much like other weddings, where the parties have no taste for finery or parade; and Mrs Elton, from the particulars detailed by her husband, thought it all extremely shabby, and very inferior to her own. 'Very little white satin, very few lace veils; a most pitiful business! Selina would stare when she heard of it.' But, in spite of these deficiencies, the wishes, the hopes, the confidence, the predictions of the small band of true friends who witnessed the ceremony, were fully answered in the perfect happiness of the union. (p. 378)

At the end as at the beginning, Jane Austen leaves the material details of her constructed world to be supplied from the experience of her readers. What she supplies is the double judgement. Mrs Elton has been characterized throughout the novel as a snob with unerringly bad taste. In the opening, the community of those with defective judgement was left open, since as many as possible were to be educated, like Emma, into correct standards. Now the two communities are polarized and the boundaries drawn, and those who choose wrongly are given the companionship of the dreadful Mrs Elton and her equally dreadful sister for eternity.

Jane Austen's tone is heavily ironic as she repeats without comment Mrs Elton's judgement: 'in spite of these deficiencies'. Irony, which here operates because the reader is by now in no doubt as to Jane Austen's opinions, functions as a form of negation, though the judgement is not negated because it is obviously foolish, but only because its source is Mrs Elton. The judgement which follows, that the witnesses were 'true friends' and that the union was blessed with 'perfect happiness', is not on the face of it any less foolish, but it is presented without irony, since the means by which irony can be constructed by Jane Austen have been used up in the first half (she cannot appeal to the taken-for-granted assumptions of her group to repudiate the first judgement, and then construct an ironic perspective by repudiating that group within the very same sentence).

As a result we are left, in the mimetic plane, with the happy and cohesive social group who celebrated the wedding, and a married couple who enjoy a lifetime of perfect happiness. But this world is sketched in with minimal detail. What is more substantial is the society in the semiosic plane that comes to this judgement or that asserts these sentiments. Austen is as concerned with semiosic meanings as Ionesco. The crucial difference is that she has elided the intractable material realities that might disrupt the certainties of her community, where Ionesco delights in maximal intractability. The consensus of her community is built around the values of order and conformity, where Ionesco allies his audience with critics of order and consensus. Ionesco's project paradoxically involves more and sharper contact with reality, if less with common sense, where Jane Austen's 'realism' is largely constructed and validated by 'common sense', as this was understood by her group. But to see that this common sense was not simply life as experienced by the group, we need simply to remember that *Emma* as published was dedicated to the Prince Regent, who greatly admired her work and knew at first hand that not all unions lead to 'perfect happiness'. As of course even the unmarried Austen knew perfectly well.

Jane Austen's kind of realism was very different in aims and methods from the realist theatre of the Norwegian dramatist Henrik Ibsen. Ibsen abandoned poetic drama in 1869, when he was aged forty-one, and from then onwards wrote prose dramas dealing with contemporary social issues, many of them concerned with the emancipation of women and with the constraints and double standards of Norwegian middle-class life. *Hedda Gabler* for instance, first performed in 1890, is a study of a woman of the same class as Emma, just married as the play opens to a man as sensible as Jane Austen could have wanted, Jorgen Tesman, a mediocre scholar but regrettably from a lower social station. Ibsen described his sets meticulously, with far more detail than Austen gave to describing a scene. The opening is described in the following terms:

A large drawing-room, well furnished, in good taste, and decorated in dark colours. In the back wall there is a wide doorway with its curtains pulled back. This opening leads into a smaller room decorated in the same style as the drawing-room. In the right wall of this outer room is a folding door that leads into the hall. In the opposite wall, left, is a glass door also with curtains pulled back. Through its panes can be seen part of a verandah outside and autumn foliage. In the middle of the stage is an oval table with a cloth on it and chairs round it. Downstage, against the right wall are a large, dark porcelain stove, a high-backed arm-chair, a padded foot-rest and two stools. Up in the right corner are a corner sofa and a little round table. Downstage, left, a little way from the wall, is a sofa. Above the glass door, a piano. On each side of the door way at the back stands a whatnot with terra-cotta and majolica ornaments. Against the back wall of the inner room can be seen a sofa, a table and a chair or two. Over this sofa hangs the portrait of a handsome, elderly man in a general's uniform. Over the table a hanging lamp with a soft, opal glass shade. All round the drawing-room are bouquets of flowers in vases and glasses; others are lying on the tables. The floors in both rooms are covered with thick carpets. Morning light: the sun shines in through the glass doors. (Ibsen 1961: 263)

As a written text this has the same high modality as Ionesco's stage directions, and for the same reason: Ibsen takes for granted the known reality of the realist stage and the community of the theatrical profession built around this shared knowledge. But the opening takes for granted another area of shared knowledge, knowledge of what constitutes 'good taste'. These are the values of an elite within the middle-class of the period, presented by Ibsen with a seeming lack of awareness that such values are normally specific and transitory. Such effortless familiarity with dominant notions of 'good taste' positions the producer, the production and the audience in an insidious complicity with these values which constitutes a bond of solidarity between them.

The first sentence gives the overriding message of the set, through the key-words 'large', 'well furnished', 'in good taste' and 'decorated in dark colours'. Size is a transparent signifier of power, and transparent signifiers have high modality. In order to contain all these items of furniture this stage would have to be very large by the standards of this tradition. Yet however large it was, the stage would be encumbered by the items, which would continue to intractably occupy space, blocking the gaze of the audience and the free movement of the actors. Unsurprisingly a set as elaborate as this is unchanged throughout the play, its elaboration determining its rigidity. At one level it is a symbol of the material constraints on the existence of someone like Hedda Gabler. But it is an especially powerful symbol because it is constructed out of such tangible and recognizable material items, which are directly experienced as constraints on audience and actors and production as well as on the fictitious characters.

The setting, if reconstructed according to Ibsen's specifications, has a very high modality, higher in some respects than the characters themselves. The effect of this is to skew the reality-values of Hedda's whole world. Her house was presume has other spaces, including bedrooms and other private, intimate spaces, and there is a world outside, gardens (a painted backdrop or some other signifier glimpsed through the glass door in the back room), the town (from where characters come and go into this room), Italy (where she spent a six-month honeymoon) and so on. But all these other places have lower modality for a performance than the two rooms in which the action of the play unfolds. That action itself has higher modality-value than the action that is reported or supposed to occur off-stage.

The result of this modality-operation is that domestic public life, the part of life lived within the confines of the well furnished bourgeois drawing-room, comes to seem the overwhelmingly determining social reality for Hedda, the only place in which she truly exists. Yet events in other less real spaces continually impinge on this space. In the course of the play Tesman's rival as a scholar, Ejlert Lovborg, is said to have produced a masterpiece inspired by Thea Elvsted, but the jealous Hedda persuades him to kill himself with her pistol, and she burns the manuscript. The possible scandal that she believes will ensue puts her in the power of Judge Brack, who has long wanted to have an affair with her. These events constitute the plot of the play, such as it is; not highly plausible yet constructed as real by the characters in the play, who thus confer on it some (though not all) of their own ascribed reality.

The final scene of the play is set in the same room, this time at evening. Hedda has retreated to the inner room and pulled the curtain. Tesman has set up a relationship with Thea, who will now be his inspiration instead of Lovborg's, and Judge Brack is sitting in the sofa, with Tesman's complicity, waiting for his part of the triangle to begin:

> *Tesman* (*at the writing table*): I tell you what, Mrs Elvsted. You shall move into Aunt Julle's and I'll come over in the evenings. And then we can sit and work there. Eh?
> *Mrs Elvsted*: Yes, perhaps that would be the best plan –
> *Hedda* (*in the inner room*): I can hear perfectly well what you are saying. But how am I going to get through the evenings out here?
> *Tesman* (*turning over the papers*): Oh, I'm sure Judge Brack will be kind enough to come out and see you.
> *Judge Brack* (*in the easy chair, calling gaily*): Willingly! Every single evening, Mrs Tesman. We shall have a very pleasant time together here, you and I.
> *Hedda* (*clearly and distinctly*): Yes, that is what you are looking forward to, isn't it, Mr Brack? You, as the only cock in the yard.
> (*A shot is heard within. Tesman, Mrs Elvsted, and Brack jump up.*)
> *Tesman*: Ah! Now she's playing with the pistols again.
> (*He pulls the curtains aside and runs in. So does Mrs Elvsted. Hedda is lying lifeless, stretched out on the sofa. Confusion and cries. Berte comes in distractedly from the right.*)
> *Tesman* (*shrieking to Brack*): Shot herself! Shot herself in the temple! Think of it!
> *Brack* (*half-collapsed in the easy-chair*): But merciful God! One doesn't *do* that kind of thing!   (p. 364)

Modality-levels are not constant throughout this scene, nor in every code, and such variability is the rule in modality. Tesman for instance speaks in a clichéd manner here as always, but the clichés do not always have the same modality. His vague phrase 'work there' (of his future relationship with Thea) and the equally unspecific 'come out and see you' (tacitly giving permission to Judge Brack to move in) as semiosic acts have high modality, precisely because the words themselves are presumed to have low modality. These are the kind of euphemisms that the current common sense would expect of a man like Tesman negotiating a double irregular liaison, within this utterly respectable place. This 'common

sense' would know about the existence of irregular relationships as structural within the bourgeois system of marriage of the period. It would also
know that the conventions of polite language were such that these
arrangements were unspeakable here, so that this language with this content has a negative modality. So by the rule of double negation, the fact
that this presumed reality is unspoken in this low-modality discourse
serves to confirm its plausibility.

When Brack exclaims at the end 'One doesn't *do* that kind of thing!'
his language is equally clichéd, but its modality is subtly different. Firstly
it is an exclamation, which is a marked form of intonation, not the taken-
for-granted intonation that confirms the untroubled presence of expected
realities. Again it has a high modality as a semiosic act, as the 'real'
response of a Brack to something so unprecedented in his world. But
where 'common sense' effortlessly supplies and thus validates the
unspoken behind Tesman's discourse, it does not do so for Brack's meaning. Clearly people *do* do such things, and what is signified is the modality
deficiencies of this kind of language, as faced with this kind of reality.

The shifts in modality are organized by a structure of three levels, each
with its own truth-value. The most basic level is the prison of bourgeois
domestic existence, signified with overwhelming power by the set, and by
the clothes, actions and discourse of all the actors. The second level is the
strategy of accommodation, the unacknowledged set of double liaisons
which the characters invoke. This is assigned a lower modality-value in the
play, since we never see it or any reliable signifiers of its possibility. It is in
fact constructed by the method of double negation: since it cannot be
spoken of in the language of inauthenticity it must be true.

Finally there is Hedda's suicide. Unlike the double liaison this is
enacted on stage, authenticated by the bang of the gun, but it occurs
behind a curtain. This indirect presentation is not the only negative aspect
of the modality of the incident. In fact the negative modality of the
presentation is necessary in order to create an overall positive modality,
since the action is itself implausible by 'common-sense' criteria. Brack is
quite right. Women in real life (as understood by the common sense of the
day) do not usually walk off after that kind of conversation and shoot
themselves. The negative modality of the act needs to be counteracted by a
negative modality in the presentation in order to make it relatively acceptable. Even the realism of the pistol shot is a theatrical risk, liable to disrupt
the illusionism of the episode.

Hedda's act comes from the traditions of melodrama, not real life. As
such it has a fictional modality, so that this level has a weaker modality
than either of the other two. The meaning of this act is her affirmation
that there must be an alternative to bourgeois marriage or bourgeois
adultery. That is, her affirmation is a negation of the two possibilities
offered asymmetrically by her world. But although that affirmation is

foregrounded by its position in the play it is still negated by the surrounding modality-structures. And since the possible alternative has been negated, the power of the world has been reaffirmed.

The play thus declares a critique of bourgeois domestic life, especially from a woman's point of view, yet also represents the alternatives as non-viable. A double negation is of course not the same as an affirmation, so that Ibsen cannot be seen to be reinforcing the dominant order to the same degree as Austen, yet the power of his realism comes from the sense he constructs that reality could not be otherwise. Austen approves of the dominant order and disparages efforts to resist it. Ibsen disapproves of the dominant order, but cannot conceive of how it could be resisted. Change is more likely to come from Ibsenian realism than from Austen, but only marginally. It is easy to see why writers committed to social change could become impatient with the conventions of realism, seeing them as too closely implicated with existing conditions to be compatible with radical change.

Modality as symptom

Modality is the end product of a series of semiosic acts, so that a reading of modality is a reading of the semiosic process itself. Modality markers constructed by producers of texts are implied claims about the semiosic process. Many of the cues used by readers are seen by them as actual traces of the semiosic process, transparent signifiers which therefore have a high modality themselves. Producers of texts can make misleading claims, and readers can make wrong guesses, but even so modality is a prime site for symptomatic readings of texts. Modality is the key to what a writer/ speaker 'really meant'. Analysis of modality takes us immediately into the dialogic context and process in which that meaning was constructed, allowing us to reconstitute the poles between which it moved, its dynamic and trajectory. Historians and others who attempt to read truth from literature or from any other document need to attend closely to modality. Modality not only masks the truth they seek, it carries its own equally important social meanings.

What, for instance, did Ibsen 'mean' in his play *Hedda Gabler*? He constructed characters, plot, setting and speeches, but as we have seen, each of these is modified by different and shifting levels of modality. The speeches, so easy to quote, are all the views of a constructed character, not necessarily of the dramatist. Yet in spite of these necessary qualifications, the speeches and everything else do ultimately proceed from the dramatist, through whatever structures of mediation. It is as unprofitable to cut literary meanings entirely off from material social agents and realities as it is to accept them as direct and reliable records. And the fact that drama typically inserts such views into a dialogic context provides more not less evidence for a reconstruction of meaning processes and the modality of a message.

Hedda Gabler provides a typical instance. At a crucial point in the play in Act 2 there is a dialogue between Hedda and Ejlert Lovborg. Ejlert refers to a secret love affair they had when young, carried out under the nose of her father, General Gabler, which ended when Ejlert made open advances to Hedda, and Hedda threatened to shoot him with her father's pistol. Hedda calls herself a coward for being afraid of the scandal that would have ensued:

> *Hedda*: And I'm a coward. (*She leans nearer to him, without meeting his eyes, and says more softly*). But now *I* will confess something to *you*.
> *Lovborg (eagerly)*: Well?
> *Hedda*: That, my not daring to shoot you down –
> *Lovborg*: Yes?
> *Hedda*: That wasn't my worst piece of cowardice . . . that night.
> *Lovborg (looks at her a moment, understands and whispers passionately)*: Ah, Hedda! Hedda Gabler! Now I see a glimpse of the hidden foundation of our comradeship. You and I! Then it *was* your passion for life –
> *Hedda (quietly, with a sharp, angry glance)*: Take care! Don't assume anything like that. (pp. 317–18)

In this exchange, Lovborg clearly believes that Hedda has admitted that she was in love with him and did want to accept his advances, but out of cowardice did not want to say so. So the attempted shooting was an inverse act of love, expressing love by its opposite, by its negation. The refraining from shooting, then, was a negation of this negation, which she presents as a double act of capitulation, not an affirmation, since both times it recognized the overriding power of social constraints.

Hedda does not say this directly, and in fact seems at the end to deny it. However, Ibsen has constructed a dialogue that invites a symptomatic reading from both Lovborg and the audience, drawing on their common systems of interpretation, based on long experience of discourse in everyday life. Ibsen's text is in Norwegian, but I will analyse the English translation to illustrate the methods of symptomatic reading of deliberately constructed symptomatic language. Ibsen's actual text contains comparable moves: Norwegian systems of modality and discursive strategies are close to those of English.

Hedda begins with a statement, 'And I'm a coward', which seems to have a high modality, though 'coward' is the term used by Lovborg of her, and an actress could as it were put quotation marks around it to distance Hedda from it, and thus empty it of much of its positive modality. She is then described as 'leaning towards' Lovborg, which is a normal proxemic signifier of solidarity in the semiosic plane and therefore a transparent

signifier of high modality, as is the soft voice. Both these mark the following statement as carrying higher modality (and by contrast they detract
from the modality of the preceding one). But she does not meet his gaze, a
signifier which cancels the solidarity of her physical proximity and introduces an equivocation into the modality of the statement.

Hedda's confession, when it comes, is not exactly full and frank, and it
is the hesitations and suppressions which carry her primary meaning. Her
first half-sentence, 'That, my not daring to shoot you down – ', bears
many traces of extensive transformational activity. The dash indicates a
pause whose length, in performance, signifies the extent of her self-
repression of meaning, and also her dependence on Lovborg to complete
it. The projected core of the utterance is 'I shoot you down', as a meaning
without modality, the present thought of that past occasion. Its subsequent history is something as follows: H: I shoot you down ⇒ I dare to
shoot you down ⇒ I do not dare to shoot you down ⇒ I did not dare to
shoot you down ⇒ my not daring to shoot you down. In this history, 'dare'
plays an interesting role, since it is precisely the affirmation of courage that
she seems to admit she lacked at the time. Yet in the sequence, 'dare'
comes as a weaker affirmation than the unmodalized thought/act of
shooting. We see from this that it is an affirmation that implies a preceding negation of the act of shooting. This 'dare' attempts to overcome a
prohibition by 'society' or by the ever-present Father, General Gabler,
whose portrait in the inner room still maintains its gaze over the action of
the play. Then the prohibition reasserts itself to negate the 'dare', and
then the negated dare is situated in the past. But the final step removes
many of these markers of modality. The agent, 'I', is transformed to the
possessive 'my', and the pastness of the act is also removed.

Her next speech is just as obscured by semiosic transformations. 'That'
refers to the not shooting, which is compared to another not stated 'that'
which is the only trace of the deleted profession of love, which was
unspeakable then and is still unsaid. 'Cowardice' is a repudiation/
negation, from the point of view of a heroic/military code of ethics (which
Lovborg has also brought into play), of the non-action which the same
code of ethics seemed to have required. 'Worst' then intensifies the
negativity of the judgement on the action, and as a strong negative combined with the initial negative (not declaring love) constructs it as a positive. This is what Lovborg (after a short pause to allow the complex
processing to occur) reads as her declaration of love. Hedda immediately
seems to deny this interpretation, but with such complex modal operations (merely 'Don't assume that', not 'It isn't true') that Lovborg and the
audience would not be unreasonable to not entirely believe her.

From this excavation we can reconstruct Hedda's buried text, her core
philosophy. True courage is the affirmation of love: she should not have
renounced Lovborg. But courage and a form of love are also present in the

destruction of love through the death of the lovers. The events of the play provide some confirmation that this philosophy has validity as an explanation of Hedda's behaviour and the meanings she attaches to her life. After the renunciation of heroic love and heroic death, Hedda is faced with the bourgeois marriage system, loveless marriage followed by equally loveless adultery. Her suicide following the suicide she persuades Lovborg to commit thus has meaning as a return to the heroic stage of negative choice. By this stage in her life the direct affirmation of love is no longer possible, so by killing herself with her father's pistol, the same weapon that once she threatened Lovborg with and which she gave him to kill himself with, she has transformed herself to Lovborg as victim. The suicide becomes an affirmation of heroic, anti-bourgeois love.

As a philosophy this may seem somewhat jejune, presented in this form. But Ibsen has not presented it in this form. He has given us the modalities and transformational processes of Hedda's speech in context, from which we have an implied narrative of semiosic processes. In this narrative we see that her dialectic practically excludes Lovborg, and instead incorporates the prohibitions and values of the patriarch, her father the General, at every level. Even when she is alone with Lovborg, her father is a potent third, symbolized in the scene by his portrait. Loving for Hedda is defiance of the patriarch, yet repudiation of the claims of love is 'cowardly' and therefore does not conform to the aristocratic values of the patriarch. Killing one's lover or oneself is heroic obedience to the patriarch, in keeping with his values, yet by negation it also expresses love, and loving is forbidden. And murder and suicide are 'not done', and so they too are forbidden by the patriarch. Hedda is caught in a double bind which is held locked in place by the contradictory law of the Father, in a dialectic which Lovborg is excluded from and whose existence he is not even aware of.

From this analysis we see one major premise of symptomatic readings of modality. What is strongly negated or heavily modalized is not necessarily untrue for the person concerned. Strong negation and heavy modalization are likely to indicate a meaning that is highly problematic and strongly contested, one whose affirmation is difficult to assert but also (since it has resisted so many repressions) highly potent, highly desirable. The unmodalized mimetic content at the end of the chain of operations (the simple affirmative) remains significant, as the indispensable starting point and source of energy of the semiosic process itself. We do not know whether or in what sense it is held to be true, but we do know that it is important, for diagnostic purposes. And so are the forces that hold this meaning in check, as revealed by a symptomatic reading.

These of course are Hedda's presumed meanings, not Ibsen's. The attribution of them to Hedda is a further modality operation on the part of Ibsen, whose modality value depends on the presumed relationship of

Ibsen to his character. He was a middle-class male, she a female of a higher social status, and he was a dramatist and a radical, she a character. All the differences in this semiosic syntagm create distance and weaken the modality of the meanings. A final distance that I have ignored for the purposes of this analysis is created by the act of translation: in this case it has been Una Ellis-Fermor the translator's construction of Hedda's modality that has been examined, not Ibsen's. Yet as with Hedda's own modality structures, s symptomatic reading is only able to generate suspicions, not confirmations or certainties. For those, we have to go to other kinds of texts, with different kinds of modalities.

Literary and dramatic texts are not the only kinds that invite a symptomatic reading of their modalities. The documents that historians of ideas analyse can never be understood in isolation. They consist of statements whose full meaning and effect can only be understood by reference to their semiosic context, the dialogue to which they contribute, the meanings and 'common-sense' understandings that they mobilize. Dramatic texts provide good models for analysis precisely because no individual statement in a play can be taken in its own terms, even though the play constructs only a version of the terms of a debate and cannot be relied on to represent them faithfully or without ideological intent.

Polemical tracts are notoriously one-sided texts, and for this reason they are typically assigned a lower modality as documents. But precisely because they are more visibly and directly implicated in some ongoing debate a symptomatic reading of modality structures is especially revealing. As an example I will take one of the most famous and influential manifestos of the nineteenth century, *The Communist Manifesto* by Karl Marx and Friedrich Engels, first published in German in 1847, official English translation published in 1850. The *Manifesto* dealt with the premises of Marxist thought, but here I will look only at a passage that deals with the same themes as Ibsen's play, the issue of sexuality and the nature of bourgeois marriage. Marx and Engels are debating objections against Communism:

> But you Communists would introduce community of women, screams the whole bourgeoisie in chorus.
>
> The bourgeois sees in his wife a mere instrument of production. He hears that the instruments of production are to be exploited in common, and, naturally, can come to no other conclusion than that the lot of being common to all will likewise fall to the women.
>
> He has not even a suspicion that the real point aimed at is to do away with their status as mere instruments of production . . .
>
> Bourgeois marriage is in reality a system of wives in common and thus, at the most, what the Communists might possibly be reproached with, is that they desire to introduce, in substitution for a hypocritically concealed, an openly legalised community of women. For the rest, it is self-evident that

the abolition of the present system of production must bring with it the
abolition of the community of women springing from that system, i.e., of
prostitution both public and private. (Marx and Engels 1968: 50)

This passage is full of markers and traces of modality. On the one hand
there are many intensifiers, whose ostensible meaning is to mark especially
strong modality but which in a symptomatic reading come to signify the
opposite, i.e. a site of uncertainty, a position under attack. References to
'real', 'really' and 'reality' commonly carry this force, as do words like
'naturally' and 'self-evidently'. Here the reference to the 'real point', for
instance (in the German, *es sich*, the thing-in-itself), is a claim about a
deep motive and a logical distinction that the enemy would have very
great suspicions about. This motive and distinction, however, are not
declared directly. They are given the modality of affirmation by a double
negation. They are offered as what the bourgeoisie would not suspect or
believe. Since the bourgeoisie by definition carry negative modality, the
statement acquires positive modality, at least for readers who assign this
modality to the borgeoisie.

The passage uses this strategy consistently, constructing a positive
modality by a process of double negation which relies on the bourgeoisie,
as the enemy, having a constant negative value. But the constructions of
this kind have considerable complexity. Take for instance the opening
sentence: 'But you Communists would introduce community of women,
screams the whole bourgeoisie in chorus.' The core phrase here is 'community of women' (in German *Weibergemeinschaft*), itself a transform of
'(males have (sexual relations with)) women in common', the imputed
agent of this transformation being the bourgeoisie. So the core meaning,
not explicitly stated, is an image of total promiscuity. The German form is
a compound noun, which has the usual effect of reifying the entity and
distancing the prior actional form.

This meaning is then subjected to a series of qualifying modalities.
'Will introduce' gives a future modality, which at the same time denies
that it is true in the present. 'Would' weakens the future modality,
making it more hypothetical. 'You Communists' is both the hypothetical
agent of the verb, and also an indicator of modality, since it establishes the
negative relation between the constructed speaker and the statement,
making it an accusation, which has a lower modality value. The German
word *ihr* ('you') defines the relationship, and hence the modality, in a
more specific way than does the English: it is an intimate plural, signifying
simultaneously familiarity and contempt.

This whole structure is then positioned by the clause that follows. Any
reference to semiosic acts (e.g. 'I think/say/believe') normally weakens
modality, and the process of weakening is intensified the more hostile/
unreliable the producer of the text is presumed to be. 'Screams' (*schreit*)

describes the kind of excessive affirmation that is normally read symptomatically, as an indication of irrational excess. 'The whole bourgeoisie in chorus' (*im Chor*) works in a more complex and subtle fashion. For a whole group to agree is normally a positive modal indicator. Here, in so far as the group has a predefined negative modal value the collective nature of the statement intensifies the negative modality. 'Chorus', however, has a negative modality for a different reason. Whatever group speaks 'in chorus', in current English usage as in nineteenth-century German, speaks in what is labelled as a low-modality code, the specially marked non-everyday form of the song or chant. By claiming that this accusation is spoken in the chorus genre Marx and Engels are assigning it that modality.

The result of this series of modal operations is complex and ambiguous, given its semiosic context. The core notion of 'community of women'/ (indiscriminate promiscuity) is attributed to Communists by the bourgeoisie, but this attribution is constructed by Marx and Engels. In a totally polarized polemical context, such as these modality structures rely on, Communists are presumed to read with exactly opposite modality judgements to the bourgeoisie. From this point of view whatever the bourgeoisie say is by definition false. So if we assign these values to the modality complex, the notion of a community of women is a false accusation against the Communists; this is simply a typical lie of the bourgeoisie. A bourgeois reader, however, would be presumed to negate the negative value assigned here to the bourgeoisie, and conclude that the claim is ultimately true, that Communists do advocate 'community of women' and that this set of counter-accusations is simply an elaborate smokescreen. That is, Marx and Engels should expect their enemies to believe the claim, and their allies to deny it.

Friend and foe alike would scan the text in vain for a clear statement of Communist proposals about sexuality, women and the family. The Communists 'might be reproached' with 'desiring' (not exactly proposing) an 'openly legalized community of women' – the language is as euphemistic as Hedda Gabler's, in the German as in the English, and the meaning of the proposal depends on the meaning of the prior state of affairs which it proposes to negate. But it must refer to some kind of sexual liberation, the right of all, women as well as men, to free expression of their sexuality. This is similar to the unstated core of Hedda's philosophy, whose relationship to Ibsen's own beliefs was as we saw not entirely clear. And for Marx and Engels as for Hedda and possibly for Ibsen himself it proved impossible to declare in any public form. What both could declare was a critique of bourgeois marriage. In Ibsen's play no husband and no wife is monogamous, and Marx and Engels can say, with only a slight modality-tic, that 'Bourgeois marriage is in reality [*Wirklichkeit*] a system of wives in common.' For both, the critique is sayable, though it is marked as a site of difficulty. Affirmation of free sexuality, however, finally proves impossible, for the German revolutionaries as for the Norwegian radical.

A final paradox is that the buried meaning in this text is designed to be more accessible to the enemy, the bourgeoisie, than to the working-class allies. So the extreme polarization on which the modality structures seem to depend collapses, because the bourgeoisie are not always wrong and the proletariat/loyal Communists are not always right. On this topic, the working classes of Marx's day were more Puritan than some sections of the bourgeoisie, and clear calls for a sexual revolution would have alienated support for the political and economic transformation that the *Manifesto* proclaims. Marx and Engels knew about the radical sexual proposals of the Utopian socialists who preceded them, whose radicalism influenced them though they distrusted their utopian idealism. In an earlier draft, *The Principles of Communism*, written by Engels, presented in the form of a catechism, there is this statement:

Question 21: What influence will the communist order of society have on the family?
Answer: It will make the relation between the sexes a purely private relation which concerns only the persons involved, and in which society has no call to interfere. (Marx and Engels 1975–80: vol. 6, 502)

This answer opens the possibility of a multiplicity of kinds of sexual relationship, many of them going outside the bounds of conventional monogamy. It is the brief legitimation of a transformation of sexual relationships to match the transformation of political relationships that communism proposed. But as many feminists have pointed out, though both Marx and Engels were seriously committed to this domain of revolution, neither they nor their readers or followers were yet ready to give such proposals the modality of achievable reality. The *Manifesto* therefore had to include this meaning and also neutralize it. Its presence even in so masked a form was a tribute to the tenacity with which Marx and Engels held to it, while the extent of its masking was an indication of their sense of the overwhelming hostility it would arouse.

This is the kind of 'truth' a symptomatic reading can recover: the site of battles that were important, not necessarily who was fighting or what it was about or who won. Analysis of modality processes reveals claims and deceptions, not truth or reality. It also points to the specific terrain of semiosic struggles, what aspects of 'common sense' cannot be brought into dispute at a particular time, for a particular group. And always a symptomatic reading scrutinizes a text but also goes outside it, searching out other texts to confirm or confound its suspicions and increase its certainty: never confusing any text, literary or other, with reality itself, but never abandoning the effort to trace the mediations and follow the dialectic by which its meanings came to have the form they did.

Modality and intervention

Literature's record in changing the world is not exactly impressive. This is unsurprising, since its typical function from the point of view of any ruling group is precisely to allow the expression of critique and aspiration in a safe form. The linchpin in systems of control of literary meaning is the modality apparatus that pre-assigns a low modality to literary texts as a general category, although as we have seen there are different modalities assigned to different genres and to different aspects of individual texts. This apparatus is enforced through reading regimes which become taken-for-granted strategies for both writers and readers, the contract that bonds them into a consensus community.

But this arrangement is never entirely stable, since it is a compromise between the interests of the dominant to confirm the dominant order and the interests of many others, including writers, that oppose it. The balance can always shift, and the truths contained by literary texts can suddenly have a new effectivity, becoming part of a process that mobilizes people and mounts a powerful challenge to 'reality' itself.

As an instance of this kind of process I will look at the phenomenon of the protest song of the 1960s, as exemplified by Bob Dylan's 'A Hard Rain's A-Gonna Fall', first performed in 1963. Dylan's songs in general, and this one in particular, formed a rallying point for youth protest in America in the 1960s. This protest was directed against the political consensus about American imperialism at home and abroad, the imperialism of the Cold War and support of right-wing regimes in Asia and elsewhere such as Korea and Vietnam, a consensus whose central premise was the 'common sense' of the need for the Ultimate Deterrent of a nuclear arsenal.

The success of this protest should not be exaggerated. The 1970s saw America's withdrawal from Vietnam but not the disbandment of the CIA or the ending of American military involvement in Central America. Not until 1987 was what seems a genuine reduction in nuclear arms achieved, through a treaty signed by a Republican president, and the strains of Bob Dylan were no longer heard throughout the land as President Reagan's pen touched paper. I do not want to make excessive claims about the effectivity of these songs or this moment. Yet undoubtedly the meanings carried by these songs were politically potent at the time, and the whole phenomenon becomes a valuable site for the study of the conditions and possibilities of literary interventions.

The first verse of this song is as follows:

> Oh, where have you been, my blue-eyed son?
> Oh, where have you been, my darling young one?

> I've stumbled on the side of twelve misty mountains,
> I've walked and I've crawled on six crooked highways,
> I've stepped in the middle of seven sad forests,
> I've been out in front of a dozen dead oceans,
> I've been ten thousand miles in the mouth of a graveyard,
> And it's a hard, it's a hard, it's a hard, and it's a hard,
> And it's a hard rain's a-gonna fall.
>
> (Dylan 1973: 66)

In its original and most potent form this text was a song, not even officially a literary text, but literature and song are adjacent semiotic forms with considerable affinity and overlap. Both are mega-genres with an overall modality value, and they include component genres each with their own modality value. Song itself ostensibly has an even lower modality-value than literature, and this initially seems curious, given the potency that this song in particular and other songs have had. We will see in a moment how this paradox arises.

The most distinctive markers of song in Western culture are at the same time transparent signifiers of their characteristic modality. Song delivery is always marked in some way by its difference from natural everyday speech, and this deviance is itself a signifier of departure from the 'common-sense' norms inscribed in everyday speech. Song-speech is normally more resonant ('musical'), purer in sound, louder, and slower, with more marked intonation patterns (tunes) and greater distortion of the sound values of speech. It is also often accompanied by musical instruments which further obscure the clarity of meaning and make rational meanings more inaudible. These characteristics give a general formula for the modality of song, as an emotional intensification and focusing of everyday meaning, less rational and more powerful and therefore (normally) more unreliable.

Dylan's delivery is recognizable as song-delivery, but it is a deviant form of it. His voice is resonant, loud and intense, but not musically pure, and less distorted than is the norm for song. These qualities signify not in themselves but against the norms of song. What they signify is rebellion (against the conventions of song) and authenticity, relative fidelity to the truths of speech, even though in fact Dylan's song-style is more distorted than most speech. In the 1963 version of the song he has no backing other than his own mouth organ and guitar accompaniment, again in context a signifier of authenticity.

Dylan's voice quality is so distinctive that it is also a complex signifier of his own identity and meaning as a singer. The modality of the song is not simply in the words, whoever sings them, however they are sung. Dylan's persona is the pivot of a semiosic syntagm which was constructed by many texts proclaiming him the 'voice of his generation'.

A crucial role in this process was played by the performance-texts in which the songs were embedded. The experience or reputation of major concerts became a powerful meaning in this overall complex. The size and nature of the audience completed the semiosic syntagm of Dylan-in-performance. A huge audience of enthusiastic young people represented not simply numbers but energy and the consciousness of mass identity, of participation in a collective. Large numbers of records sold, as with popular singers like Perry Como or Bing Crosby or Elvis Presley, backed up by the higher-modality popularity of extensive air-play on radio, contribute to the modality of a singer and a song. Dylan's record sales were not as large as theirs, but the modality-value of his concert performances more than made up for the gap. Audiences constructed by record-sales are made up of replicated individuals, and hence have only an abstract, low-modality existence, but a mass audience is a concrete reality, and it is this mass audience which provided the modality core of the construction of Bob Dylan. The current form of videoclip which plays a crucial role in the construction of the meaning of contemporary rock stars has a relatively low modality, and would not allow the same intensity of meaning that a mass concert could generate.

The text of the song constructs a dialogue, which provides a frame for the song as a whole. Each verse begins with a question by the Mother, followed by a series of mysterious answers by the son, concluding with the refrain, 'It's a hard rain'. This form is highly traditional, recalling early ballads, specifically one of the best-known of all ballads in English, 'Lord Randall', in which the mother asks a series of questions to the dying Lord Randall which progressively reveal that she is responsible for his death.

Normally the use of a past genre like use of a past tense lowers the modality of a text. But Dylan is not simply using an old form. It was crucial to the modality of this song that it was an original composition and that Dylan was its composer. Even the fact that it was freshly composed was important to its modality: it does not have the same impact or the same modality 'now' (e.g. in 1989) as it had then, even as sung by Dylan himself. But in addition to the high modality of the very new, it had an enhanced modality from the oldness of the traditional form. The fusion by Dylan of the very old and the totally new creates the most powerful modality of all, the timeless present, giving the category of a truth that is as true now as it has always been, sustained by the weight of past generations as well as the present.

The allusion implies that the Mother asking the questions is complicit in the death and horror that the poem describes, now on a cosmic not a personal scale. The answer as a whole adopts a traditional riddle form, giving a series of statements that seem to evade a clear sense. The different answers have different modalities, and even the component words have different modalities, depending on the general modality-value of the contexts they are associated with. The specific numbers, for instance, have a high modality, since counting is a high-modality activity in our society, but a phrase like 'misty mountains' has the relatively low modality of poetic language. Normally in a text a few such words can give a modality-value to the text as a whole, but in this case the contradictory signals leave the overall modality-value problematic.

The riddle form constructs a doubled text with a double modality-value. The individual clauses seem almost nonsense, which has very low modality-value, but the real meaning they conceal has correspondingly high modality, for those that can decode it. The strategy constructs a double community, those who understand/believe and those who are excluded by incomprehension or disbelief. The strategy is similar to that of Theatre of the Absurd, where a powerfully cohesive community is created by a shared belief in the profound importance and ultimate mean-ingfulness of a seemingly absurd text. Here as there the strategy is sus-tained by attributing great power to the one who alone knows, at some level, the 'sense' of the non-sense, and whose mysteriousness underpins the cohesion and power of the group.

The mysteriousness of the verse acts sets up a contrast with the clarity of the chorus. The previous statements were in the past tense. The chorus is in the present, even though it is describing a future disaster. 'A-gonna' is not a departure from everyday speech but a defiant affirmation of its forms and modalities. 'Hard rain' was not ambiguous or archaic, for its audi-ence: it referred to radioactive rain after a nuclear blast, a phenomenon not known to Lord Randall or his mother. The repetition itself enhances modality, by a process that advertisers know and use. Repetition typically has the effect of making the next occurrence of the item easy to predict, giving it a right to appear in that context, a truth-to-context which is a transparent signifier of general truth, even though what is repeated three times is not always three times as true.

But in considering the effect of this song it is important to stress that its function is quite different from that of an advertisement. The core proposition, that the future is threatened by a nuclear holocaust, was not in doubt with Dylan's audience. On the contrary it was the central premise in the 'common sense' which united them as a group. Its common-sense status thus gratuitously reinforced the modality of the chorus, creating modality-overkill. Within modality, belief and solidarity are so interdependent that each constructs the other. But where Marx and Engels relied on the solidarity of their Communist readers to create belief in their views, Dylan's song used the excess of belief to construct an especially intense state of solidarity. Dylan's text could mobilize people not because it was able to persuade them of a truth but because it could draw on a prior reservoir of acts of persuasion to draw them together. And it was especially powerful because it did not have to try very hard to enhance the modality of its claims. On the contrary, as we have seen, its modality values are complex, ambiguous, and unstable:

in some respects closer to Ionesco or even Austen than to Ibsen or Marx.

With Dylan's song as with all literary texts, the modality-value is a function of modality claims in the text plus the general structures of modality genres and 'common-sense' assumptions of particular groups at particular times. A textual analysis on its own is therefore unable to account for the power of Dylan's text in its original context, or for the definite but different modality and effects it would have for different audiences in different context – as for instance an English class in Britain in 1989, with students who were babes in 1963. This is why it is common for texts which had an extraordinary impact in their day to seem rather stiff and wooden or implausible and ineffective to later readers. In order to have had such an impact they must have worked both with and against the modality structures of the reading regimes of the day, invoking the invisible mass of an oppositional 'common sense' to charge their content with the highest possible reality-value, while seeming to adopt low-modality forms and content in deference to the received position of literary modalities. As that invisible mass invisibly recedes, such works can be left with only their selfconscious, self-protective disclaimers, announcing their new irrelevance to a new generation who cannot but believe them.

The same thing happens, however, with every literary text to some extent. All literary texts play a complex game with modality. They use markers of unreality to allow contact with their truths and construct illusory realities to enhance their power, giving rise to the contradictory and unstable modality-characteristics of literature that have caused such puzzlement since the days of Plato. So complex is the game and so subtly do its rules change and its players twist and turn that all attempts to codify the truth of literature are continually at risk. But this is because the issues of 'truth' and 'reality' are always at stake in every act of semiosis, in literature as in life. They are important enough to justify our continuous attention, unless for reasons of our own we choose otherwise.

SOURCES AND CONTEXTS

The category of 'modality' is derived from linguistics, where the work of Halliday 1976, 1985 provided the basis for the social theory of modality developed in Kress and Hodge, *Language as Ideology*, 1979. See also Kress, 'Tense as Modality', 1977, Hodge, 'Cliche and reality-control: the Modality of Duckspeak', 1986b, and Hodge and Tripp, *Children and Television*, 1986, for the development of modality systems in children.

Outside linguistics, Bateson's theory of schizophrenia includes a major contribution to the understanding of systems and functions of modality (1973). See also Laing, *Knots*, 1972. Foucault's concepts of 'power/knowledge' and 'truth effects' provide a useful social and historical framework for studying modality systems as they operate in particular discursive formations: see e.g. *Power-Knowledge*, 1980.

In spite of a two-millennia obsession with the problem of reality, literary theory has not taken much note of the category of modality. See the chapter in Ruthrof, 1981 'Fictional Modality: a Challenge to Linguistics', for a useful discussion. Discussion of the problem of 'reality' in literary criticism has mainly focused on the insidious practices of realism: see e.g. Belsey 1980 and Eagleton 1983. Within Marxist literary criticism the opposing positions were articulated by Brecht, whose theatrical practice was designed to deconstruct the taken-for-grantedness of the dominant conventions of bourgeois realism (Brecht 1964) and by Lukacs, as in *The Meaning of Contemporary Realism*, 1963, which argues that the classics of bourgeois realism had a firmer grasp of historical and social truth than modernist and later realist texts. On the potentially radical role of fantasy see Jackson, *Fantasy: The Literature of Subversion*, 1981.

In the teaching of English in schools, the liberation of literature from reality through the category of 'imagination' coexists with an insistence on the palpable reality of concrete 'personal experience', as in the writing pedagogy of Britton 1975: see Mares, ' "Personal Growth" as a Frame for Teaching Literature', 1988, for a critique. Bettelheim's *The Uses of Enchantment*, 1976, made an influential case for the role of low-modality forms such as fairy stories in children's development.

A number of influential critics have diagnosed a pathology of modality systems in modern post-industralist consumer society. See e.g. Baudrillard, *Simulations*, 1985, for an apocalyptic version of this case, and Eco, *Travels in Hyperreality*, 1986, for a more focused account of the 'post-modern condition'.

History as a discipline has had to recognize the problem of 'reality' in theory and practice. This is reflected in the polemic about 'empiricism', with its assumption that the truth about the past is easily knowable, requiring only the careful accumulation of data, but even a classic of historical method such as Carr's *What is History?*, 1961, recognizes the practical need for scepticism about sources, such as the category of modality enables. On some of the modality operations characteristic of historical writing as a disciplinary practice, see the classic analysis by Barthes, 'Historical Discourse', 1967. On the historiographic assumptions and discursive practices of the 'classic' historians of the nineteenth century see White's *Metahistory: the Historical Imagination in Nineteenth Century Europe*, 1973.

On Absurdist theatre, see Esslin, *The Theatre of the Absurd*, 1969. For a semiotic discussion of modalities of performance and the 'performance text' see Elam, *The Semiotics of Theatre and Drama*, 1980. A sophisticated treatment of the modality of film is Douglas, *Film and Meaning*, 1988. On the category of 'irony' in literary criticism Muecke's *Irony*, 1970, is still useful. For a recent literary critical discussion of Austen's 'irony' see Odmark, *An Understanding of Jane Austen's Novel: Character, Value and Ironic Perspective*, 1986. Weinsheimer's 'Theory of Character: *Emma*', 1979, develops sophisticated doubts about the stability of common-sense notions of character, but in the process removes the ideological meanings of the text from its originating social context. But see Poovey 1984 for a subtle feminist analysis that situates Austen's language and technique in its contemporary semiosic context. On Ibsen's realism and its aims, see Williams, *Modern Tragedy*, 1966. On Marx and Engels and their views on the family and women, see Waters, *Feminism and the Marxist Movement*, 1972, and Vogel, *Marxism and the Oppression of Women*, 1983. On the relations between these traditions and anarchism see Ehrlich, *Socialism, Anarchism and Feminism*, 1977.

7
Narrative and Society

Narrative is an all-pervasive form, existing in countless texts at every level of every society. Etymologically the word comes from the Latin *narrare*, to tell a story, which in turn probably derives from *gnarus*, knowledgeable about. 'Narrative' retains this potent link between knowing and telling which is central to its ideological effectiveness, since it seems to guarantee a transparent form of telling in which the form of speech closely matches its object. This object is itself regarded as transparent, the taken-for-granted concrete world of actions, processes and events, along with the patterns of causality and linkages that make sense of it.

Traditional literary criticism fully recognized the existence and importance of narrative. It has developed terms, concepts and strategies for analysing and discussing its literary forms and effects. New theories of narrative have emerged in the last fifty years which have extended the scope of the category and allowed some crucial connections to be made, especially outside the texts of the canon, but these developments have not consigned all previous ideas to oblivion. On the contrary, some of the key terms of traditional criticism, such as 'plot', 'character' and 'setting', have a very long ancestry indeed, and they still form part of an everyday understanding of this everyday form. A theory so deeply sedimented may need to be retheorized by a new paradigm, but it cannot safely be ignored.

In this task of connecting with and reworking earlier traditions, it is useful to go back at least as far as Aristotle, whose *Poetics*, written in Greece in the fourth century BC, has proved immensely influential in Western criticism, providing some of the most durable critical categories in common use. Aristotle was mainly concerned with one genre, tragedy in its classic Greek form, and his terms have had to be adapted to other genres at other times. His key terms were plot ('mythos') and character. He also added four others: setting ('spectacle'), 'thought' and 'diction' (which together correspond to 'discourse') and finally, specific to Greek drama in performance, what he termed 'melody', his undeveloped but useful attempt to incorporate non-verbal components and para-texts into a comprehensive account of literary phenomena.

Aristotle regarded plot and character as inseparable, but saw plot as the more potent signifier of the meaning of texts, at least for Greek epic and tragedy, the genres he was most concerned with. Not all genres foreground narrative, and not all traditions of criticism have preferred the kind of narrative that Aristotle himself favoured, a plot bound by rigorous causality into a beginning, a middle and an end with no loose strands hanging over. But in spite of their specific ideological inflections, Aristotle's basic categories have been durable because they are positioned near the centre of what do seem to be semiotic universals: people and their attributes, physical and semiosic actions, contexts and paratexts, as they would be rephrased in social semiotics. In traditional literary criticism Aristotle's terms tend to be used taxonomically, without systematic or explicit concern for either society or meaning. But from a social semiotic perspective we need to understand clearly how they carry meaning, and how that meaning is intrinsically social and ideological in form and function.

In spite of the prominence Aristotle gave to plot, the point of anchorage of the social meaning of texts is the set of people and relationships that they represent: something like 'character' in traditional criticism, though shorn of the particular ideologies built into that term. The basic meaning of characters is not given by their individual subjectivity but by the categories that make them social individuals, who are assigned their social value by paradigmatic sets which organize members of that social group: categories including national or ethnic identity, class, gender, and age and many others. But meaning only exists in syntagms, not in paradigms alone. The minimal syntagm which has social meaning is either a relational syntagm, linking a person to a quality which has been assigned a social meaning, or an actional syntagm, linking a category of person to a category of action, physical or semiosic, which has been assigned a social meaning.

People and actions, then, as Aristotle recognized, together form the primary constituents of narrative and the basis of its social meaning. To this we can add setting, context or domain as the third primary category, the physical dimensions of space and time which inexorably determine material existence, as they are assigned a social meaning by particular social groups. These three categories apply to every unit of text that can represent actions, from words, phrases and clauses, all the way through to texts, oeuvres, series and genres. In so far as these mimetic syntagms of action can all be organized by the same set of paradigmatic categories, they can all have a commensurable form, which will then mediate a complex social meaning that is active across all levels of the text. The term used in semiotics for this commonality of form is *homology*, which in this case refers to a pattern of identities and differences between syntagms of different kinds, at different levels of a text or semiosic structure.

Homology also establishes two other systems of linkage that are essential in analysing the social meaning of narrative. One is between the mimetic and the semiosic plane, seeing the narrative event as itself a syntagm ordered like a narrative, organized by similar sets of paradigmatic categories. The other linkage is between both these planes and the social world itself, in so far as this is organized into syntagmatic regularities that make sense of social identity and social existence. This is a set of ideological forms structured like narratives, narratives that are the prescriptions for a life, that give it shape and direction and closure, inscribed in notions of 'career', 'life plan' and ritualized progressions through the various stages of a 'life cycle'. This last syntagmatic level is decisive for the social meaning of narrative, since it is the recurring signified or reference point of the mimetic plane and the essential site of every semiosic process. From this follows a basic premise for the social analysis of narrative: the social categories that organize the levels of narrative must first be understood in relation to the dominant categories and syntagmatic forms of social life, as these operate through the semiosic context of specific narratives.

The social meaning of myth

The category 'literature' that has organized literary criticism for at least two centuries uses the term 'narrative' of a narrow range of genres, primarily novels, short stories and narrative poems. These literary narratives are typically complex and sophisticated texts produced in societies so well known and familiar that the relevant social categories seem too obvious to mention, so taken-for-granted as to be invisible to readers or critics. In this section I will concentrate instead on kinds of narrative that challenge and extend these normal and normalizing assumptions about the meaning and function of narrative forms.

I begin with the category of myth. In some usages this is not an unfamiliar term in traditional criticism. On the contrary it has been an inexhaustibly exciting and resonant term, invoking a mysterious substratum of 'primitive' (primal) culture as mediated through thousands of years of Western literature and art. Myth in this numinous sense seems nothing like the myths collected and published by anthropologists working with actual 'primitive' peoples. Typically as published these are stripped of all the verbal elaborations that marked their cultural performance, reduced to their 'content' as short, opaque and alien texts, unreadable as literature and not easy to interpret as social or historical documents either. In this form it seems inexplicable how the groups concerned could value them as highly as they seem to do, claiming that they carry core social meanings vital to the survival of their culture. Between the nebulous plenitude of Western archetypal myths and the impoverished fragments of contemporary non-Western myths the genre itself has become unavailable for serious study in the English curriculum, in spite of its continuing prestige. The depth of the fissures in the concept is extraordinary and in urgent need of explanation. We require a strategy for reading the social meanings of myths, in terms of which we can specify what we need to know about their social conditions and contexts and what dimensions of the text carry their social meaning and therefore must be incorporated or indicated in transcriptions and translations. We can then begin to understand the social functions of the treatment of 'myth' in the traditional curriculum, as a potent absence which removes at a stroke both the social history of contemporary English narrative and the continuing vitality of non-Western narrative forms.

It was from the anthropological study of 'primitive' myths that structuralism made its most significant contributions to the theory of narrative. Here the key figure is Lévi–Strauss, from whose formidable, controversial and not always consistent body of work I draw the following propositions that feed into a social semiotics of myth. Firstly he explored the 'cultural logic' that enabled what he called 'the savage mind' to construct the social meaning of times and places, objects and activities as these occurred in a range of socially significant texts: myths, rituals, art, laws and customs. His postulation of this underlying logic, inscribed in a set of paradigmatic categories and their transformations, was his most crucial contribution to semiotics, the indispensable basis for his analysis of myth and society. He emphasized the protean nature of this cultural logic, its capacity to apply effortlessly to new instances, and assimilate them to familiar patterns and meanings. In particular he saw a consistent homology that linked meanings in the sphere of economics (exchange of goods), sexuality (exchange of women, as he termed it) and discourse (exchange of meanings/ knowledge). He was primarily concerned with semiosic events incorporated into the mimetic content of narratives (the posing and solving of enigmas, transgressions of knowledge as signifiers of other forbidden exchanges) but his homological structure provides the basis for a theory of the process of narration as itself structured like a narrative. In these terms it becomes possible to read the meanings of narrative and narration within a single framework, dealing with the same areas of social life.

Lévi–Strauss's cultural logic also established a linkage which is an essential stage in establishing the social meaning of verbal narrative. An earlier form of analysis of myth (as spoken narrative) had opposed it to ritual (as enacted narrative), treating most surviving myths as uncomprehending rationalizations of a vanished ritual. Lévi–Strauss treated the two types of text as transformationally related in the present of analysis, with neither type of text having privileged status. This move allows us to examine the complex transformational and functional links between the two forms in a given instance as a vital step in keying verbal texts into texts that control social behaviour. I will depart from Lévi–Strauss in expecting that in practice, in most instances, the ritual text in this complex will have a higher status for a group than associated myths, since rituals are inscribed in bodies, a high-modality medium, and they are normally policed more carefully than verbal narratives. But this is an empirical claim which needs to be examined in every instance, not a principle of analysis.

One of the functions of myth in Lévi–Strauss's view is to address the most fundamental oppositions confronting the culture, as problems of its logic and dilemmas for its social order. These problems are so fundamental that in his view they cannot actually be solved, so that myth's function is only to appear to solve them, deploying semiosic sleight-of-hand. Myth therefore provides evidence of the terms of these problems, rather than stable solutions, though the speciousness of what is accepted as a solution is part of its social meaning. There is one important class of ritual texts that have similar qualities and functions. These are what have been termed 'rites of passage' (Van Gennep 1961). These rituals confront the inconvenient social fact that every community and every individual is subject to change which cumulatively threatens the illusion of stability of the social order, and the fiction of the identity of the social individual. They do so by taking as raw material the narrative given erratically by biology, and transforming it into a carefully segmented narrative, in which the moments of risk where change is acknowledged to have occurred are organized by specific rituals whose function is to police the anomalies created by maturation and other changes of status, clarifying ambiguities and clearly marking and legitimating transitions. The form of these rituals typically reflects this function. First individuals are separated from their former identity and set of relationships, then they are inserted into a ritual domain where their old identity is destroyed and they 'die', to be reborn into their new identity and status, and finally they are incorporated into the community clearly marked by their new identity.

Rituals therefore encode primary categories of the society concerned. But since they are designed to cope with the breakdown and reconstitution of these categories they are not simply a reflection of 'normal' values. In practice they have a particular modality-value, in order to carry out their contradictory task of acknowledging transgression while affirming order. Myths serve a parallel function, often working in close conjunction with rituals, complementing and elaborating or reshaping their forms, sometimes incorporating fragments of myths as in-texts, transformed and inserted into particular moments of the narrative itself.

To illustrate how such myths may work I will look at the following short narrative, which I will transcribe in full, since conventions for transcribing and paraphrasing such texts are an issue, and this particular text would not otherwise be accessible for most readers. It is a story told by an Aboriginal,

David Downs, in his own Walmatjarri language to Joyce Hudson, a linguist who recorded and transcribed it in the Kimberley region of Western Australia in the 1970s. The translation is mine, drawing on Joyce Hudson's invaluable grammar and commentary.

'Galburdoo the Water Snake'

1

Me, I am *pinarri*, expert about Galburdoo.

It devoured me one hot season.
No rain.
I saw a wind come from the east,
stirring the water,
swirling it round.

We dived,
we fell,
many men in the water.

Galburdoo devoured me
as I dived.

They saw me
and said one to another
'Where will he come up?'

Galburdoo was small
and entered the body of a snake
(you can see this in the picture).

He followed me,
my uncle grabbed me, my mother's brother.

He dragged me into its stomach,
Galburdoo, Lamboo.

Many people were there.

After that I was nothing.

Now I am *pinarri* in water.
I can go down deep,
and come up far away.

2

It devoured me like this.
I went down in the river
and they lost me.

We clung to the south bank,
and climbed trees,
and jumped into the water below.

They threw me into the middle of the river –
'I can't swim!
'I'm a bushman,
I'm not *pinarri* with rivers!'

Then it devoured me.
Down, down into the water I went,
west, downstream,
and I saw the sand on the river's bed.

Down, down I went,
dark, whirling around.

Then my brother grabbed me,
Spider.

The others almost cut themselves for grief,
but they found me, to the west,
they helped me out,
and showed me off, like this.

It was him who saved me,
Spider.

Near there I came up,
he took me by the hand,
and we two returned.

And they cried out then,
they almost cut themselves for grief.
They found me after I'd come up,
far to the west.

3

There was another time, going from Christmas Creek.
I'll tell you the story.

On my way from Christmas Creek I went through the river.
I went carrying meat on a stick.

I went into the water like this.
This water is nearby.
I like it.

I went down in the darkness,
moved on,
and came up again,
just travelled on,
carrying the meat.

It didn't devour me, the water.
It's deep,
but me, I am *pinarri*.

David Downs, the narrator of this story, is an adult Aboriginal male, telling it to an adult White female, who collected it in the early 1970s in order to publish it in a scholarly form (for White middle-class scholars) and to preserve a language and culture which at one time seemed threatened with extinction, and which in the 1970s was showing signs of resilience. The meaning of this semiosic transaction, then, was as part of a strategy of resistance to a process that has been described as cultural genocide. This has been a dominant theme in recent histories of Aboriginals in Australia (see e.g. Reynolds 1978). Aboriginals had not simply been dispossessed of their lands. Their basic social patterns and cultural forms were also subjected to a range of attacks. Before the coming of the Whites, Aboriginal identity was sustained by traditional cultural forms, the rituals, myths and customs that organized their social life into families, kin groups, totems and tribes. Without these, many Aboriginals became demoralized, sinking into a culture of poverty and hopelessness. As an index of this, figures for suicide among Aboriginals are still of epidemic proportions. It is for such reasons that Aboriginals see the recovery of their traditional culture under their own control as having a key role to play in sustaining a sense of social identity and purpose.

This summary description indicates a context in which a sociologist or a 'people's historian' might situate this text. But although these macro categories are relevant to the semiosic participants, they do not seem obviously relevant to the mimetic content of the narrative. The story seems on the face of it to describe three incidents which happened to David Downs, all involving water and the risk of drowning. As a description of incidents from everyday life, we can immediately recognize the presence of another kind of text with another modality, one in which monstrous water-snakes swallow and regurgitate boys, the modality of myth and ritual which allows magical events to occur. But it doesn't declare itself to have any grand status as myth. If it were produced as a piece of writing in an English classroom, it would have seemed simply a quaint and fanciful autobiographical sketch.

One way of situating such a text in its own framework of meaning is to attend closely to the language used at key points in the narrative, openings and closings and other transition-points, since these are precisely the points where the meaning of the narrative is itself at risk for the narrator and the culture. This is where homologies are at their most dense and most functional, linking microstructures (words, phrases, clauses, episodes) with major macrostructural elements. This is therefore where the exact language of the text needs to be most carefully scrutinized, in its original form, where the issue of translation is at its most acute. In this text, every word in the first line is dense with significance, in the way that literary criticism expects only of works of high literary status. The first two words of the story in Walmatjarri are *marni ngaji*, both of which can be translated as 'I'. In Walmatjarri as in many other Aboriginal languages, the first person pronoun can be incorporated into the verbal group, or it can be made explicit (*marni*) or it can be emphasized (*ngaji*). By using this emphatic and marked form, David Downs is foregrounding his own ego in a way that is uncharacteristic of Aboriginal culture, but entirely in keeping with the purposes of this text, announcing that the meaning of the narrative that follows is his acquisition of his own identity, his own clearly marked ego structure. And the 'knowledge' of Galburdoo that he goes on to describe is a decisive moment in his acquisition of a social identity.

The key word *pinarri* in Walmatjarri cannot be translated by a single English word. It derives from *pinna* meaning 'ear' or the activity of listening. So *pinarri* indicates a kind of knowledge that comes through listening to others, not from direct experience. The word has the same kind of authority as *gnarus*, the root of 'narrative', drawing on the conditions of oral culture that are common to both. In both cases, this is not regarded as unreliable hearsay knowledge, but on the contrary as reliably transmitted social knowledge, communicated by one who is authorized to know: the only legitimate way of 'knowing' traditional myth and ritual in Aboriginal society. The word thus has the sense of 'instructed', almost 'passed an examination in relation to'. The narrative that follows, then, describes the tests that David Downs has passed.

The text goes on to describe three separate incidents, three occasions when he nearly drowned. Each of these has the same underlying frame, a syntagmatic form that is repeated in each. For formal analysis the problem is to see how this essential frame is to be located and isolated by what can be termed *syntagmatic reduction*, but in practice this does not prove difficult, since the underlying frame is endlessly repeated, an organizing principle for both speakers and hearers, readers and writers of texts. The process of syntagmatic reduction is an intervention into a semiosic process which is not innocent, but nor is it fundamentally different or alien from the other interventions that semiosic activity continuously involves.

This abstract frame consists of a sequence of three syntagms. First David Downs, young, male and Aboriginal, nearly drowns. This is consistently translated into another syntagmatic form in which he is swallowed by the Water-snake Galburdoo. Then he is saved, first by his maternal uncle, then by his brother Spider, and finally by himself. We can set out the syntagmatic frame as follows:

1 X (Downs) nearly drowns in water
2 Water/monster nearly kills X
3 Y saves X

This frame allows us to assemble an inventory of the significant characters in the narrative, and from this we can derive the categories which are operative in the narrative, which are the key to its social meaning. These are also not coincidentally the primary categories that organize 'rites of passage' in traditional Aboriginal society. The incidents follow a significant sequence. Each time Downs is older, and the person who saves him is closer in age and more equivalent in status, with himself as an adult being the limit case. The most prominent category here is age, which organizes the individual narrative and its sequence, making each episode a 'rite of passage' through which David Downs's social identity is repeatedly constructed. The second category is blood or kinship. The first helper is a maternal uncle, a relationship which anthropologists call avunculates, one that is of great significance in Aboriginal society as in many others. The maternal uncle is a male who is allied to the mother and whose social meaning and function therefore is to mediate between male and female allegiances. The maternal uncle plays an important role in the rites of passage through which Aboriginal boys are initiated into their adult status.

The second saviour is David Downs's own brother, again a male related by blood through a common mother, this time someone of his own age, representing consanguinity but not power. And David Downs, who is his own saviour in the last episode, has the same mother as himself. Thus we see that although no woman appears to play a role in the narrative, gender is very much at issue as a covert category in Downs's construction of his adult identity. And though the gender of Galburdoo is not specified (Aboriginal pronouns are not marked for gender) Galburdoo is clearly a local manifestation of one of the most significant figures in Aboriginal mythology, the Rainbow Serpent, a creative who is often bi-gendered but is associated especially with female fecundity. In this case David Downs drew an accompanying illustration which shows graphically the womblike nature of Galburdoo's interior. In each incident the drowning is a reverse birth, or a death and a birth, following the classic formula for Aboriginal initiation rituals. The ritual (and David Downs's narrative) thus describes a passage from a destructive maternal involvement to a state of detachment as self-sufficient male, while using the imagery of the process of birth which is a female site of power.

There are other persons who play a role in this story. First there are David Downs's companions, Aboriginals who in the first instance were indifferent to his fate and in the second actively caused the problem by throwing him in too deep. On this second occasion they then grieved for him, cutting themselves in the traditional mourning rituals for the dead. These individuals are Aboriginal and male but not specified as linked by blood and a common mother, and the role they play is equivocal. In the final incident David Downs is alone, the author of both the risk and the rescue, positioned at a slight distance from Aboriginal society.

The place where he is coming from is also significant in these terms. Christmas Creek is the name of a location to which Downs gives the Aboriginal name but which was a town constructed by Whites. This is one site where by implication the opposition between Aboriginal and White is touched on. Another point is in the second incident, where Downs cries out 'I'm a bushman, I'm not *pinarri* with rivers!' The word translated here as 'bushman' is in Walmmatjarri *pujman*, an Aboriginal loan word, their pronunciation of 'bushman'. So at this point in the narrative he is constructing his adult identity as given by White society, announcing that his competence as a 'bushman' does not include an Aboriginal competence with rivers or the skill of swimming. He evidently labels swimming as an Aboriginal activity not a White one, in spite of White Australians' pride in their swimming ability, because in his experience it is a knowledge that Aboriginals learn from Aboriginals, not from Whites. The narrative thus assigns to learning to swim the status of a prized Aboriginal activity, the mastery of which confirms his status as an Aboriginal. The rite of passage is a progression from juvenile status, under the influence of women, to autononomous male status, and also from dependence on White knowledges to an Aboriginal autonomy, a full Aboriginality which also includes self-sufficiency from Aboriginals as well.

Christmas Creek and the bush itself mark two poles of the context of the narrative. There are other ways in which the spatial context is assigned meaning. East and west are mentioned a number of times, with a consistent value. East, where the sun rises, is a transparent signifier for birth, origins, and west, where the sun sets, signifies death, in this story as in White Australian idiom. In this part of Australia rivers run roughly westwards into the ocean, thus reinforcing this value, so that downstream signifies death also. Downs repeats 'deep' to describe the river or water hole at its most deadly, so that 'deep' clearly has this significance too: up = life and down = death.

In this way an element of context can contribute meaning to the actional syntagms that make up the narrative. For instance, the cause of the second incident is the game that the youths are playing beside the river. The game consists of climbing trees (up) and jumping into the water (down). The meanings of up and down give this activity a meaning that is homologous to the movement of the narrative, a game of life and death, even though the 'death' is only a small risk.

This game, no doubt a common and enjoyable one for the young David Downs and his friends, is incorporated into the narrative as an in-text, a highly recognizable text from everyday life, with its own recognizable modality-value, the modality of 'play'. The game is in effect play-suicide, while the playful throwing him into the middle of the river is a play-murder, which nearly became more real than anyone intended. The homology of structure assimilates the incidents to the pattern of the overall narrative, while the different modality-value distinguishes them from both the accidental death by drowning that we presume nearly occurred, and also the symbolic death that is at the centre of the ritual. The central activity in each section has a social value in addition to a characteristic modality, and this becomes part of the meaning of the narrative. The first incident is an accident, occurring to a young boy while playing, the second concerns an older youth who is already a *pujman*, in conditions of play, but the third is work. Moreover, it is man's work (in the gendered division of labour in traditional Aboriginal society collecting and carrying *kuyi*, meat, is man's work). It is also Aboriginal not White work. So in the conclusion David Downs is moving confidently from the Whiteman's world (Christmas Creek) to an Aboriginal space in the bush, performing Aboriginal tasks as competently as he can perform in the Whiteman's economic sphere. The story overtly records his achievement of Aboriginal identity, while not renouncing his status (such as it is) within White society, though for David Downs the significant journey is back into Aboriginality, leaving White society as something that can be left to coexist.

The narrative weaves together texts from three distinct domains, myth, ritual and everyday life, mapped onto each other by a common set of paradigmatic categories. Each has its own kind of truth, but the effect of Downs's narrative is to obscure the difference so that overall the story has a curious and contradictory modality, mingling the factual and the magical in a way that is disconcerting for White readers. And though sequence and progression are fundamental principles of organization, the semiosic action of his narrative keeps on departing from sequentiality. This difference between sequence in the text and in the events described is a common one which is recognized in narrative theory in the opposition between 'text' and 'story', but the key to the meaning of this discrepancy is to understand the meaning of both structures, and the transformations that link them. For instance, at the beginning of the second section (which is marked in my translation but not in Downs's original story) Downs starts with the central moment ('It devoured me like this') before he goes on to describe how this came about. Later he mentions the grief of his mates twice, the second time after he has already described their delight when they had found him. This kind of play with sequentiality asserts the coexistence and interpenetration of two ordering principles, one of which is linear and progressive, the other which is circular, a pattern of recurrences. So by the end of his story David Downs represents himself as having achieved full status as a man and an Aboriginal, yet each episode also recorded his seemingly definitive achievement of the status of being 'expert' about Galburdoo. The final words of the narrative repeat the opening almost exactly, to achieve the kind of closure that is associated with high art, but which in practice has a common ideological meaning in both Aboriginal and Western culture.

We can now return to the semiosic transaction which constituted this story, and see its significance. David Downs is constructing a narrative which is neither a traditional myth, although it involves a figure from myth, nor a lifestory, a 'trustori' as it would be termed by Aboriginals in the area (see Roe and Muecke 1983). His own story is recast by incorporating as in-texts both a mythic narrative and a masked account of a traditional ritual. This ritual, like all Aboriginal transition-rituals, constructs a strongly gendered identity, and its details are forbidden knowledge to women in traditional society. For Downs to tell this tale to someone who is White and a woman is therefore a double transgression, only possible if he can give her an honarary reclassification as not-really-woman, or if he can trust that she will not recognize the real content of the tale: that is, if he can incorporate her into a new Aboriginal identity, or can rely on her own self-exclusion through ignorance. Clearly these are contradictory moves, although they correspond to contradictory elements in the situation itself, where the act of recording the story is both support and appropriation.

The social meaning of this text includes the meaning of its semiosic activity. The mimetic content gives some of the key categories at risk – age, gender, kinship and race – though some of these are occluded and implicit. It also offers the narrative of a successful transition, one which signifies the construction of a stable identity in which oppositions and contradictions are incorporated and resolved. Because it draws on texts (myths and rituals) which have high authority within Aboriginal society it derives authority from those texts, though we cannot know this from Downs's text on its own. These rituals were designed to sustain both structure and change, allowing change within a specific space so that outside that space the social structures would remain unchanged. But the traditional rites of passage were not designed to allow movement between Aboriginal and White culture, or to construct an identity which is a stable and meaningful resolution of those powerful oppositions. David Downs's narrative achieves this kind of mediation. It is an individual act of mediation, a private ritual, which is a contradiction in terms, certainly for Aboriginal culture where rituals are socially constrained acts of mediation. Yet this text is not an assault on these traditional categories and genres, but a response to the difficult situation in which Aboriginal culture and Aboriginal individuals like David Downs find themselves. For the historian or sociologist or anthropologist, the text is revealing not because of the 'facts' that it contains (there aren't any giant water-snakes lurking in the rivers of the Kimberleys) but because of the nexus it shows between traditional structures of ritual and myth, and the active construction of social identity to cope with the pressures of non-traditional reality. It does not represent the processes of cultural genocide directly, but it does show what is at stake for Aboriginal people in that struggle. It is not a culturally prestigious text within either Aboriginal or non-Aboriginal society, but this only gives it greater value as a text to be incorporated into an English curriculum.

Fractured narrative

Classic narrative tells a story, a series of events that unfold inexorably from beginning to end. In this sort of narrative the implacable logic and its sheer visibility as rendered by the narrative form are core meanings carried transparently by these qualities of form. In other well known kinds of narrative, of which Greek tragedy and detective fiction provide clear instances, the classic narrative form is filtered through a narrative process that systematically distorts it, constructing a semiosic narrative that moves the reader from a state of powerless ignorance to a condition of equality with the narrator. This transformational work becomes a transparent signifier of the meaning of this form. But in many other cases the transformational work of narration does not have such an insistent quality, and it does not operate on such a monolithic underlying structure. In these cases, the genres are often not treated as narrative at all. Lyric poetry for instance normally eschews straightforward narrative, representing instead subjective thoughts and images and feelings that arise in response to some theme or situation. But these texts still ultimately draw on and are interpreted in relation to an understood social material world, organized through narrative syntagms that have simply been more drastically rearranged than is the case with classic narrative. It is still a form of narrative analysis that is required to bring out the social meaning of these occluded narratives.

As an example of such narratoids I will take a poem by Sylvia Plath entitled 'Lady Lazarus', written in 1962. The poem begins:

> I have done it again.
> One year in every ten
> I manage it –
>
> A sort of walking miracle, my skin
> Bright as a Nazi lampshade,
> My right foot
>
> A paperweight,
> My face a featureless, fine
> Jew linen.

The poem, for those who know the relevant pre-text, is 'about' a failed suicide attempt, not her first. Within a year she was to make another attempt which would be successful. These two 'facts' are each a narrative fragment, each of them a semiosic syntagm that is produced by a different text outside this poem. One was known to Plath when she wrote the poem, the other not, but both are constructed out of the same paradigmatic ingredients, within the same syntagmatic frame which they share with the poem. The homology binds the mimetic and the semiosic plane into a complex social meaning which is in some respects not a meaning that Plath herself could produce or control, because the terms through which she constructed 'her' meanings were inevitably social, not merely individual.

As with the Downs text, it is useful to sketch in the terms and the social categories that seem to organize the semiosic plane. Sylvia Plath's situation when she wrote the poem was defined by markers of nationality and class. She was an American living in England, married to though estranged from an Englishman. Her parents were of Germanic extraction, her father an émigré from Germany, his mother the daughter of Austrian migrants to America. As German-speakers, a minority group in America, both experienced hostility and prejudice, especially during the First World War. Plath also has identity in terms of micro-categories: age (exactly thirty), gender (female) and familial status (mother and wife/non-wife).

Sylvia Plath labelled the kind of semiosic act that her poems were in the following terms, in a letter to her mother written on 21 October 1962, within three months of her death:

> Don't talk to me about the world needing cheerful stuff! What the person out of Belsen – physical or psychological – wants is nobody saying the birdies still go tweet-tweet, but the full knowledge that somebody else has been there and knows the *worst*, just what it is like. It is much more help for me, for example, to know that people are divorced and go through hell, than to hear about happy marriages. Let the *Ladies Home Journal* blather about *those*. (Plath 1975)

In this text she is constructing both a persona and a purpose for her writing. The persona is someone with 'full knowledge' (in Downs's terms, *pinarri*), and this knowledge is she claims a source of comfort to the group of people like herself who are experiencing the transition-point of passing out of marriage. And because this experience is an ultimate, she feels able to claim identity with the Jewish victims of Belsen: an identity which would be problematic in social terms, since Jewish survivors from Belsen would not recognize a real community with an American woman of Germanic ancestry.

This identity is distinct from the identity that she constructs for herself in the poem, 'Lady Lazarus' as the title refers to her. This title is a highly compressed syntagm. 'Lazarus' refers to a narrative in the Bible, as the name of a man whom Christ raised from the dead. That narrative becomes an in-text for her own narrative, linked to it by homology and opposition. Lazarus died, and Christ raised him from the dead, where Plath nearly killed herself but recovered (rose from the dead, assisted by unstated helpers). Christ and Lazarus are both male, but Plath as both agent and object of her death/salvation is female, 'Lady'. The term assigns her not only gender but also class.

There is another Lazarus mentioned in the Bible, a beggar at a rich man's gate, who when he dies will be taken to the bosom of Abraham the Patriarch, according to Christ. And the rich man will beg in vain for favours from Lazarus, whom when living he despised. Within this narrative there is a transformation of Lazarus from extremes of death and life and poverty and wealth. If the narrative is one of the pre-texts of Plath's poem, then she repeats this transformational process, with death as the marker of inversion of social categories and normal modalities.

If the title overtly constructs some of the determinants of 'character', and in the process invokes a contradictory set of narrative pre-texts, the first line works in a complementary way, constructing a narrative frame which implies or leaves positions open for a contradictory cast of characters. 'I have done it again' pivots around the empty pro-verb 'done', which could refer to either of the two actional syntagms, her killing herself or her resurrection. The text labels the action as an achievement ('manage', 'miracle') giving the phrase a self-gratulatory tone, but in the real-life pre-text there is no obvious achievement. The failed suicide constructs a new identity as a successful resurrectionist. But the form of the claim implies a number of contradictory semiosic acts, and different categorizations of the speaker. 'Miracle' is religious language, so that the speaker is a Christ, a worker of miracles. But the context, here and later in the poem, implies a showman in a circus (another male role), an exhibitor of freaks who claims credit for their bizarre deviance from the laws of nature ('The peanut-crunching crowd/Shoves in to see/Them unwrap me hand and foot').

This text is now a poem, a text in a privileged, high-status genre, constituted by a semiosic transaction between a high-status speaker, the poet, and high-status hearers/readers, though this was not yet the case when she wrote it. This semiosic syntagm has a homologous structure with that of the showman-crowd. Instead of the discreet and cultivated audience of poetry-readers, Plath constructs a vulgar, aggressive and insensitive circus crowd as her audience. It is the same kind of transformation, involving the same categories, gender and class, as we saw with 'Lady' and 'Lazarus'.

Already we can see the outlines of the basic syntagmatic frame of this text: a semiosic frame in which the subject and object of semiosis fuse in an ambivalent relation with the audience, and a mimetic frame in which acts of destruction and preservation blur together, and destroyer/saviour and victim/beneficiary are also conflated. Because of the radical instabilities in both mimetic and semiosic planes, the central character, the poet/showman/saviour/victim as active/passive, male/female, rich/poor has no certain identity, only the capacity to incorporate contradictions.

The text refers to three suicides, one every decade, the present one occurring in her thirtieth year. In this way the category of age is made relevant. The poet implies that the timing was deliberate, thus making each act a rite of passage, just as David Downs did with incidents that were not actually intended as rites of passage either. The connection with an initiation rite was not constructed by Plath purely for this occasion. In 'Initiation', written ten years earlier for an earlier 'performance', she observed: 'And she knew that her own private initiation had just begun' (Rosenblatt 1979: 94).

The events in the present narrative have the classic structure of a rite of passage, a 'death' followed by a 'birth'. Sylvia Plath as celebrant of each rite establishes her identity as priest, and as initiand she is concerned to construct an age-related identity. But where the traditional kind of rite such as Downs alludes to is concerned to manage transition from one status to another, so that identity before and after the rite is left distinct and separate, in the 'rite' that Plath invents, her identity both before and after is essentially the same, ambiguous and ambivalent. The modality of the 'rite' is also different in the two cases. Rites of passage in Downs's Walmatjarri tribe are socially sanctioned, with strong authority and high modality. Plath's 'rite' does not have any social status. It is an individual stategy for negotiating identity which changes nothing, where Downs drew, if idiosyncratically, on the 'proper' means of marking a new social identity. The social meaning of reference to ritual is not a constant. It depends on the social meaning of those rituals, for those narrators in that specific society.

Where Downs's narrative explicitly marked the context of space and time of the events, Plath seems not to, apart from the reference to ten-year cycles. However some of her metaphors act as micro-narratives which imply significant contexts. 'My skin/Bright as a Nazi lampshade' triggers a narrative of the holocaust, an incident in which a Nazi commandant used the skin of a Jew as a lampshade. This incident repeats the form of the primary syntagmatic frame, with the Nazi as destroyer and preserver (in so far as he restores the beauty and brightness of the skin of the jew, if not her life). The Nazi is thus transformed to a macabre anti-Christ. His miraculous power is his ability to turn a living human being into a thing of beauty or display, as in their different way the showman and the poet do. Since Plath is the author of this metaphor she is the semiosic agent of this transformation, responsible for this horrific image of her own skin as a lampshade, her own transformation into an object of aestheticized disgust.

The term 'Nazi' invokes not only a narrative and an agent but also a context in space and time: Germany under Hitler, the concentration camps where Jews were exterminated, and the privileged spaces where Nazis lived surrounded by objects of high culture, music, art and literature. This refers to events of her youth (she was born in 1932), events that came to construct the meaning of her parents' German identity, and her own in so far as she is German as well as American. The metaphor is a semiosic action that crosses this gulf and cancels her German identity (as oppressor) by adopting a Jewish identity (as victim), the status of oppressed minority that her father had experienced in America precisely because he was German. But Plath reconstructs herself on both sides of this equation as both Nazi and Jew, victim and agent of destruction, in an identity in which extremes of antagonism coexist without resolution.

The poem that follows consists of twenty-eight three-line stanzas. Its organization is non-narrative, in that the sequence of events does not determine the order of the poem. In this respect it is different in degree not kind from David Downs's text, where the narration respected the overall order of events but also moved backwards and forwards in time. But the overall orderliness of the progression in Downs's text is a transparent signifier of progress itself, the progress that is made by the initiate to a new status and identity. Plath's refusal of narrative is a transparent signifier of her lack of belief in an objective order which represents 'progress' and can underwrite her new identity.

The poem does however have an ending which has a structural place in terms of the semiosic plane:

> Ash, ash –
> You poke and stir.
> Flesh, bone, there is nothing there –
>
> A cake of soap,
> A wedding ring,
> A gold filling.
>
> Herr God, Herr Lucifer,
> Beware
> Beware.
>
> Out of the ash
> I rise with my red hair
> And I eat men like air.

The first two stanzas repeat part of the syntagmatic frame, the act of destruction, but this time there is no ambiguity, no conflation of destruction and preservation. The agent of destruction is 'you'. Formally this pronoun has no gender-marking, but in terms of the narrative this is a Nazi, a male, a doctor (earlier she has referred to him as 'Herr Doktor . . . Herr Enemy'). Her own identity likewise is now single, as dehumanized victim, a commodity ('cake of soap, 'gold fillings') and also the wedding ring that marked her married status, which survives her imagined death.

The second two stanzas mark the emergence of a new identity. This persona addresses the Enemy, now transformed to an ambiguous divine being, God or the Devil (but unambiguously German and male). 'Beware' is an imperative, marker of self-confident power in the semiosic plane, declaring her power over this powerful being, whose power she had previously only been able to match by assimilation. The second stanza describes at last an authentic resurrection, her rebirth as a female with red hair signifying passionate sexuality, a destroyer of men whom she devours like air – like Galburdoo who devoured boys like water, though Plath's source is likely to be the figure of Lilith from Jewish mythology, a female demon who devours new-born children unless they are protected by an amulet. In the course of the poem she has negotiated a new identity, which like Downs's is a gendered identity, though for her even more than for Downs, gender is the insoluble problem.

We return to the fact of her suicide and its contribution to the meaning of the text. The opening 'I' asserts the presence of an ego. Like Downs's *marni ngaji*, initially it is empty of social content but rapidly fills up, under pressure from the semiosic syntagms that intersect at this point, whose meaning is this very pressure of contradictory specifications anchored and over-determined by the meanings of Plath. For traditional literary criticism these meanings are illicit, outside the meanings of the text as poetry, but for other contemporary readers they are the reassuring ground of the narrative experience (see for instance Alvarez's celebration of Plath as heroic suicide, 1974).

Plath's society did not provide her with the authoritative structures and texts that Walmatjarri society offers Downs. Her use of Christian myth only proves the point, since her use of it shows that it has been emptied of its sanction and truth-value. But the semiosic work of fusing categories has another meaning. Most of the poem constructs an identity that is not viable because it tries to incorporate unassimilable oppositions, saviour/destroyer, Nazi/Jew etc. This quality is a transparent signifier of an impulse to achieve solidarity across barriers of hostility. It represents a rage for cohesion, for an impossible alliance between Germans and Jews, parents and children, men and women. The 'solution' is thus doomed from the outset, since it achieves an identity which is itself the problem: the problem of isolation, non-solidarity, exclusion.

The meaning of popular forms

Popular literature and popular culture occupy an uneasy position even within the emerging paradigm of English. Although it is clear that the previous paradigm strongly excluded such texts from the curriculum, it isn't equally clear what exactly would be included in the curriculum, or why. The arguments parallel the debate within History about the role of 'people's history' and its attempt to restore meanings that have disappeared from the record or been marginalized and buried under the well preserved loquacity of the dominant. One contribution that the social analysis of narrative can make to this project is to provide ways of reading the social meanings so densely coded in texts like Downs's story, which would otherwise lie unnoticed, silenced by its seeming triviality and encased within a minority discipline (Australian Aboriginal linguistics).

But the social analysis of narrative must also be able to address popular genres produced for mass audiences in the present or in the past. It is important to recognize that there are important continuities between these mass forms and texts like Plaths's poem, if they are produced at the same time in the same general social formation. Plath's text is in some respects 'popular', in that it has had very wide currency, reproduced in anthologies and taught in countless English classrooms. But neither the 'popular' nor the 'people' are homogeneous or unitary entities. Poetry remains an elite genre which only achieves this kind of reach when it is inserted into the reading regimes of the education domain. We need to complement this kind of semiotic phenomenon with a study of popular genres as they are enmeshed in popular modes of production and reception, and connected to basic ways of constructing meaning of broad sections of the community, even if not of 'the People' itself.

In contemporary Britain and Australia the Romance genre as packaged by Mills and Boon publishers achieves a readership of a kind and on a scale that makes this a significant phenomenon. These books are targeted at a strongly gendered market: written by women for women about women. Individual texts are relatively cheap, with new titles issued regularly every month. They are also widely available even more cheaply second-hand, since they are not designed as individual texts to be kept and re-read. They are highly formulaic, repeating a single narrative frame from text to text, especially within the sub-categories that Mills and Boon has established ('Presents', 'Romances', 'Harlequin' . . .). The women who read these books range in age from sixteen to forty-six, but the women whom they are about are always unmarried women between the ages of eighteen and twenty-four. The narrative describes the traumatic development of their relationship with a man, but at the end of the novel marriage is certain but has not yet occurred, and is not always mentioned. Clearly these novels are concerned with the construction of a gender identity, one that bears on the dominant institution of marriage, so the exclusion of marriage as a ritual/ rite of passage is surprising. These stories do not attempt to describe or legitimate the dominant ideology of a woman's role as wife or mother or domestic water. Their focus instead is on the period of transition that precedes marriage, constructing this rather than marriage as the rite of passage in the construction of gender identity.

The readers, however, are not assumed to be at this turning point in their own lives. These texts are not designed to accompany and model a rite of passage. On the contrary, they function rather than as Downs's text did to draw on and recall or project a well known ritual moment which gives significance to a life lived apparently in different terms to what is constructed by the ritual. For instance, one advertisement for Mills and Boon books included this special offer:

1987 Mother's Day Gift Pack

4 Marvellous *new* stories by the authors you love in a beautiful gift pack!
. . .

Go on – treat yourself to a feast of extra reading pleasure – it makes a great gift for a wonderful Mum.

This wonderful pack will be available in March, so why not order your copy *now*, so you won't be disappointed.

Simply complete the coupon below and return it to us. Don't forget to enclose cheque or money-order for $14.00 (post-free), or fill in the bankcard details to take advantage of this very special offer.

The terms of this offer are revealing. We note that the pack includes four books: there is no suggestion that any of them is special or unique. Even the price is no bargain, since these books would cost $14.00 over the counter. The only discount is the free postage, eliminating the need to go out of the house to the newsagent to purchase them. The legitimating occasion is Mother's Day, which is a recently constructed ritual occasion, fixed in May to coincide with traditional spring festivals in the northern hemisphere. Its function is to celebrate and legitimate a powerful gender identity for women, their role as mother, procreator and nurturer of children: compensation/reward to a woman for filling this role, to be offered by the normal beneficiaries, children and husband.

The gift pack is offered as another such reward, but this one is subversive. This is not a gift from others to the woman: it is something that she will buy for herself, a private self-indulgence that no one else in the family need know about. 'Go on' semiosically constructs a close female ally, urging her female friend to be a bit naughty. 'A great gift for a wonderful Mum' then reads like a parody of what others (father-husbands, children) will or ought to say, but probably will not get quite right. This weakens its modality and negates the force of the ideological message that it seems to carry. The strongly female identity that it constructs is clearly distinct from and even antagonistic to the identity of woman as wife and mother, while having a functional relationship to it.

The particular text in this genre that I will look at is *Love in the Dark*, by Charlotte Lamb, released in paperback in Australia in April 1987, although Lamb, one of the more popular and successful writers in the Mills and Boon stable, had published it in England in the previous year. Its central character, through whose consciousness the action of the novel is presented, is Stephanie Stuart, who at the beginning of the novel is working competently and happily as a receptionist in a hotel at Wyville, a decaying seaside resort somewhere in Britain. She is almost engaged to be married to Euan Cameron, a wealthy local man who is a successful doctor, when her life is disrupted by the re-entry into it of Gerard Tenniel, a handsome, wealthy and successful lawyer who once loved her, and who now knows her guilty Secret and uses his knowledge to hold her in his power. The novel describes her long resistance to his ambiguous advances. Only in the last four paragraphs of the 183-page novel does she acknowledge that she loves him, and they are united at last in the kind of embrace that could lead only to marriage, although the text is too discreet to mention the word.

In order to anchor the mimetic world of this text in a social reality I will begin with the cast list of characters, though as always the meanings of plot and character are interdependent. The two most salient social categories organizing this list are, unsurprisingly, gender and age. The central character, Stephanie, is of course female, aged twenty-three in the present of the text, and eighteen at the time when she first met Gerard. She has a fond brother, Robert, a doctor aged thirty-one, married to a nurse, Gwen, whose age is not given, and at the start of the novel Stephanie lives with her brother and his wife. Stephanie's father is dead, and her mother is living in Australia. Euan Cameron, the other suitor, is the son of a wealthy and powerful Wyville matriarch. Unlike the other main characters, his exact age is not given, but he appears to be the same age as Gerard, whose age is given as thirty-seven. As the novel commences, Euan's sister Elspeth is holding an engagement party. Her fiancé, John Barry, is an ambitious young architect working in the family firm. Gerard has no parents or sisters living, only a female cousin, Julia, who is almost as close as a sister, an independent career-minded person, with a boy friend (conveniently in Rio) and a full social life.

Stephanie's 'secret' concerned an incident which occurred when she was in Australia aged eighteeen. She worked on a station in Queenland as a nanny for the Burgess family, comprising Theo Burgess, aged slightly over forty, Viola, his neurotic wife in her late twenties, and their two young children. Viola, jealous of Stephanie's relationship with Gerard, attacked her. Theo intervened, and Viola shot him. But in the trial that followed, Viola claimed that the quarrel was about Stephanie and Theo not Gerard, and Stephanie did not deny it, since that might have brought Gerard's good name into disrepute. As a result, she had the reputation of having had an affair with a married man, which Gerard believed and couldn't forgive, since she felt unable to explain to him what she had done or why.

In this set of relationships there is one structure that keeps recurring: a brother-sister dyad in which the brother and sister are emotionally close, and one or other is married or nearly married to someone who seems to have a cool, rational relationship. Stephanie's brother Robert is a clear instance. He is married to Gwen, a nurse in the same hospital where he works, but he hardly ever sees her:

> His wife worked in the same hospital but all too often on a different shift, so that she and Robert practically had to make an appointment to meet for lunch once a week. Gwen always said that they had been able to see more of each other before they got married than they did now. (Lamb 1987: 11–12)

So Stephanie helps with the cooking and caring for her lovable brother, while the happy couple scrimp and save for the day in two years' time when Gwen can stop work to have a baby. This passage outlines the unsatisfactory conditions of this kind of marriage, and the phrase 'practically had to make an appointment' functions as an implied quotation to construct the semiosic situation of a disillusioned wife complaining to a female friend. This is a 'normal' happy marriage, and though Gwen does not want to shoot Robert (not yet, anyway) this is not represented here or anywhere else in the novel or the genre as a desirable or satisfying condition of existence.

Marriage, then, is not presented in an idealized form, as a more desirable state than a single life. Nor is Gerard easily distinguished from Euan as a potential mate. Both are the same age, of the same high status (successful lawyer, successful surgeon), wealthy and well connected, career-oriented but reasonably considerate towards Stephanie, and both are in love with her. For the knowledgeable reader there is never any doubt whom she will choose, but since in social terms there is no difference between them, the choice is socially meaningless. That is, the object of choice is meaningless; what is meaningful is the process of choice.

The difference, of course, is love: she loves Gerard, and though she is 'very fond' of Euan she does not really 'love' him. Love is a central signifier in this genre, and we need to understand it as a social meaning, not simply a psychological absolute. The title of this novel is a weak pun that reveals something of the complex meaning of love. At first glance, 'Love in the Dark' sounds unproblematic, since the dark is a common and satisfactory place to find it. But 'in the dark' also refers to Stephanie's ignorance of her own and Gerard's feelings, and Gerard's about hers. Knowledge and ignorance are semiosic states, affected by semiosic action. In this novel as in others in the genre, the main action in the narrative itself is semiosic. The progression is a journey from a kind of knowledge through an absence

of knowledge to a new state of understanding. At the end Stephanie like
David Downs is *pinarri*, an initiate.

The metaphors that conventionally construct the state of love in the
genre are very close to the classic terms of a rite of passage myth. At one
point Stephanie debates with Gerard about her feelings for Euan.

> She could rely on Euan; he was calm and dependable. She had understood
> that if Euan did propose it would be because he was utterly certain that she
> was the kind of wife he wanted.
>
> 'Have you ever been in love?' Gerard asked softly.
>
> Stephanie froze, looking up helplessly into the dark-pupilled grey eyes.
> They held some hypnotic attraction for her; she was afraid she might drown
> in their depths. He wasn't comfortable, like Euan; he was far from predict-
> able or manageable. He was possessed of some inner power she couldn't
> describe; a dynamic energy she could feel even without touching him. She
> saw it surging in his eyes and was drawn to it, helplessly fascinated, like a
> moth fluttering towards the brightness of a flame even though it knows it
> will burn up, be utterly destroyed.
>
> She must not let that happen to her; she mustn't let him pull her over
> the edge. She closed her eyes abruptly, shutting out the sight of his face.
>
> 'No,' she said, her voice raw. 'No, never.' (pp. 110–11)

The metaphors Lamb uses are clichés which would be avoided by a writer
with 'literary' aspirations like Sylvia Plath, and despised by critics trained
in literary sensibilities. However their familiarity contributes to their
modality effect in this kind of text. Precisely because they are so predictable they possess the guarantee of a commonly accepted truth. Stephanie
'froze', the absence of the heat which has conventionally been associated
with the flames of love for centuries. The question is a semiosic act,
demanding that she declare the truth. Her answer is another semiosic act,
the words a lie though her tone of voice announces clearly enough to
Gerard and the reader what she really feels.

The metaphors construct love as a kind of death: first (like David
Downs) a death by drowning, then the opposite, death by burning like a
moth in the flame. The two micro-narratives have a common structure, in
which the two opposites (fire and water, heat and cold) have an equivalent
value, each as a kind of death. This structure is homologous to the structure of Downs's and Plath's very different narratives, because death is a
common transparent signifier of negation and separation. And as with
Downs's text, the structure of clichés has a greater authority precisely
because it is so familiar a set of meanings.

Euan is praised because he is so rational, but within the space of the
genre this value is inverted, and Euan is unacceptable because he is so

rational. But rationality like love is not a purely psychological quality. Euan's rationality is in practice his unwillingness to change his existing situation. The choice between Euan and Gerard is not one between two different marriage prospects, but between two different kinds of relationship. Euan is a friend and colleague of brother Robert, who approves of the match, and marriage to him would mean immediate incorporation into an extended family including his formidable mother, plus his sister Elspeth and her new husband. It also means the close-knit run-down provincial community of Wyville, instead of the freedom and excitement of metropolitan London. Stephanie's new status and identity that she achieves at the end of the novel involves a formal transfer of allegiance from the 'traditional' extended family structure, and from an identity derived from a position in this traditional structure, to a new position and identity as a member of a dyad, the autonomous couple in the modern nuclear family. This transfer requires her formally to choose. It also involves some ritual actions by the males concerned. Her brother punches Gerard, who does not retaliate, thus marking his recognition of Robert's right while maintaining his own. Then Gerard punches Euan, who does not retaliate, acknowledging Stephanie's new status as no longer his possession.

Apart from these two incidents, and the murder, the action of the novel is semiosic not physical, hinging upon the 'secret', Stephanie's part in the murder and the trial, which she dare not reveal to Euan because the scandal would either shock him or ruin him or both, or so Stephanie says. The unfolding of the narrative is also a semiosic action, this time involving Charlotte Lamb and the reader. In the opening words of the novel, Stephanie is introduced: 'Stephanie Stuart handed her key to the woman on the other side of the reception desk, smiling politely' (p. 5). This is the standard form for the beginning of these novels: the central character is introduced by name, performing a typical action in her everyday context. The character thus becomes immediately recognizable in everyday terms, someone who is known to the reader but in a non-intimate way. There is a semiosic bond, but it is a weak alliance.

The narrative then introduces two kinds of distance between reader and character. The 'secret' is introduced early, but the reader is not told what is paralysing Stephanie, what crime she has committed. So Charlotte Lamb withholds this knowledge from the reader just as Stephanie withholds her fuller knowledge from Gerard. But Stephanie refuses to acknowledge her feelings for Gerard, even though the terms of her refusal make it absolutely clear to the reader how she feels and how the story will end. Until the 'secret' is fully explained, the reader is 'in the dark', separated from Stephanie by this ignorance, but until Stephanie acknowledges her love the reader is superior to her, an initiate presiding over Stephanie's painful and hesitating journey towards her new status.

The novel ends with this decisive semiosic act, whose social meaning is clearly articulated:

> She and Gerard belonged to each other. Even if she hadn't said it aloud her body was telling him so now, the heat of desire melting her flesh, burning through her senses. His hands were aware of that, she heard him breathe thickly, felt the heat in his face as his cheek brushed hers.
>
> 'Darling,' he said again, and he was asking her to admit it, to tell him. He was urgent because of the waste of five years, urgent as she was, because they needed to touch, to merge, to be one.
>
> 'I love you,' she said, and after that neither of them said anything for a long time. (p. 187)

This formulaic conclusion specifies Stephanie's new identity, at the completion of her rite of passage. Firstly it is explicitly a property-relationship: she belongs to a man and she owns a man in a mutually excusive bond. It is the relationship that the marriage ceremony exists to ratify, and phrases like 'to be one' recall that official ritual. There is also a completed semiosic transaction, after all the incomplete ones: with words as well as with bodies. But after the formal affirmation the semiosic transaction is broken again at the level of speech, by the couple, who do not talk 'for a long time', and by the author, who does not say what they are doing during this long time.

Obviously the reader, in her role as an initiate, can interpret the euphemism, knowing that Stephanie's initiation is only complete when she becomes a sexual being (until then she had been a virgin, she assured Gerard, who assured her that he was not). The silence at this point, then, is not a refusal of relationship, but on the contrary a closure. The compact of silence now includes all three female participants (writer, reader and object) in a bond of female solidarity, and excludes non-initiates. Stephanie's journey is only a fiction, but that fiction mobilizes a parallel journey for the female reader. Stephanie achieves the status of initiate, but the reader reconstitutes her own gender-identity by occupying the position of Stephanie's guide and mentor. That identity is inextricably attached to the meanings constructed by the marriage rite, because that rather than the state of marriage is the primary referent text. The identity reconstituted is that of bride not wife, bride as sexual being and equal partner, not wife as housekeeper, mother and undervalued contributor to the wealth of the household. But brides only exist in ritual space and time. Outside that domain they become wives because they once were brides. The logic is inexorable, even though the identities are so different. Special ritual occasions have been constructed which allow that special status and identity to be restored: wedding anniversaries, birthdays, Mother's Day.

Mills and Boon romances offer another opportunity for reconstructing this special status, for $3.50 a time.

Charlotte Lamb represents the construction of a 'normal' gender identity, and at the same time reconstitutes the rite of passage through which women in our society pass into the 'normality' of married life. This kind of text reinforces existing gender structures, even while incorporating a clear knowledge of the limitations in the life that those structures offer to women. The criticism of conventional married life that does appear in it only serves to strengthen its modality and thus confirm its ideological effects. Sylvia Plath's poem represents instead a failed rite of passage, to a confused gender identity which proved too fragile to survive. But both texts were written by women who live in the same kind of society, faced by the same kinds of contradiction. Where Plath tried to incorporate the contradictions into a complex new persona, Lamb allowed the contradictions to exist between the moment of her text and the everyday experience of her readers. From the point of view of social semiotics, each text is replete with social meaning, bearing on common sets of problems and experiences, but the meaning of each is incomplete in itself. Social meaning by definition is the meaning of groups, not just individuals, and it is found in processes not just in texts, processes whose ramifications inevitably go outside any individual text or genre or domain.

SOURCES AND CONTEXTS

A useful introduction to the large field of contemporary narrative theory is Rimmon–Kenan, *Narrative Fiction*, 1983. Important texts in the development of this tradition are Propp's classic *Morphology of the Folk Tale*, 1968, and Lévi-Strauss's articles, collected in *Structural Anthropology 2* 1963 and *Structural Anthropology* 1979. For the notion of 'story grammar' see Prince, *A Grammar of Stories*, 1973. Other important contributions to the structuralist analysis of narrative are the essay, 'Structural Analysis of Narrative', in Barthes 1977; Greimas, 'Elements of a Narrative Grammar', 1977; and Todorov, *The Poetics of Prose*, 1977.

Studies of narrative process include Booth's influential contribution to the Anglo-American tradition, *The Rhetoric of Fiction*, 1961, and from more recent developments within Russian structuralism Uspensky's *A Poetics of Composition*, 1973. Much feminist theory of narrative is concerned with the narrative process: see e.g. de Lauretis, *Alice Doesn't*, 1984, on the Oedipal 'plot' of the narrative process of the Oedipal text, and Gallop, *The Seduction of the Daughter*, 1982, for the 'plot' of Freudian transference and its construction of women.

The category of narrative has been recently foregrounded by historians, through the controversy that arose around Stone's 'The Revival of Narrative: Reflections on a New Old History', 1981. But Stone's article was contentious because he used it to attack a range of tendencies that he disagreed with, using what he treated as the self-evidence of the category of narrative, not because he was actually influenced by any contemporary theories of narrative: see Murphy, 'Telling Stories, Telling Tales: Literary Theory, Ideology and Narrative History', 1984, for a critique. Mulvey, 'Changes: Thoughts on Myth, Narrative and Historical Experience', 1987, deploys a more sophisticated theory of narrative to reflect on kinds of 'plots' historians use to make sense of the past. See also White's category of 'emplotment' to characterize the discourse of historians (1973). Lyotard in *The Postmodern condition*, 1984, has influentially analysed modern and 'post-modern' epistemologies in terms of narratives and refusals of narrative. For an example of use of narrative texts and structure in a 'people's history' see Taussig, 'An Australian Hero', 1987, which attempts to construct a demythologizing 'dialectical fairy tale' around an ordinary life.

The importance of the genre of narrative in English classroom practices does not need demonstrating. It occupies a key role in Britton's notion of the 'poetic function' which he felt was neglected in the language curriculum outside the subject English (see *Language and Learning* 1972). See also Rosen, 'The Importance of Story', 1986, and Reid, *The Making of Literature: Texts, Contexts and Classroom Practices*, 1984.

On the history of European assaults on Aboriginal Australian culture and society, and Aboriginal strategies of resistance, see Reynolds, *The Other Side of the Frontier*, 1978. On covert strategies of resistance by Aboriginals, see McGuinness and Walker, 'The Politics of Aboriginal Literature', 1985, and for Aboriginal myths of adaptation to European cultural forms see Hodge 1986a. For a wide-ranging application of Van Gennep's model, see Turner's stimulating *Dramas, Fields and Metaphors: Symbolic Action in Human Society*, 1974. On Plath's life and death, see e.g. Alvarez, *The Savage God: a Study of Suicide*, 1974, which constructs Plath's suicide as heroic, and Butscher, *Sylvia Plath: Method and Madness*, 1976, which treats it as irrelevant to the literary value of her work. On the concept of initiation in her work see Rosenblatt, *Sylvia Plath: the Poetry of Initiation*, 1979. On the contemporary popular romance and its gendered audience, see Radway, *Reading the Romance: Women, Patriarchy and Popular Literature*, 1984, and Snitow, *Powers of Desire: the Politics of Sex*, 1983.

8
Literature and History

'English' and 'History' are separate subjects or disciplines in schools and universities in the English-speaking world. This book is written on the contrary premise that these two subjects are essentially aspects of a single enterprise. And although 'English' departments tend to be larger at all levels of the education system, it is clear that conceptually 'English' is a part of 'History', not the other way around. History is impoverished by losing the branch of it studied as English, and so is English by its isolation from the rest of History. In this chapter I will be concerned about the reasons for the separation as well as strategies for overcoming it. Otherwise the interdisciplinary impulse will yet again run into puzzlingly insubstantial yet immovable barriers.

One part of the paradox is that 'English' already includes a practice of History, one that is in its way powerful and persuasive but unacknowledged. Many of the texts studied in English come from the past. This category of text tends to survive very well, compared to other texts from past literate societies, so they ought to have value to anyone interested in the past. They have another important quality: they have wider circulation in the present than most other texts from the past. They are treated as privileged texts which can be read almost directly (with some guidance from experts) as windows into the past. The version of history that they carry therefore has a very high modality, which gives them an ideological potency that is greater for being so masked. So readers of literature need to take other versions of history seriously, to have some check on the versions offered through 'English'. Conversely, other branches of History need to recognize the strengths as well as the duplicities of their secret competitor.

Within the study of literature during this century, there have been two broad ways of foregrounding history. One can be labelled 'literary history'. For this tradition, the chief device for anchoring the enterprise in time has been the concept of 'period', which allows a stable taxonomy of texts, so that scholars have a principle of relevance which enables them to subdivide issues, tasks and texts in a coherent and continuing enterprise. The second tradition can be labelled 'literary criticism'. This approach is concerned with the evaluation or revaluation of specific moments or authors or texts within or outside the current canon. For this tradition, the historical concern has been to track the definitive emergence of the New in a kind of revolution, a revolution of 'taste' or 'sensibility' in which the relation to the modern is a decisive criterion of value, positive or negative.

Neither of these enterprises is incompatible with each other or with current historiographical principles. The terms 'period' and 'revolution' which seem to divide them in fact derive from a common meaning: 'period' from a Greek word meaning 'moving around, returning to a given point', and 'revolution' from a Latin word with a similar meaning. If 'period' in English now refers to a stop, and 'revolution' to a violent or dramatic movement ahead, that is simply because they encode different attitudes to a historical process conceived in the same terms: as a progression through turning points, which mark a rupture in the smooth and linear movement of history. The 'periods' which organize literary texts in literary history (Elizabethan, Restoration, Romantic, etc.) recognize moments of change in literary production, which function as the boundaries holding the system in place. Claims about revolutions in art or literature imply global theses about the meaning of history which require further investigation precisely because they are so global. In that further investigation there is both the need and the scope for a reintegration with the rest of History.

There is an interesting parallel to this ambivalent concern with revolutions and turning points within contemporary historiography. In his *Archaeology of Knowledge* Foucault (1971) has posited a contradictory double movement in the theory and practice of contemporary historians. On the one hand he notes an impulse to find regularities that underlie apparent change, so that ever longer stretches of phenomena reveal their essential principle of continuity. On the other hand he sees a tendency to discover breaks, ruptures, discontinuities. The first trend concerns the basic material conditions and causes of human action and history. The second concerns semiosic activities, the sphere of culture and discourse, thought and meaning. Foucault's resolution of the opposition is to project a multi-levelled scheme organized in series and series of series, so that a discontinuity at one level may be part of a continuous series at another.

There is another important strand in contemporary historiography that is not adequately accommodated by Foucault's theories of series-of-series. This is the 'people's history' project, which points out that the historical record is systematically skewed in favour of the dominant, so that the lives and meanings of a significant proportion of society are disregarded or misrepresented. This project attempts to read against the grain of the dominant record, to recall traces of the voice of those who were written out of history. Where possible it tries to tap the oral tradition through which much of that history was transmitted. As this project gathers momentum, it tends to find continuities rather than discontinuities in the conditions of life of ordinary people of the past. The excitement of a history of breaks and ruptures, it seems, is a luxury that not everyone can afford.

The theory of social semiotics employed in this book is considerably influenced by Foucault's work. But there is a need for a more precise and more materialist theory of both change and continuity than even Foucault's work provides. In terms of this theory, the systems of regularities that change so bewilderingly across a rupture mark the presence of strong logonomic systems. The operation of these systems will be an important social fact but it is one that must be understood in terms of processes of domination, accommodation and resistance. This context will insert itself into the system itself, which will be incomprehensible without recognition of what it exists to control. A logonomic system operates through genre systems and knowledge regimes, constraining production and reception regimes. These must be sustained by specific agents, working with specific means of control, effectively directed at specific others, or they will not exist at all.

The illusion of homogeneity of views at a specific time can only be achieved through a structure of domains, which control contradiction by isolating it, and then removing domains of dissidence from public view. These domains construct anti-worlds and anti-meanings, but these are neutralized by modalities of the logonomic order which attempt to assign them a negative value, so that their inversions are inverted, to leave the dominant version of reality standing upright once again. These modality-strategies are designed to cope with pressure, but they are not guaranteed success. To competing groups, whose strength is acknowledged by the ceding of rights to a domain, the values of the anti-world express an alternative truth.

So the theory of domains therefore points to a strategy for resisting the dominant record of history, as contained in its most authoritative documents. Texts from low-modality domains can be scanned for their alternative versions of truth, prised free of the labels of untruth that protected their existence and allowed them to survive. These domains include the domains of popular religion and popular culture. They also include domains of high culture, literature and art.

If the illusion of uncontested homogeneity is something specifically constructed by a dominant group, then there is also something suspicious about the neatness of the 'turning point', which suddenly irrupts into history and then discreetly withdraws. The grammatical form of the concept obscures the issue of agency: history it seems is a car without a driver, veering sharply right or left for its own mysterious vehicular reasons.

Turning points, ruptures and fissures all mark the presence of transformations of some kind, which must have had their own agents and purposes. To explain them and to situate them in the social processes by which history is constructed we need a theory of transformations with the categories of agent, purpose and context, a theory that can trace connections across the different levels of the Foucauldian series of series, a theory that can recognize the disruption of the texts of the dominant by the texts of other histories.

In the rest of this chapter I will not address all aspects of the relations between 'Literature' and 'History' as objects and disciplines. A social semiotic approach deals with all kinds of text in all genres and media, and in this book I have argued for a wider scope for 'English' that would include all the texts that 'people's history' looks to as its new set of documents. But the 'people's history' approach looks with stern disfavour at the kind of text that constituted the main content of the traditional English curriculum. It notes its elite status and connections and presumes that it is therefore a contaminated and useless source. Undoubtedly as mediated by the reception regimes of traditional literary criticism and traditional social and political history these texts are so useless as not even to be dangerous as historical documents. But this excision of literature from History is part of the very strategy which the people's history project attempts to resist. It is strategically too important simply to ignore, because it is the linchpin of the broader strategy that maintains the separation of English and History as disciplines. Literature, even the literature of elite groups, is normally marked by the modality of unreality which allows it to express alternative or oppositional meanings that otherwise are often suppressed from the public record. It is protected by domain rules which mark out sites where writers and readers can explore the transformational processes that ultimately solidify into 'turning points'. Naturally it incorporates texts of the dominant, and is contained by reading regimes that assure that the oppositional meanings are not fully recognized or acted on. But even these mechanisms of displacement and control can be read as historical meanings, available more clearly in literary and artistic texts than in most other types of text. It would be foolish to exclude literature from History, just as foolish as to exclude all the other rich sources of buried texts.

Turning points

In spite of its simplifications, the concept of turning point has value for historical practice. It is no accident that the most influential historians since Hegel have tended to focus on moments of transition. Foucault himself tried to avoid what he saw as the grand simplifications of the

Marxists, and his theory of series-of-series was intended to discriminate between different kinds of 'break'. But his own work has as a central aim the location of major breaks, periods of transition which were decisive for the construction of modern thought and society. In this section I will use a study by Foucault as the starting point for an exploration of the explanatory power of the notion of turning points or ruptures in a transformational theory of history.

In *Discipline and Punish* (1979) Foucault located a major change in European notions of punishment in the early decades of the nineteenth century. Before the change, torture and the spectacle of punishment played a crucial role. Afterwards, these centrepieces in the technology of punishment seemed disgusting and obscene to the vast majority. The changes were discursively constructed (by polemicists such as Beccaria, Servan, etc.) and contested (e.g. by Muyart de Vouglans). More decisively, they were embodied in sets of material texts, new genres of juridical behaviour governed by new rules (kinds of sentence and explanation of sentences, and places and conditions under which sentence was passed).

Foucault formulated four rules which he claimed should guide those investigating such phenomena. They should consider them as a complex social function; as a political tactic; as part of a broader discursive formation; and finally as an 'effect of a transformation of the way in which the body itself is invested by power relations' (Foucault 1979: 24). These rules are vital principles for a social semiotic approach. The 'complex social function' reminds us that such phenomena are constructed by a number of agents for different and competing purposes, with different tendencies. 'Political tactic' points to the specific concerns of the dominant as major authors of the set of texts, as one function that cannot be ignored. The concern with the 'broader discursive framework' brings in the alliances with other groups in the construction of hegemony, and shifts and parallels in different semiotic forms and media. For instance, in the overall economy of semiosis, Foucault is in effect claiming a shift from visual to verbal forms by the state (from communicating via occasional spectacles to continuous verbal discourse) and a transformation in the semiosic position of the dominated, from active spectators of regal display to passive objects of the bourgeois gaze, whether as criminals or factory workers or students at school. And finally the problematic relationship between power, bodies and semiosis that links these disparate areas of social life also applies across the field of social life, at all times and in all societies.

In these terms the Foucauldian theme can be investigated in other societies and periods. I will look at its application to classical Greek culture, as a claimed site of the 'turning point' that constituted Western literature and culture: in particular in the genre of tragedy, whose 'birth' was an epochal event according to Nietzsche, and the text *Antigone* by Sophocles, regarded by Hegel as the finest example of the 'tragic collision'. In such an investigation it is possible to look at the relationship of social theme and semiosic form from either end: to see how a specific theme is refracted in semiosis, or to examine a semiosic form to trace some of the themes that intersect in it. But the two approaches are complementary, and in this brief study I will draw on both.

Sophocles' *Antigone* was produced as a tragedy for theatrical performance in Athens in 440 BC. As always, analysis of texts should start by reference to semiosic conditions and generic qualities. Greek tragedy was a highly constrained semiosic activity. Plays were performed in a specific space, the theatre of Dionysos, at a specific time, the festival of Dionysos in early spring: a spectacle designed for a sacred space and time, with its own modality. These conditions were a specific transformation of various ritual predecessors. The agent of this transformational process can be tentatively labelled: the rituals had fallen into decline when Peisistratus, the first tyrant of Athens, revived the practice in basically the form it had for the next century. To understand this event we need to know the significance of the institution of the tyrant in Greek political life, and its relationship to the 'democracy' that succeeded it from 510 BC. But this preliminary specification of agency already points to the site where we can heed Foucault and examine tragedy as a political tactic as well as a complex social function.

The earlier forms out of which the pre-tragedy was transformed are even less well known. Presuming that these fertility rituals had something like the form and content of rituals elsewhere, they represented a death that guaranteed a birth and fecundity. The enacted death of a god would have been accompanied by the actual death of one or more animals. Even in Sophocles' time, the festival of Dionysos began with the sacrifice of a bull, signifying male strength and fertility. At an even earlier period, some scholars argue, the festivals may have included human sacrifices.

The who and when of these earlier transformations are no longer discoverable, if they ever existed. But it is clear that slaughter of humans or even animals would constitute a spectacle of terror of the kind that Foucault analysed for a much later period. And something like this pre-text is still recoverable from a classical tragedy like *Antigone*, and not only from its conditions of production and the signifiers built into them. Aristotle's famous if much disputed definition of the tragic effect specifies the central emotions in a spectacle of terror: a tragedy he claimed should attempt to arouse 'fear and pity in order to produce a purification/purging (*katharsis*) of such emotions'.

I will not add here to the attempts that have been made to explain what Aristotle really meant by *katharsis*. It is sufficient to recognize that the emotions proper to punitive spectacle are certainly relevant, and when we examine the characteristic plots and conventions of tragedies like *Antigone* we can see why. *Antigone* represents three deaths in the course of its action, and refers to two more immediately prior deaths that precipitated the action of the play, those of Polyneikes and Eteokles: five-sevenths of the ruling family of Thebes.

This is noble carnage on a scale that would rival the spectacles of aristocratic death at the height of the French Revolution. Yet by the rigid conventions of Athenian tragedy, not one of these deaths is enacted on stage. All death and torture is described, not seen: it is literally 'obscene', off-stage, excluded from discourse. This is the definitive end-point of the series of transformations which perhaps started from the ritual of a royal human death, whose meaning at every point is the transformation of the physical action of physical bodies into discursive action: struggles through language about actions which are violent, brutal and spectacular. Yet this is drama not narrative, because there are still bodies there, constrained to speak and struggle through speech with a loquacity without precedent in any previous culture. The transformations that constituted Greek tragedy are thus analogous to those that Foucault traced in nineteenth century Europe.

The action of Sophocles' *Antigone* is built around an ancient punitive spectacle. The tragedy arises because Kreon, ruler of Thebes, defies custom by forbidding Antigone to bury her brother Polyneikes, establishing an edict that no one is to bury or mourn a man whom he, Kreon, has declared to be an enemy of the state. Antigone, Kreon's niece, defies the order and is condemned to die, but many people object to the decision, including Kreon's son Haemon, who is betrothed to Antigone. Antigone is not judicially murdered: she is walled up in a tomb, but hangs herself before she starves to death. Haemon then commits suicide, as does Kreon's wife Eurydike. Kreon repents his edict, but too late to save the slaughter. His experiment to introduce a spectacle of terror (an unburied body torn by dogs and birds) is a catastrophe. His nerve fails him in setting up the judicial murder of his niece, but even his compromise proves a dangerous strategy. The text seems to invoke a mirror image of the change that Foucault studied, a failed attempt to introduce the kind of spectacle of punishment that withered in the early nineteenth century.

At first glance it is not easy to link the action of the play with contemporary issues of justice. There were laws regulating the conduct of funerals, aimed particularly at restricting excessive displays of public grief by women, but these were left to senior males in the family to enforce, and capital punishment would have seemed excessive. The Greek legal code was not generally given to spectacles of punishment, a phenomenon that was known about but repudiated by the Greek states. Herodotus, for instance, transmits a representative Athenian horror and fascination with the spectacles of punishment practised by the Persians, and he foreshadows Foucault in linking these with a despotic form of government, to be contrasted strongly with Athenian 'democracy'.

However, there was one aspect of the Athenian judicial process which did involve torture, and which strikes later commentators as curious and anomalous. This was the practice of allowing slaves to be tortured, as guarantees of the master's truth. Reports of evidence given under these conditions were accepted as valid evidence in the court, and although masters had absolute rights over their slaves as property which could be 'damaged' by this procedure, in the documents that have survived they are normally criticized for exercising this right, as though it proved that their case was weak.

The custom seems extraordinary as a judicial tactic, and so it is, but this very extraordinariness makes the assumptions on which it is based more easy to recognize. It signals a displacement of state power over bodies onto the bodies of slaves, which serve to guarantee the discourse of their masters. It is so cumbrous and unsatisfactory as a technology of power that its explanation must lie somewhere else, in the overall economy of power in Greek society. It is this wider sphere which is the obvious source of the other problem of Greek judicial methods. Trials were brought by individual litigants, and decided by juries who sometimes consisted of something like a mass audience. In the famous trial which convicted Socrates of heresy there were five hundred and one jurors. Such a semiosic structure is a transparent signifier of a shift in the location of power in the system of justice, from a concentrated power to punish to a diffused (and expensive) power to judge. Socrates' death was unspectacular (a quiet and private death by hemlock): it was the trial which was the spectacle.

Socrates' body was coerced by the sentence (though there is good reason to suppose that he was expected to escape into exile); but so were the bodies of the mass of jurors, constrained into constructing a message about the democratic nature of the Athenian state. This state was not democratic in at least three important ways. It excluded slaves, it excluded women, and it masked the continuing power of a small number of still powerful and wealthy older families, amongst whose duties was included the support of performances of tragedies at the annual festival of Dionysos. Athenian theatre was one of a number of institutions by which power was mediated, all of which involved discursive displays in front of a body of judges, whose votes were decisive, and whose acts of deliberation reaffirmed the power of the citizens against the concentrated power of the aristocracy.

In Sophocles' play, Antigone's crime is purely semiosic, a 'victimless crime'. It is not a visually spectacular act (she simply sprinkles dust over the dead body of her brother). What she does do is to challenge Kreon's control over semiosic production: who can say what about whom in this state, who can discursively construct value for the living or the dead. The punishment that he imposes is not spectacular, but is constructed by him in ambiguous terms:

Away with her, and having walled her up
In a rock-vaulted chamber, as I ordained,
Leave her alone at liberty to die,
Or if she choose, to live in solitude,
The tomb her dwelling. We in either case
Are guiltless of this maiden's blood.
Only on earth no lodging shall she find.
(1968: 885–90)

In this speech Kreon declares the terms of his crisis of judicial power. His power is defined by its operation purely through words ('as I [ego] ordained'). Through words he acts on the bodies of others who are to execute his will. But even these his agents cannot act directly on the body of the criminal. They are to 'leave her alone', so that her death is not to be attributed to them and thus to Kreon. But Kreon now uses the so-called 'royal we' (hemeis), the plural signifying power and the transcendence of his individuality: he has become society, so that he cannot repudiate the actions carried out by his agents.

Yet the power which denies its contact with bodies can still touch and hurt illicit bodies. Antigone is a female and therefore not a citizen in Athenian terms, but of the royal house and not a slave. Kreon claims that he is 'guiltless' (hagnoi), a word from religious discourse meaning 'unpolluted', but as secular power he is unable to control a religious labelling of his action. And in practice his punishment not Antigone's is the central activity of the play. His punishment is exercised on other bodies – his wife and son and niece – but this is like torturing a slave's body to assure a master's truth. The final words of the play by the chorus make this target clear:

Swelling words of high-flown might
Mightily the gods do smite.
Chastisement for errors past
Wisdom brings to age at last.
(1350–3)

The concern of the gods, it seems, is wisdom, a correct attitude of the mind: the mind of an elder (who is of course male). Kreon's fault was his words, and these are punished by blows of the gods: blows administered to bodies that he owns, which therefore reach his mind.

Thus far we have worked from a pre-established problematic back to a text. It is also proper to work the other way, from the issues as the text establishes them, to those issues as they emerge in society, in so far as we can know them. Hegel's concept of the 'tragic collision' seemed to follow this route. With *Antigone* for instance he located the essential point at issue between Antigone and Kreon as a conflict between two competing systems of right: right based on the family (*oikos*) and right based on the state (*polis*). The conflict in these terms can then be taken back to a 'turning point' in Greek society, the transition from a legal system based on family and kinship obligations to one which recognized the overriding right of the state.

It is clear from studies of Greek law that there was conflict between *oikos* and *polis* and that the powers of the state were expanding at the expense of the private household during the period when Sophocles was writing his plays. However, if there was a 'turning point' in this process it seems to have occurred many centuries previously, during the so-called 'Dark Ages'. But one value in having Sophocles' text is that we can see the categories used within it to construct this conflict: the intersection in the text of key terms from other discourses that encode dominant relations of the time. These terms themselves are like complex texts, since they hold together major blocks of meaning in a socially validated but unstable and contested form. To be able to see these terms function under conditions of conflict is to have access to important moments in social semiosis from the past.

At the centre of the play is a crucial debate between Kreon and his son Haemon. This debate is crucial because within a patriarchal order the disobedience of a woman is an external problem to be dealt with, but the revolt of the son threatens the order itself. In this debate, Kreon begins defensively (he has ordered the death of his son's prospective bride) and he invokes the unity of power in both *oikos* and *polis*.

> What evils are not wrought by anarchy!
> She ruins states, and overthrows the home,
> She dissipates and routs the embattled host;
> While discipline preserves the ordered ranks.
> Therefore we must maintain authority
> And yield no tittle to a woman's will.
> Better, if needs be, men should cast us out
> Than hear it said, a woman proved his match.
>   (672–80)

The supreme problem here is 'anarchy' or lack of rule, which is given feminine gender. 'She' is equally a threat to *polis* and *oikos*. But defeat within the sphere of the *oikos* is even more disgraceful, and this is defeat at the hands of a real not a metaphoric woman. Precisely because the *polis* has superseded the *oikos* the family becomes a site of challenge to its order. But we also see that this issue masks the issue of gender, banished from the *polis* and even more dangerous because it still survives in the *oikos*.

Haemon's response is to appeal to democracy and tradition:

Haemon:	I plead for justice, father, nothing more,
	Weigh me upon my merit, not my years.
Kreon:	Is not this maiden an arrant law-breaker?
Haemon:	The Theban commons with one voice say, No.
Kreon:	What, shall the mob dictate my policy?
Haemon:	Tis thou, methinks, who speakest like a boy.

The core of Haemon's case is obscured by this translation. The argument pivots around two ambiguities: one over *neos* (either 'young' or 'new/ innovatory'), the other over *polis* (either 'the state' or 'the body of citizens'). His opening comment is: *Ei d'ego neos*, literally 'Even if I am young/new'. *Neos* describes equally his youth (in relation to his patriarchal father) and his innovation (in opposing his father). His final criticism of Kreon repeats this ambiguity: Kreon is *agan neos*, 'too young', or 'too much an innovator'. So both stances are labelled by Haemon as innovations, to be regretted or deplored, even though they are in opposition: autocracy or rebellion. Haemon then appeals to the popular will. Kreon's innovation is to oppose this kind of appeal. The word translated here as 'mob' is *polis*, the state in whose name he had opposed Antigone and demanded unquestioning obedience. But Haemon is being equally devious, since Kreon's charge which he denied is clearly true: he has been influenced by a woman, who has also persuaded citizens of the *polis* of the justice of her cause.

Kreon learns two main lessons from the action of the play. One is in the sphere of the *polis*, where he comes to understand the role of discourse in constructing and enforcing his own power. The other is in the sphere of the *oikos*, where he recognizes the presence of forces, again constructed through discourse, which he must respect, including the power of women and perhaps even of slaves. In each sphere we see the operation of the same contradiction, where power is the control of bodies exercised through words, so that the non-powerful (women and slaves) alone have the capacity to act. In so far as Athenian men did of course still perform acts, in war and peace, this principle served to deprive them and their action of status.

At this point in the play, then, we have not a single 'collision' but a cluster of oppositions. Each of these can be associated with a 'turning point' of some kind, since the alignments involved shifted consistently over time. The position of women in Greek society, for instance, seems to have slowly deteriorated during the classical period, till Aristotle can describe women as barely different from slaves. We are not able to reconstruct the stages of this history or nominate the moments or events that marked significant points of deterioration, but the innovation (respect for women) that Haemon silently sides with in his support of Antigone seems to be a transformation against the direction of history. The analysis has a number of implications for a study of literary texts as records of 'turning points'. The first is that the crises represented in the text are often remote in time from the society of the text. The text rewrites history, making sense of existing conflicts by reference to a constructed past. This version of the past cannot be dismissed as purely a fiction. It almost certainly incorporates an oral history tradition to which women and slaves were able to contribute in a way that was not possible in the contemporary literary tradition. Oral history constantly and silently reshapes the record but it is also remarkably tenacious about some matters. Scholars were astonished when Schliemann's excavations of Troy and Mycenae demonstrated the accuracy of Homer's text. Herodotus the 'first historian' was labelled 'the father of lies' because he incorporated so many oral reports, some of which have been spectacularly vindicated by later discoveries as more reliable than the 'common sense' of his literate critics. Sophocles and his audience drew on a rich oral tradition which has now been lost, except in so far as it has left traces in written texts such as this.

But the text must also have incorporated texts and meanings from its present. Sophocles and other Athenian citizens physically moved each day between *oikos* and *polis* and back. The movement would have been organized by a set of transformations linking the two domains, to be negotiated in different ways by every member of Athenian society. If the *oikos* was labelled as the more primitive, it nonetheless could not be ignored. Relations within the *oikos* did not consist solely of the simple relations of power and obedience prescribed by the official morality and inscribed in the legal code. Within this domain, relations between women and men, old and young, parents and children, owners and slaves were a complex and shifting mix of power and solidarity, dependence and hostility. So the domain of the *oikos* was a site where the non-dominant could still present and transmit some meanings and rights from their past, in a form that was active in the present. For dominant and non-dominant alike, these alternatives coexisted along with transformations linking them, transformations that would have the same basic form whether they functioned to link different epochs in the past, or different groups, ideologies and domains in the present. So these versions of history encode a formula for relations in the present, especially as inscribed in representations of a crisis or turning point.

It is clear that a text like *Antigone* is too dense and impacted a structure to be directly available as 'evidence' on its own. It is for instance a highly unreliable guide to the official status of women in classical Greece, whose hopes for a better future at law have had to wait for more than 2,000 years. In this respect it has a negative modality, constructing an anti-world and celebrating a victory that no social historian should trust as a factual record. Yet within its domain of ritual/drama it replays struggles and transformations within the occluded domain of the family which were never definitively won or lost, which remained on the agenda for millennia. These struggles have left traces in other texts that have survived, in documents that social historians recognize must be scanned intensively if a comprehensive picture of the past is to be reconstituted, as the people's history project desires. But these other texts are themselves partial and incomplete, recording aspects of a dynamic process without its essentially dynamic character. It is an explanatory context such as this that literary texts like *Antigone* can have so crucial a role to play, though not in isolation, and certainly not as privileged texts within an autonomous literary canon.

Even so, my practice of applying terms from Foucault and Hegel may seem fundamentally unsound and anti-historical. Certainly it's the case that if history moves inexorably forwards from one turning point to another, each shutting the door of the previous epoch, then earlier societies and their literature and culture would rapidly become incomprehensible and irrelevant. But if history is constituted by continual struggles with shifting outcomes, then it becomes possible and necessary to see below the pattern of breaks and ruptures that marked each mighty victory, to study the struggles and strategies out of which those victories were constructed, and into which they were always liable to collapse. And if this is how history moves then patterns of homology and repetition between ancient Greeks and modern Europeans are not surprising or disconcerting or without significance: especially if we are able to insist at the same time on the specificity of the conditions in which those homologous forms appeared, and explore the contemporary consciousness of such struggles through their traces in verbal and other texts.

Decentring a classic

Antigone survives because it is a classic, whereas the discourse of opposition as spoken by Greek women and slaves has been lost. English has inherited the strategy of organizing its own discourse around the concept of classics, so we need to understand the nature and function of classics if we are to read English as itself a way of reading. The term 'classic' comes from the Latin *classis*, meaning a group of people called together: either a social class, or a group of students. Both meanings continue to act in 'classic', which refers to texts which are socially impeccable and well adapted to educational use.

This etymology serves as a warning about the purposes built into the strategy of using classics as the focus for a semiosic regime. The strategy consists of a series of transformations of the set of texts from the past. First the classic texts are abstracted from their original context, obscuring the network of transformations that constituted them in the first place, and making them stand for this whole body of texts. In effect this gives them sole responsibility for constructing the meanings of their age, then deprives them of the supporting texts that would have enabled them to carry out this function. Then they are inserted into a new context dominated by the needs of the present: ideological functions of the school classroom. In this context they are cut off from their own history, and this opens the way for two alternative strategies. One is to assert the identity of the past with the present, united by the timeless truth of the classic. The other is to insist on difference, constructing a version of the past as the key to the meaning of the classic. This key is controlled by the authorized guardians, and their version of the past rebukes the imperfections of the present by its vanished perfection. But either way history is mystified, and the real difficulties of the classic texts are exploited to reinforce the power of teachers over taught.

One powerful metaphor that has been deployed to reinforce the position of 'classics' in the curriculum has been the notion of 'centre', seen as the position which organizes the periphery, as the still point of the turning world, inside the circle yet outside space and time. The ineffable but ideological meanings of such a centre can then be used to organize the relations between classics and non-classics, between one classic and another, and finally between what is essential (permanent, stable, 'central') and what is non-essential within an individual text or corpus. So potent and seductive is this ideological concept of the centre that the term 'decentring' has come to describe an influential way of attacking the pedagogy which has been built around the notion of a 'canon' of 'classic' texts. But a counter-ideological strategy will not seek only to dismantle an existing canon. All such systems have their own inbuilt contradictions which make them a potential site for ideological intervention. The crucial weakness of such a system is that it has control only of reception regimes, not of production regimes. It is able to select from the potential body of classics, but it cannot freely construct them. Even the status of classic is a socially given category, constructed over time by an authorship that incorporates non-dominant readers and interests. Every classic was once to some degree a popular text, even though it was also ideologically acceptable. This is not irrelevant to their use as a classic: the classic use of classic texts mobilizes then transforms the pleasure of the text, such as it is, into an ideological point.

The legitimacy of a regime built around classics derives from the prior status of the classics themselves. So an attack on the regime can make use of the classic texts themselves, restoring the occluded transformations that make them mysterious, recognizing the hegemonic status of the texts and using it to reveal the processes of hegemony. This was one of the strategies followed by the dramatist Bertolt Brecht in the radical theatre he established in East Germany after the Second World War. His own plays constituted part of the repertoire of this group, but he also saw it as important to develop new readings of the classic texts of German theatre: the Greeks, the Elizabethans and the German Romantics. He attempted to fix the meanings of these readings in model performances, recorded in model books, where commentaries and photographs could transmit the semiosic messages of his production.

We can see something of Brecht's use of this strategy by looking at the first of his model books, the one he wrote for his 1948 production of *Antigone*. He explains his reasons for choosing this particular text:

> The Antigone story was picked for the present theatrical operation as providing a certain topicality of subject matter and posing some interesting formal questions. So far as the subject's political aspect went, the present-day analogies emerged astonishingly powerfully as a result of the rationalisation process, but on the whole they were a handicap; the great character of the resister of the old play does not represent the German resistance fighters who necessarily seem most important to us. (Brecht 1964: 210)

This comment reveals Brecht's equivocal judgement on the whole strategy. The juxtaposition of present and past worked only too well, mobilizing meanings from the present at the cost of obscuring the pastness of the past. In particular the aristocratic bias of the classic text proved an intractable barrier to representing the non-aristocratic resistance that Brecht believed should be celebrated. He also believed that their exclusion was itself an important meaning of his production, but one that paradoxically needed a knowledge of the otherness of the classic texts in order for it to be appreciated. 'Not everyone will necessarily realise that they [i.e. the German resistance] are not the subject in this case, but only he who does so will be able to summon the measure of strangeness needed if the really remarkable element in this Antigone play – the role of force in the collapse of the head of the state – is to be observed with profit' (p. 210). The sense of 'strangeness', the ability to construct a gap between past and present is indispensable: and it is unequally distributed amongst the audience. In so far as its basis is a sense of history and a knowledge of the specificity of the classic texts, we can see that a knowledge of the classics is still an invisible key to knowledge of the classics, just as for Bourdieu, possession of culture is the prerequisite for reading and using its texts.

It was precisely that closed circle that Brecht was trying to prise apart with his production. I will look at just two aspects of his strategy. Firstly he wrote what he called 'bridge verses' for the actors, which he described as follows:

> To keep the performance subordinate to the story, *bridge verses* were given to the actors at rehearsals, for them to deliver with the attitude of a

narrator. Before stepping into the acting area for the first time Helene Weigel said (and in subsequent rehearsals heard the prompter saying):

'So then Antigone went, the daughter of Oedipus, gathering
Dust in her pottery bowl, to cover the dead Polyneikes
Whom the tyrant had thrown to the crows and the dogs in his anger.'

The actress playing Ismene, before entering, said:

'And her sister Ismene came upon her as she did this.'

Before verse 1 Weigel said:

'Bitterly then she wept, bewailing the fate of her brother.'

And so on. Each speech or action that is introduced by such verses comes to seem like their realisation in practice, and the actor is prevented from transforming himself completely into the character: he is showing something. (Brecht 1964: 213–4).

These 'bridge verses' perform a curious function. Their mimetic content is identical with the content of what immediately follows. Because they mirror that content they foreground the semiosic difference. That difference is the difference between narration and enactment: the representation of bodies through words as against representation of and by speaking bodies. In this process, the dramatic action is constructed as the transformation of a prior verbal narrative text. But Brecht's own transformational processes here involve a double move. He has transformed dramatic action into verbal form, into a kind of paraphrase of the performance, thus carrying the process which Foucault noted to an extreme, asserting the primacy of speech not spectacle. He then establishes this as a control-text, whose function seems to be to control the bodies of the actors (who are the only ones who hear this text). This control-text specifically blocks the potential transformational work of the actors, whose effect within the conventions of illusionist theatre would have been to intensify the power of the performance by masking that particular transformational move.

But what the audience would see, in this performance, is not the transformational work but the discrepancy and sense of constraint that signals it, for those who understand. The control-text has a further meaning, which again would be concealed from the audience: it is written in the archaic, literary language of poetic drama. The constraint, then, is not submission to the control exercised by the producer-playwright, but submission to the literary tradition itself, reconstructed by the radical producer. This transformational work compresses within the space of a moment of a single production a version of the major shifts in the history of Western theatre, although in some respects it reverses that history, working backwards from a radical theatre in the present to a founding moment in the past.

Brecht also reproduced photographs from this model performance. The example we will look at shows Antigone and Ismene with Kreon and the elders (plate 4). The use of photography is apparently a helpful, neutral teaching device, showing what words could not. It is also, inevitably, a system of control of bodies: the bodies of the actors in the first performance, frozen and offered as spectacle, and the bodies of actors in subsequent productions, coerced by the definitive scheme. Brecht was aware of this assertion of power as a problem. He insisted that the models were 'by definition incomplete', and in his own practice he did not require his company to know his theoretical writings. But this move only establishes the terms of a contradiction, it does not resolve it. The negation is a type of transformation, whose meaning is given by what it acts on (power) as well as what it does (renouncing power).

Brecht's text glosses the meanings he assigns to the performance text. The stage is divided into two areas, one the well-lighted acting space, between four posts surmounted by horses' skulls, the rest in semidarkness where actors can be seen sitting on benches waiting for their cues. The movement of actors from dark to light signifies the transformational process of adopting a role, made visible to the audience. The meaning of the acting space is given only by absences – of all kinds of scenery and background that could locate it in time or space – with only the horses' skulls to assign it meaning. Brecht does not gloss these. They are left to stand as an archaic spectacle of death, signifier of incomprehensible rituals whose relation to the action of the drama is now obscure.

Brecht's efforts show the intractability of the classic text as both problem and resource. In so far as he can sustain difference, strangeness, he can create a space where transformations can be understood, transformations which imply important meanings about both past and present. Yet audiences tend to collapse history and construct an identity between past and present, which releases powerful energies which he courts as well as deplores. The semiosic tradition in which the classic text is embedded (theatrical style, literary status) constitutes a similar opportunity and obstacle. The tactic of interrupting the conventions of the tradition gives them an available history (the micro-history of the transformation of actors into their roles, the macro-history of the construction of the conventions of Western theatre). But the process of making transformations visible as an object of mimesis makes heavy demands on an audience. In practice it tends to polarize them, dividing them into an elite who can track the transformations and read history as a meaning of the text, and others who can not. This seems to contradict the radical aims of Brecht's theatre. It is true that there are real dangers in the strategy of decentring classic texts. But there is still value in a strategy which can challenge the dominant construction of classic texts and the authority of its guardians, and open up a space for the study of transformations and history.

Plate 4   Fixing a classic: Brecht's model for *Antigone*, Photograph from *Antigonemodell* 1948, the first of the 'model' books, is reproduced by kind permission of Mr Johannes Hoffmann.

Reading disciplines, disciplines of reading

The split that exists between English and History is not an oversight that could be overcome by a bit of good will from the various people concerned. It is systemic and functional, related to the way knowledge is organized within specific institutions in contemporary society, and only by understanding it in these terms can we see how it might be changed. It is difficult to present the two systems economically and convincingly, since they do not consist of two distinct, stable and homogeneous sets of practices, nor of two homogeneous and self-contained communities. But this is a legitimate task to ask of social semiotics: to provide strategies for reading 'disciplines' through specific instances, showing both their core of logonomic rules and the degrees of latitude that accommodate conflict and contradiction within them.

One place to begin is with authoritative texts that offer metacomments on the practice of their discipline. As an instance I will take the opening of Leavis' *Revaluation*, a book described on its dust jacket (1964 paperback edition) as 'among the classics of modern literary criticism'.

> The work has been done, the re-orientation effected: the heresies of ten years ago are orthodoxy. Mr. Eliot's achievement is matter for academic evaluation, his poetry is accepted, and his early observations on the Metaphysicals and on Marvell provide currency for university lectures and undergraduate exercises. (Leavis 1936: 17)

In reading a text like this for our purposes we need to go behind the immediate mimetic content, and even the specific semiosic situation, because this text like every other was a counter in a particular struggle, to be interpreted in relation to that struggle. What we need to attend to instead are the taken-for-granted logonomic rules that organize the argument. Whether or not the claimed revolution was as successful as Leavis implies, the kinds of object of the revolution are not in contention. Leavis takes for granted a canon, a set of texts and valuations of texts that control a community in the same way as canonical texts control membership of a religious group. The specific 'work' of members of this community is semiosic: constructing a revolution within the community. The passage has the form of a classic narrative, with a hero (Mr Eliot) enjoying his triumph. Mirroring this triumph is Leavis' triumph as critic of the critic-as-hero. But (since this is the beginning of the book) we will find unsurprisingly that the closure achieved by Eliot is to be deferred for his critic. If there was not work to be done, the community would lose its reason for existing.

Leavis then refers briefly to the other functions that sustain the community that is organized by a canon of texts: lectures and exercises, a circulation of texts about the canon in which teaches and students are alternately the objects of the others' inspection. The essential nature of these secondary texts is to be commentaries on the texts of the canon, demonstrations of the proper functioning of the reading regimes that define the community. It is not at all clear that there is any need or scope to produce new knowledge, certainly not knowledge of objects outside the canon.

In addition to reading meta-comments like Leavis's, we need to look at the genres of texts that organize the forms of discourse of the community, scanning them for their regularities and using these to reconstruct the logonomic systems at issue. Leavis wrote his text in 1936. He is now dead, and the 'school' he founded has dispersed, but the canon he deferred to still lives on. John Donne, the leading poet of the 'Metaphysical Poets', is still the subject of a major genre of criticism, the book-on-a-major-writer. As one instance I will take *Fulfilling the Circle: A Study of John Donne's Thought*, published in 1984 by Terry G. Sherwood.

The aim of this text is conveniently summarized in a publisher's blurb, which is a particularly useful sub-genre, worthy of more attention that it normally receives:

> This book assumes that we can understand Donne's works much better if we take them as a whole. The book also assumes that the principles of consciousness, of epistemology and psychology, are the backbone of his thought. In the light of these assumptions, Terry Sherwood concentrates on principles of reason, bodies and suffering that unify Donne's works. These principles reflect how Donne assimilated the complex spiritual and intellectual currents of his time. More important, these principles inform the centre of important works written throughout Donne's long and varied literary career.
>
> TERRY G. SHERWOOD is a member of the Department of English at the University of Victoria.

We will start at the end: the validation of Sherwood's right to engage in this discourse, through the location and status of his body, part of an English department which is part of a university. No mention is made or needs to be made of the processes of scrutiny he can be assumed to have passed to have reached that position.

The text does announce some assumptions (made by the book, not by the absent Sherwood) but these assumptions are a way of assigning a higher modality to claims that 'the book' is making. The form of these claims masks the real assumptions, so taken for granted that they do not need to be declared. 'We can understand Donne's works much better' derives from an unmodalized prior form: 'We understand Donne's works.' This as an imperative is the founding premise of the genre. And the notion of a 'centre', reference to which provides the climactic justification of the book, establishes Donne's work as the end-point of all inquiry, with its horizon sited inside this capacious set of texts.

The enterprise indicates its interest in history, its concern to place Donne 'in his time'. The key word for the relationship proposed is 'assimilated', which is simultaneously a process of reading and a process of transformation, attributed to Donne. But if we look at the book's index, to see what objects constituted Donne's 'time' as far as it is concerned, we find a surprising anomaly. Apart from Donne's works, which are massively represented, there are only five authors with nine references or more devoted to them. All these were born more than 250 years before Donne. Four of these (Plato, Paul, Augustine and Bernard of Clairvaux) are not literary writers: the only poet in the group is the Italian Petrarch. Only four English poets contemporary with Donne are listed, with a combined total of five references.

There is a complex series of transformations performed here by Sherwood (not Donne). Of two traditions that intersect in Donne's work, a literary tradition and a religious tradition, the literary has been virtually eliminated. Within the religious tradition (and in what is left of the literary tradition) all transformational activity has been eliminated, including such major 'ruptures' as between the canonical texts of the Bible and later exegesis, and between Catholic and Protestant exegesis. The strategy of reading (incorporating transformations that delete the processes of transformation and the terms of conflict) becomes a version of history (one without ruptures or breaks or moments of conflict). This unity is also imposed on the series of transformations performed by Donne over his lifetime, so that the 'whole' assumed by this exegesis rewrites Donne's own history in the same way.

The nature of the ideological performance of this text is clear enough. The title promises that it will go nowhere ('Fulfilling the Circle') and it fulfils its promise. But it does have a narrative form, one of the classic narrative forms: not a revolution but a search, a pilgrimage, whose end is to arrive at the 'centre' which was its beginning. The final chapter is titled: 'Conformity as Conclusion: *Deaths Duell*'. The archaic spelling guarantees historicity, proving that there was a time when conformity was the supreme value, even for 'revolutionary' poets.

There are good reasons why no other kind of historian would want to read a book like this. Sherwood draws substantially on texts from the past, but he removes their temporal location, and deletes all recognition of the conflicts and transformations which constitute this kind of history, for those interested in it as history. There are many references to historians of religious thought, but even these would have no reason to return the compliment, since in this book he uses these historians to explain an object which is outside their system: the works of a poet. There are no

references to any other kind of historian (social, political, economic) nor to
any objects of their discourse, and the 'history' of the period as they would
understand it is absent from its pages. So we have the paradox that a book
that appears far more scholarly and 'historical' in its orientation than
Leavis's essay is in practice just as effectively sealed off from all other
historians.

Sherwood was chosen as typical, not as incompetent. But we need to
recognize that a logonomic system does not prescribe a homogeneous
ideology, so that no one example will be sufficient. I will now look, more
briefly, at another book about Donne, this one published in 1982: *The
Poetry of John Donne: Literature and Culture in the Jacobean Period*, by
William Zunder. The argument of this book is summarized on its flyleaf
as follows:

> This INVALUABLE, lucid introduction considers the whole of Donne's
> poetry in the historical context, looking in turn at the *Satires*, the Love
> Poems, the *Verse Letters*, the *Anniversaries* and the *Divine Poems*.
>
> Against a background of radical economic, social and cultural change, the
> underlying themes, views and sentiments shown in the poems are exam-
> ined to see how far they could be said to be representative of the attitudes
> and values of the time. Dr Zunder sees John Donne as ultimately turning to
> God as a means of studying life's problems and expressing a personal and
> social pessimism characteristic of the Jacobean period. These are considered
> to be radical departures from traditional views, emphasising other-
> worldliness at the expense of social obligation.

This book promises to take conventional history seriously (politics, economics, culture) and it does so. It is half the size of Sherwood's text, and
only an introduction, yet it has forty-eight references to mainstream historians. It opens up its side of a dialogue between the disciplines. But there
are two ways in which it maintains closure. First, although it refers to
historians, it does not incorporate any of the objects of historians' discourse. The only non-literary document that it uses is Thomas Aquinas –
who loomed large in Sherwood's version of history too. Second, like
Sherwood's text its primary focus is on an object in the canon: Donne's
poetry. For Zunder as for Sherwood, explanation goes in one direction,
towards explication of the texts. The history is transformed to 'background', subordinated to the 'reading' of a literary object. As such it
would be of no interest to historians, and the disciplinary boundaries
could remain in place.

Zunder differs from Sherwood in another way, signalled by the double
use of 'radical'. The word, used of the period, marks an allegiance to
turning-point historians who claim to have located revolutions in the
period. The second use is more complex: the 'radical departure' from

tradition is a movement away from a radical social and political stance, to what is another kind of conservatism. This is essentially the same judgement as Sherwood made, but from an opposing point of view. Zunder regrets what Sherwood celebrates. But although their conclusion is the same, the narrative of their semiosic act is different, and they appeal to different factions within the community of literary criticism. Zunder heroically exposes a failed revolutionary, where Sherwood merged with the poet and the past. One enterprise is radical, the other is conservative. It cannot be said that literary criticism is purely a system for replicating a conservative view of history. But at the same time we can see how it contains that conflict within its own discursive domain, so that no other discipline, not even 'History', can understand what is at issue or intervene.

It is clear why mainstream historians would not see any value in reading literary criticism/scholarship. It is not so clear why they would not use literary texts. Donne's poetry, along with his other writings, could provide evidence for attitudes to love, marriage and religion, themes that social historians are very much interested in. In 1984, for instance, Ralph A. Houlbrooke published *The English Family 1450–1700*. Its dust jacket describes its contents in encouraging terms:

> Dr Houlbrooke draws on a wealth of fascinating, colourful and often inti-
> mate evidence – letters, diaries, autobiographies, epitaphs, the testimony
> of witnesses in court cases, and literature from Christian homilies to popu-
> lar songs – to illuminate the attitudes and aspirations of all levels of
> society. Examining this material in the context of the economic, demo-
> graphic, religious and political developments of the period, he challenges
> the fashionable notion that the years between 1450 and 1700 saw major
> changes in family structure, functions and sentiments. Dr Houlbrooke
> argues that continuity rather than change characterised family history in
> the period, and he shows that many of the elements of what we consider to
> be a distinctively 'modern' pattern of family life have far deeper roots than
> we are usually led to believe.
>
> RALPH A. HOULBROOKE is Lecturer in the Department of History at the
> University of Reading.

This book is one of a series entitled 'Themes in British Social History'. The series title marks one difference in the way the discipline of History organizes its components. 'History' is subdivided by object (social, eco-nomic, etc.) by nation and by period, as well as by theme. Taxonomic activities are more precise and more prominent in the discourse of History. The list of objects, the different kinds of evidence referred to, initially seems open to the inclusion of literary texts – in fact the word 'literature' is used, linked to Christian homilies and popular songs, though neither of these would count as 'literature' in the canonical sense. But if we refer to the index, we find that there are only four references to writers who would appear in the canon: Bunyan, Greene, Jonson and Defoe. In no case is a text from these writers discussed or analysed. Either a text is summarized as though it were a document like a diary or the evidence of a witness, or a part of a sentence is quoted out of context. In spite of the claim implied on the dust jacket, 'literature' is excluded as an object of the discourse of this historian, or at least it is tacitly redefined so that what a literary critic would include is excluded.

In some respects his framework seems similar to that of the literary critics – relating 'intimate evidence' to the 'context of the economic, demographic, religious and political developments of the period'. But there are two important differences. The period is constructed as dynamic, in a state of 'development', and his aim is not to illuminate these texts, but to use them to illuminate another object, an object of historical discourse: patterns of family life, and claims about a revolution in sentiment.

Here Houlbrooke's achievement is constructed as a heroic achievement. He 'challenges' the 'fashionable notion' that there was a revolution in the English family during this period. That is, a revolutionary narrative has been constructed about the past, but in this text the revolution in historiography that sponsored this revolutionary narrative is dismissed as merely a 'fashionable notion'. Houlbrooke's enterprise is thus constructed as a counter-revolutionary move which is even more heroic than the revolutionary move. His triumph is to defend the legitimacy of the 'modern family' on 'our' behalf, discovering its 'deeper roots' and routing those who have tried to 'lead us to believe' otherwise.

The Houlbrooke narrative in some respects mirrors Sherwood's, but this does not mean that either Houlbrooke or History is allied to a conservative ideology. Lawrence Stone, for instance, wrote *The Family, Sex and Marriage in England 1500–1800* in 1977, a major work that 'documents the extraordinary changes in attitudes towards the individual and towards emotion that took place in Britain between 1500 and 1800' (dust jacket). Stone the 'revolutionary' is Dodge Professor of History at Princeton University: Houlbrooke the 'counter-revolutionary' is merely a Lecturer at the University of Reading. Clearly we cannot label History as an unequivocally conservative discipline.

Nor does Stone avoid literary texts. He has no references to Donne, admittedly, but he has eight to Shakespeare, and draws many examples from other writers. What he does not have, however, is any reference to a literary critic. Where Zunder had many references to historians but no independent use of historical data, Stone has considerable use of literary data, but no use of literary critics. This partly reflects the unusability of critics for historians, and helps to preserve the difference between the two disciplines. But it has another effect. Because the 'experts' on literary texts are of no use to him, Stone must read them in his own way, as a historian. This way of reading is essentially realist, the same way as Houlbrooke read the few that he used. But texts which have a complex modality – like Donne's poetry for instance – cannot be easily read in this way. In fact their value for historians comes from their complex modalities, the inverted worlds they construct. So with Stone as with Zunder an attempted transgression of the boundary between the disciplines leaves a breach across which nothing can pass.

The operation of the logonomic rules that keep English and History apart turns out to be subtle and complex. The barrier is not created by distinct autonomous and coherent sets of practices. On the contrary, each discipline is fragmented in its own way, and each allows analogous sets of conflicts within it, to construct parallel narratives of revolution and counter-revolution. Nor is the barrier impermeable. On occasion, practitioners of each seem to have free access to some aspects of the other. Yet finally each has a different defining object, which cannot be incorporated into the other domain without challenging the identity of the discipline itself. And without a discipline, academics have no position, no institutional place to support the bodies that they continue to have, in spite of their status as intellectuals.

Literature as evidence

There are many ways in which English and History could be reconstituted to become parts of a single historical enterprise. But strategically one essential move is to make over the defining object of literary criticism – the canon – as the source of documents for the aims of 'History'. As an indication of how this might be done within a social semiotic framework I will take Donne, showing how he can be read not as a canonical poet but as the focus for a set of documents in a history of attitudes towards love, marriage and the family in seventeenth century England. But these documents will be treated not as records, more or less reliable, but as traces of the basic processes which constituted them. The primary concern will not be to classify elements as 'new' or 'old', or typical or unique. I will assume that the components of what has been claimed as a 'turning point' at the macro level must also have existed at the microlevel, in innumerable exchanges and events. So the analysis must try to position the event in a transformational series, showing what forces in what conjunctions precipitated the old or the new, and what meanings the various agents deployed to make sense of what they were doing.

The first step is as simple as it is indispensable: consulting standard biographical sources to locate the semiosic events in a material history. John Donne was born in 1572, his father a successful merchant, his mother a Catholic of a good family related to Sir Thomas More. Donne was brought up a Catholic but 'converted' to the dominant Protestant religion, a move that was indispensable if he was to be employed by the state or in the state Church. At the age of twenty-nine he secretly married Ann More, then aged sixteen, the niece of Sir Thomas Egerton, his then employer. Her father so strongly disapproved of the marriage that he tried to have it annulled. Donne was imprisoned in the Tower, and dismissed from Egerton's service. The marriage is usually described as 'a disaster' for Donne's career by his biographers (all males). Certainly being sacked from your job and put in prison does not sound like success. But Donne was competing in a difficult market, and it is not at all clear that his marriage upwards into the gentry class was always a disadvantage in the years that followed.

In the following fifteen years Donne was not able to advance high in any area of secular employment. Only in 1615, after he was ordained in the Anglican Church, did success come, and it did so with some speed: royal chaplain and rector of two parishes between 1615 and 1616, and finally Dean of St Paul's in 1621. But his wife Ann had died in 1617 as this career was just beginning. Having had eleven children, Ann gave birth to her twelfth, a still-born child, and died within a week. This, then, was a typical enough career and marriage for an aspiring middle-class male allied to a female from the gentry, complicated by Donne's Catholic background and the parental opposition to his marriage.

Donne's poetry, which we will be using as document, was mostly not published during his lifetime. In 1633, two years after his death, an edition was published, followed by further editions in 1635, 1639, 1649, 1650 and 1654: sufficient indication of their popularity. The first edition was accompanied by fifteen commemorative verses, many of them quite long and by distinguished authors, further indication of Donne's status as a poet. Our concern here is not to demonstrate his merit, as worthy of belonging to the canon, but to examine the ways in which his semiosic position was established by contemporaries. Here the sheer bulk of the words and the conspicuous labour that went into their composition are transparent signifiers of the value of Donne's poetry. Even more revealing as evidence, however, are the recurring structures of meaning in these texts. Thomas Carew, himself a poet, concluded his elegy with the couplet:

> Here lie two Flamens, and both those, the best,
> Apollo's first, at last, the true Gods Priest.

Sir Lucius Cary, Viscount Falkland, concluded his as follows:

> Then let his last excuse his first extremes,
> His age saw visions, though his youth dream'd dreams.

These poems repeat a theme that runs throughout the elegies: a contradiction between two kinds of discourse, religious and poetic, constructed as extremes, their characteristic speakers associated respectively with youth and age, their modality with dreams and visions. The work of the elegies then is to bridge the two, or to make that claim on Donne's behalf. Cary is explicit that the second counts as truth, whose function is to 'excuse' the dreams of the first, while Carew contrasts the 'true God' with Apollo, by implication the false god. The move repeats Sherwood's strategy, emptying out the modality-value of non-religious discourse in order to assimilate it to religious forms. Or more precisely, Sherwood repeats this move, which is prepared for by reading regimes of the time which existed to perform this task. But those ways of reading existed in order to neutralize and contain the meanings of the love poetry, as obligatory transformations that allowed the texts to still circulate. Far from vindicating Sherwood's reading, these two parallels from the past point to the need to recognize what is suppressed.

I will now look at another text (plate 5), this one taken from the other end of Donne's adult life. This is the portrait of Donne by an unknown artist, probably painted around 1595 when Donne was twenty-three. A cut-down version of the painting was used for the cover of the Penguin *John Donne: the Complete English Poems*, showing that this text still plays a role in the modern construction of Donne the poet. At the time it encoded an identity as clearly as did the elegies, but this was the identity of the young man, unmarried and marked with the signs of the melancholy lover: black hat, sensuous but mournful countenance, dishevelled clothes. Donne here as later inscribed meanings on his body, presented for the public gaze.

There is a Latin inscription for this painting, presumably composed by Donne: '*Illumina tenebras nostras domina*', 'Illuminate my/our darkness, O lady'. The words are close to a parody of a well known prayer in the English Book of Common Prayer, 'Lighten our darkness we beseech thee O Lord', with 'lady' substituting for 'lord', and a singular meaning concealed behind *nostras*. But more is at issue than a single word. Parodies of religious texts would normally be labelled as blasphemous by contemporaries, but Donne has clearly got away with it here. The change from Lord = God to Lady passes through a Catholic reading (= the Virgin) to mistress, a secular woman of flesh and blood who replaces both God and the Virgin as the object of his prayers. The use of *nostras* in a singular sense is also significant, making the individual (Donne) stand for the whole human race: an assertion of power that more than matches Kreon's.

The transformations here work in both directions, as transformations commonly do. A religious text has been appropriated to a secular meaning, but that text has also incorporated religious meanings into the description of an erotic relationship. That religious meaning has itself

Plate 5   Art as evidence: portrait of John Donne. From Private Collection. The book
jacket design is reproduced courtesy of Penguin Books.

incorporated another transformation, a Catholic transformation of the masculine Judaic God into the female Virgin; a transformation that Protestants were very aware of and were at pains to resist. The text as a whole constructs the painting as incorporating not just an individual, but a relationship, the male sitter and the absent powerful female, who is not to be identified with the viewer, since Donne's gaze looks to the right.

This work, however, is conceived within a generic form with its own modality. The relationship is understood to be unreal in two ways. The rules of gender in Elizabethan society quite clearly subordinated women to men. And marriage practices of the period imposed severe constraints on the sexuality of both men and women. Donne's unmarried state at the age of twenty-three was to continue till twenty-nine, and this was not an unusually late age for an Elizabethan male without financial security. This, then, must be read as the text of an unmarried male, expressing a set of meanings which were legitimate within this genre (portrait) and domain (young unmarried males, the Court) but assigned a negative modality. They expressed the will to power through the absence of power, and intense sexuality through ascetic or sublimated forms. The result, within this anti-world, is a relationship in which women have not simply equality but an excess of power. The most extreme fantasies of a feminist are advanced as the projection of a frustrated male's desire. Or so it seems.

Neither of these texts is part of the canon, but Donne's poem 'The Canonization' certainly is. Zunder devoted seven pages to analysing this poem, and Sherwood discussed it over nine pages. It can be dated as after 1603, therefore after his marriage, and the relationship it describes is the intense and equal relationship that Stone calls a 'companionate marriage', a 'new' form of the marital relationship that was part of the 'revolution' in family forms. But in reading it as a document, we need to be clear about the transformations that construct it, and the modality that it can be assigned.

I will start with the title, 'The Canonization'. It is the official transformation of the meaning of the poem, somewhat like the dust jacket of an academic book, and as a word it is itself a complex syntagm, a kind of text in itself whose full set of meanings incorporates a version of history. 'Canon' usually referred to a rod or rule but came to refer to an authoritative list, established by the Church, of what constituted sacred texts, sacred individuals (saints) or official members of an ecclesiastical order. 'Canonization' was a nominalization, referring specifically to an action that transformed secular individuals into sacred individuals (saints). But the agent of this action was understood as part of its meaning: the Catholic Church, whose claimed powers of canonization were the focus of Protestant anger. Donne's transformation of this transformation turns lovers into saints and their story into a new sacred text. It also inserts himself, a secular individual, as authority into the position of sacred authority formerly occupied by the Catholic Church. Thus he is challenging the authority of the Church in a distinctively Protestant way while at the same time incorporating its traditional forms into his new order: ambiguously an iconoclastic Protestant and a covert Catholic.

The poem however begins with satire, not religion:

> For God's sake hold your tongue and let me love,
>   Or chide my palsy, or my gout,
> My five grey hairs, or ruined fortune flout,
>   With wealth your state, your mind with arts improve,
>   Take you a course, get you a place,
>   Observe his Honour, or his Grace,
> Or the King's real, or his stamped face
>   Contemplate; what you will, approve,
>   So you will let me love.

Part of what impressed Leavis about this poetry was the intrusion into poetry of a speaking voice, as in the opening of this poem. Speaking voices as such are not such a difficult achievement: speakers use them all the time. But here as Leavis recognized it has an effect on the modality of what is represented. An everyday tone of voice signifies the modality of every-day life. The stanza that follows constructs a real speaker and a real listener, talking about a shared real world in which lovers grow old and the sphere of public life is both corrupt and hostile to love. Phrases like 'his Honour or his Grace' act as complex transformations to both incorporate and repudiate this world. 'His Honour' is the secular transformation of the category of honour into a title that can be bought, and 'Grace' is likewise the debasement of a potent religious category. And along with the transformations comes their presumed agent, someone with tradi-tional values who displays this process but doesn't endorse it.

With these markers of high modality goes the seeming close connection to Donne's own situation, choosing love (his 'disastrous marriage') over a career of achievement at court: except that Donne spent the first fifteen years of his married life trying to break into this corrupt scene, and only when he lost hope of gaining 'honour' did he successfully seek for 'grace'. The poem constructs neither his actual situation nor the values he acted on, in spite of the impression it gives to the contrary.

By the third stanza of the poem, the modality changes:

> Call us what you will, we are made such by love;
>   Call her one, me another fly,
> We are tapers too, and at our own cost die,
>   And we in us find the eagle and the dove,
>   The phoenix riddle hath more wit
>   By us; we two being one, are it.

So to one neutral thing both sexes fit
We die and rise the same, and prove
Mysterious by this love.

The metaphors signify a form of poetic language. But into this recognizable and neutralized anti-world comes another insertion from religious
discourse: 'we two being one', recalling Christ's words about marriage
which play a central role in the Anglican marriage service. Again Donne is
incorporating religious discourse into his construction of gender relationships. Where the unmarried Donne transformed the illicit Catholic image
of the all-powerful woman into a new map of gender roles, the married
Donne is taking an authorized religious version of marriage. It now
appears in a low-modality anti-form, poetry, though in a kind of poetry
whose modality-values have been rendered unstable. But religious discourse is a low-modality domain also, one in which a phrase like 'the two
become one' could coexist with the acknowledged fact that men and
women in Elizabethan society had very different and unequal lives. By the
laws of biology, two were more likely to become three, then four and five.
By 1603, the earliest possible date for this poem, the Donnes had one
child. By 1604 there were two, and by 1605 a third had been born.

This is a poem that announces a revolution in gender-relations which
goes beyond customary practice in the period. But it also goes beyond
Donne's own practice. It achieves its pure radical image by a transformational working over of that practice, eliminating both the older generation
of parents and kin networks which exercised a powerful and resented
influence on Donne's life, and the younger generation who were another
kind of constraint. The transformational analysis in some ways projects a
future that Donne's own style of life was only partly moving towards.
Equally illuminating, it reveals the sources that these transformations
worked with. In Donne's case it was the potentially radical version of
gender roles contained within Catholicism that he drew on. The precondition for his transformational work was the collapse of the modality
structures that had neutralized the Catholic anti-world. But this collapse
had weakened the modality-values of religion generally, and so there were
Protestant forms of Donne's work too.

But the 'new family' was a text that was co-authored by women as well
as men. Although Donne's poetry constructs a place for women as equals
in the relationship, this is very different from a woman's construction of
the terms of that equality. The problem illustrates the crucial problem of
the canon as a source of evidence, the massive gender and class bias that is
built into it. There are only a few women who were published in this
period. Of those, none has been admitted into the canon. The closest has
been Anne Bradstreet, who is assigned a position on the margins. But if it
is to serve as evidence the canon must urgently adopt an equal opportunity

policy, including affirmative action. And the case of Anne Bradstreet is a good place to start.

I will look briefly at one poem, 'A Letter to her Husband, absent upon Publick employment', a poem that was not published in Bradstreet's lifetime, but has since been praised for introducing a new 'domestic' note into English poetry. It begins:

> My head, my heart, mine eyes, my life, nay more,
> My joy, my Magazine of earthly store,
> If two be one, as surely thou and I,
> How stayest thou there, whilst I at Ipswich lye?
> So many steps, head from the heart to sever,
> If but a neck, soon should we be together.

Anne Bradstreet was the daughter of Thomas Dudley, one of the most important men in the New England colony. Like Ann More with Donne, she had influential connections and a power base in her own right. Unlike Donne, her background was strict Puritanism. A historian could use a poem like this one to illustrate the views of a pious Puritan gentlewoman, expressing a version of the companionate marriage along with a mild grizzle that her dear husband was away too often. Closer attention to the transformational moves and modalities of the text makes it a considerably more interesting and revealing document.

Firstly we can note the same biblical phrase that Donne used: here 'If two be one, as surely thou and I'. But where Donne asserted this without qualifying modality-markers ('we two being one'), leaving genre and domain to neutralize its meaning, Bradstreet reinforces it with modality-markers from everyday language, 'as surely thou and I'. But such heavy markers of modality signify the problematic status of the proposition, propping it up against doubt or opposition. Similarly 'If' attaches a hypothetical modality to the statement, by everyday standards of reality. This 'thou' is not an imaginary lover, but the actual Simon Bradstreet, absent from an actual Ipswich. Where Donne asserted an absolute and unreal unity by drawing on the anti-worlds of religious and poetic discourse, Bradstreet is attempting to take the proposition with naive literal-mindedness, and finding that she can't. So neither John or Ann Donne could really complain if reality did not conform to his picture of it, but Anne Bradstreet can, and does.

But the opening words of the poem are not realistic: they are an extravagant claim that he is her body, itemized as head, heart, eyes and life. They are easily recognizable as poetic discourse, with the modality of poetry. But the last couplet quoted treats this conventional metaphor unusually seriously, producing a sentence that is difficult to interpret. The meaning seems to be as follows: Your being away ('so many steps' between us) serves to sever head from heart; if only you were closer, it would be like a neck connecting head to body organically. The tortured syntax is appropriate for the brutal image that is constructed out of these conventional ingredients. With the breaking of the unity promised by marriage, her loss of her husband is a loss of her own body, which has been transformed into him. This alienated body is further split within itself, decapitated and dismembered. Simon Bradstreet had only been carrying out his normal masculine functions as a public figure. But the anti-worlds of poetry and religion, taken too literally, have constructed painful expectations, and with these have come a sense of self-division and self-hatred, anger towards the absent male-as-body redirected at the present body, her own. The pious Anne Bradstreet suffered most of her married life from sickness and depression. This poem indicates not simply that like a good and loving wife she missed her husband when he was gone. Rather, the demands she made on the relationship were the source of anger and self-hatred even when he was there. The 'companionate marriage' had its costs, especially within a continuing structure of material inequalities.

Conclusion: social semiotics and the interdisciplinary project

This chapter and the book itself so far have been engaged in a double compromise, with both 'English' and 'History' as they are at present constituted. Their separate developments and histories and the different logonomic rules that organize each as a distinct 'discipline' are potent social facts, not to be ignored in the name of an illusory project of unity. I still believe that the effort to stitch them together is exciting and productive for students of either. However, it does not seem satisfactory as an end in itself. English and History are not like Yin and Yang, two matching halves of a single pre-existing whole. Each is engaged in its own necessary struggle, with its own accounts to settle with its past. Until it does so, each will obstruct the other as much as it helps, especially if it constructs the other as conveniently fixed and homogeneous.

The legacy that English has left to 'New' English as its successor is an approach that is ponderously unserious, elegantly safe: clinging to a respectable pleasure of the text, engaging only in shadow boxing with real issues and real forces of the kind that threaten or deform lives. Its most urgent task is to cope with 'literature' from the present in all its media and all its forms as these express and are constrained by social forces and social agents. Only from this basis can it have much to offer History as a study of these processes in the past. The need is not to eliminate the study of texts that form the canon, but to replace the tunnel vision of the past, controlled through the concept of a canon, with a broadly based practice that is situated socially and historically. This is not to say that the study of literature from the past should be deferred or disvalued, even for the moment. Rather, the basis for that study of the past needs to be secured by attention to the present.

History's continuing problem is rather different. It lies in its remorseless obtuseness, its imposition of innumerable constraints on its practitioners as a substitute for any powerful and enabling forms of analysis: as though the overwhelming problem for History is too many people reading too much into a past that contains too many documents and too many interpreters. It is no accident that the 'people's history' project is one of the most exciting areas of historical inquiry, because this is one area where the paucity and opacity of documents makes over-reading at last a virtue. Paradoxically, part of the attraction of the very different reading regimes of quantitative history is again the difficulty of the texts that it works with: the rich complexity of ordinary lives, reduced to a few fragmentary statistics. But the kinds of reading required for these enterprises have no models in the practices of English, old or even new. Even the texts of a 'people's history' are as far outside the scope of English as of normal History. The 'popular' of 'popular literature' seems to refer to a different manifestation or perhaps a different form of 'the people', and the approaches that are being worked out within the new English seem to have no immediate application to this form of History. A union with English is no more obviously a liberating influence for History than the converse.

The role of social semiotics as expounded in this book, then, is not to urge a marriage between English and History, but rather to make such institutional re-arrangements irrelevant. In different ways the New Histories and the New English need a more powerful and precise understanding of the social construction of meaning, in the present as in the past, a past which begins a nanosecond from every now. In terms of this framework, the myopic focus of traditional English on its chosen texts will appear manifestly inadequate, so that a reading of the kind of text that historians read or write will seem immediately essential, and not something that has to be carefully negotiated through History as its official guardian. Conversely, the current limitations imposed on historians by History will seem a barrier not a virtue, to be transcended not enforced, and the mysteries surrounding literary texts will fade away. It is at this level that both English and History have a common need: for a powerful and comprehensive textual strategy that can analyse the social production of meaning, across the full range of relevant texts. This book was written to meet this kind of need for both historians and literary critics, whatever different aspects they may wish to draw on for their different purposes.

SOURCES AND CONTEXTS

In considering possible links between 'History' and 'English' it is important to recognize that each is a set of sometimes contradictory and competing practices, not the unitary and monolithic discipline that they may appear to be from the outside. It is not the place here to give a comprehensive map of the different kinds of history and the possible linkages. Blum 1985 argues that among the kinds of 'New History' that have emerged, social historians have shown most interest in literary texts and texts from popular culture that provide evidence on forms of consciousness, *mentalités* (e.g. Arißes 1981). She also notes the significant use of literary texts, including popular traditions, by major Marxist historians Hill, Hobsbawm, Thompson and Williams (whose inclusion in this list is testimony to his achievement in overcoming disciplinary divisions). *History Workshop Journal* publishes work in 'people's history' that draws on the methods and materials of the new 'English', as does *Radical History Review*, its American counterpart, and the links could be much stronger.

At the other extreme, 'Cliometrics' and the rage for quantification would appear to be resolutely opposed to anything as 'soft' as texts and readings of texts: see e.g. Laslett's (1971) polemic against *Romeo and Juliet* and the whole tribe of critics for misleading everyone about the Elizabeth on age of marriage. But see Hodge 1984b for the case that the two kinds of evidence, statistical and literary text, are complementary, each insufficient on its own. Floud 1984 argues a similar case in 'Quantitative History and People's History: Two Methods in Conflict?', that the current ideological hostility between these two schools is excessive and counterproductive.

The situation within History can alter when concerned with different broad periods, owing to differences in the surviving material or the mode of organization of the discipline. So within Classics, it is unsurprising that an economic historian like Finley, *The Ancient Greeks*, 1963, draws extensively on Homer or a social historian like Humphreys 1983 uses the Greek tragedians extensively. Sharpe in 'The Politics of Literature in Renaissance England', 1986, makes a similar point about this period, making a strong plea to practitioners of the 'new historicism' to attend to literary issues and materials. He commends to historians the innovative work being done by literary scholars such as Greenblatt in *Renaissance Self-fashioning from More to Shakespeare*, 1980.

Greenblatt draws on the work of Foucault, whose own work constitutes a major contribution to the history of discursive formations, a project that opens up new possibilities for what is called intellectual history or history of thought. See also the work of La Capra *Rethinking Intellectual History: Texts, Contexts, Language*, 1983.

Historians who have drawn productively on a form of turning-point theory include not only Hegel from the nineteenth century, but also Burckhardt, Nietzsche and even Marx and Weber. In the twentieth century, Lukacs, *The Historical Novel*, 1962, and Benjamin 'The Work of Art in an Age of Mechanical Reproduction', in Benjamin 1970, have both offered accounts of turning points that have been influential on literary critics. Althusser's intensive reading of Marx's *Capital* developed a methodology for positioning that text precisely in relation to what he claimed was a turning point in Marx's own intellectual development, as well a turning point in the history of thought (Althusser and Balibar, *Reading Capital*, 1970). Louie's *Inheriting Tradition*, 1986, shows how disastrous a crude and doctrinaire version of Marxist periodization was to the history of thought in post-revolutionary China. But a notion of turning points organized the Essex literature and history conference project published as *Literature, Politics, Theory*, Barker et al., 1986.

On ancient Greece, see Andrewes, *The Greeks*, 1967, and Anderson, *Passages from Antiquity to Feudalism*, 1974. On Greek legal institutions and practices, see MacDowell, *The Law in Classical Athens*, 1978. On the relations between *polis* and *oikos* see Humphreys 1983. On Donne's social and political ambitions and insecurities, see Danby 1965, and Aers and Kress 1981. On competing theories of the invention of the modern nuclear family see Poster, *Critical Theory of the Family*, 1978. The definitive biography of Anne Bradstreet is by Elizabeth Wade White (see e.g. Wade White, 'The Tenth Muse' 1983). See also the feminist interpretation by Martin, *An American Triptych*, 1984.

Bibliography

Achard P. 1980, 'History and the Politics of Language in France'. *History Workshop Journal* 10: 175–83.

Aers D. and Kress G. 1981, 'Darke Texts Need Notes: Versions of Self in Donne's Verse Epistles'. In *Literature, Language and Society in England 1580–1680*, D. Aers, R. Hodge, and G. Kress, Dublin: Gill Macmillan.

Afferbeck Lauder (J. Morison) 1965, *Let Stalk Strine*. Sydney: Ure Smith.

Althusser L. 1971, *Lenin and Philosophy*. London: New Left Books.

Althusser L. and Balibar E. 1970, *Reading Capital*. London: New Left Books.

Alvarez A. 1974, *The Savage God: a Study of Suicide*. Harmondsworth: Penguin.

Anderson P. 1968, 'Components of a National Culture'. *New Left Review* 50.

Anderson P. 1974, *Passages from Antiquity to Feudalism*. London: New Left Books.

Andrewes A. 1967, *The Greeks*. London: Hutchinson.

Anobile R. 1982, *Star Trek 11: The Wrath of Khan, a Photostory*. London: Methuen.

Applebee A. 1981, *Writing in the Secondary School*. Illinois: NCTE.

Ariès P. 1981, *The Hour of Our Death*, trans. H. Weaver. London: Allen Lane.

Arieti S. 1981, *Understanding and Helping the Schizophrenic*. Harmondsworth: Penguin.

Aristotle 1985, *Poetics*, trans. S. Butcher. London: Macmillan.

Arnold M. 1875, *Culture and Anarchy*. London: Smith, Elder.

Arnold M. 1901, *Letters*, ed. G. Russell. London: Macmillan.

Arnold M. 1954, *Poems*, ed. K. Allott. Harmondsworth: Penguin.

Ashplant T. 1988, 'Psychoanalysis in Historical Writing'. *History Workshop Journal* 26 102–19.

Atkins G. and Johnson M. 1985, *Writing and Reading Differently: Deconstruction and the Teaching of Literature and Composition*. Kansas: Kansas University Press.

Auerbach E. 1953, *Mimesis*. Princeton: Princeton University Press.

Austen J. 1946, *Emma*. London: Oxford University Press.

Bakhtin M. 1968, *Rabelais and his World*, trans. H. Iswolski. Cambridge, Mass.: MIT Press.

Barber C. 1959, *Shakespeare's Festive Comedies*. Princeton: Princeton University Press.

Barker F. et al. 1986, *Literature, Politics, Theory*. London: Methuen.

Barnes B. 1982, *T. S. Kuhn and Social Science*. London: Macmillan.

Barthes R. 1967, 'Historical Discourse'. In *Structuralism: A Reader*, ed. M. Lane, London: Jonathan Cape.

Barthes R. 1968, *Elements of Semiology*, trans. A. Lavers and C. Smith. New York: Hill and Wang.

Barthes R. 1977, *Image-Music-Text*, trans. S. Heath, London: Fontana.

Bateson G. 1971, *Steps to an Ecology of Mind*. London: Paladin.

Batsleer J. et al. 1985, *Re-writing English: Cultural Politics of Gender and Class*. London: Methuen.

Baudrillard J. 1981, *For a Critique of the Political Economy of the Sign*, trans. C. Levin, St Louis, Miss.: Telos Press.

Baudrillard J. 1985, *Simulations*, trans. P. Foss, M. Patton and J. Beitchman. New York: Semiotext(e).

Beattie A. 1987, *History in Peril: May Parents Preserve It*. London: Centre for Policy Studies.

Bell I. 1985, *Defoe's Fiction*. London: Croom Helm.

Belsey C. 1980, *Critical Practice*. London: Methuen.

Benjamin W. 1970, *Illuminations*, trans. H. Arendt. London: Jonathan Cape.

Bennett A. 1983, 'Texts, Readers, Reading Formations'. *Literature and History* 9 2: 214-27.

Benveniste E. 1971, *Problems in General Linguistics*, trans. M. Meek. Coral Gables: University of Miami Press.

Berger J. 1973, *Ways of Seeing*. London: Viking Press.

Bernstein B. 1971, *Class, Codes and Control*. London: Routledge and Kegan Paul.

Bettelheim B. 1976, *The Uses of Enchantment*. Harmondsworth: Penguin.

Birch D. 1988, *Language, Literature and Critical Practice: Ways of Analysing Text*. London: Routledge and Kegan Paul.

Blake C. 1984, 'Where Are the Young Left Historians?' *Radical History Workshop* 28: 114-23.

Blake W. 1966, *Complete Writings*, ed. G. Keynes. Oxford: Oxford University Press.

Blum A. 1985, 'The Uses of Literature in nineteenth and twentieth Century British Historiography'. *Literature and History* 11 2: 176-202.

Booth W. C. 1961, *The Rhetoric of Fiction*. Chicago: University of Chicago Press.

Bordwell D. and Thompson K. 1979, *Film Art: an Introduction*. Reading, Mass.: Addison Wesley.

Bourdieu P. and Passeron J. C. 1977, *Reproduction in Education, Society and Culture*, trans. R. Nice. London: Sage.

Bowen J. 1986, 'Practical Criticism, Critical Practice'. *Literature and History* 13 1: 77–94.

Bradstreet A. 1962, *Prose and Verse*, ed. J. Ellis. Gloucester, Mass.: Smith.

Brecht B. 1964, *On Theatre*, trans. J. Willett. London: Eyre Methuen.

Briggs A. 1986, 'Language and Social History: a Review Essay'. *History Workshop Journal* 22: 181–4.

Britton J. 1972, *Language and Learning*. Harmondsworth: Penguin.

Britton J. 1975, *The Development of Writing Abilities 11–18*. London: Macmillan.

Brontë E. 1946, *Wuthering Heights*. Harmondsworth: Penguin.

Brooks C. 1968, *The Well Wrought Urn*. London: Methuen.

Brooks C. and Warren R. 1976, *Understanding Poetry*. New York: Holt, Rinehart and Winston.

Burke P. and Porter R. 1987, *The Social History of Language*. London: Cambridge University Press.

Bush D. 1962, *English Literature in the Early Seventeenth Century, 1600–1660*. London: Oxford University Press.

Butscher E. 1976, *Sylvia Plath: Method and Madness*. New York: Seabury Press.

Cain W. 1984, *The Crisis in Criticism*. Baltimore: Johns Hopkins University Press.

Cannadine D. 1987, 'British History: Past, Present – and Future?' *Past and Present* 116 Aug.: 169–91.

Carr E. H. 1961, *What is History?* Harmondsworth: Penguin.

Carter R. 1982, *Language and Literature*. London: Allen and Unwin.

Chadwick O. 1975, *The Secularization of the European Mind in the Nineteenth Century*. London: Cambridge University Press.

Chilton P. (Ed.) 1985, *Language and the Nuclear Arms Debate*, London: Frances Pinter.

Chomsky N. 1957, *Syntactic Structures*. The Hague: Mouton.

Cixous H. 1980, 'The Laugh of the Medusa'. In *New French Feminisms*, ed. E. Marks and I. de Courtivron, Brighton: Harvester.

Corcoran B. and Evans E. 1987, *Readers, Texts, Teachers*. New York: Boynton Cook.

cummings e. e. 1968, *Complete Poems*. Bristol: MacGibbon and Kee.

Danby J. F. 1965, *Elizabethan and Jacobean Poets*. London: Faber and Faber.

de Bono E. 1967, *The Uses of Lateral Thinking*. London: Jonathan Cape.

de Certeau M. 1986, *The Practice of Everyday Life*. Berkeley: University of California Press.

de Lauretis T. 1984, *Alice Doesn't: Feminism, Semiotics, Cinema*. Bloomington: Indiana University Press.

Defoe D. 1927, *The Shortest Way with Dissenters*. Oxford: Blackwell.

Defoe D. 1949, *Selected Writings* ed. J. Boulton. London: Cambridge University Press.

Defoe D. 1965, *Moll Flanders*. London: Pan.

Derrida J. 1970, 'Structure, Sign and Play in the Discourse of the Human Sciences'. In *The Structuralist Controversy*, ed. R. Macksey and E. Donato, Baltimore: Johns Hopkins University Press.

Derrida J. 1977, 'The Law of Genre'. *Glyph* 7: 201–32.

Dixon J. 1967, *Growth through English*. Oxford: Oxford University Press.

Donne J. 1971, *The Complete English Poems*, ed. A. Smith. Harmondsworth: Penguin.

Douglas I. 1988, *Film and Meaning*. Perth: Continuum Publications.

Drabble M. 1985, *The Oxford Companion to English Literature*. London: Oxford University Press.

Dylan B. 1973, *Writings and Drawings*. London: Jonathan Cape.

Eagleton T. 1975, *Myths of Power: a Marxist Study of the Brontës*. London: Macmillan.

Eagleton T. 1976, *Marxism and Literary Criticism*. London: Methuen.

Eagleton T. 1983, *Literary Theory: An Introduction*. Oxford: Blackwell.

Eco U. 1986, *Travels in Hyperreality*. New York: Harcourt, Brace and Jovanovich.

Ehrlich C. 1977, *Socialism, Anarchism and Feminism*. Baltimore: Vacant Lots Press.

Elam K. 1980, *The Semiotics of Thetre and Drama*. London: Methuen.

Eliot T. S. 1921, *The Waste Land*. London: Faber and Faber.

Emig J. 1983, *The Web of Meaning*. New Jersey: Boynton Cook.

Empson W. 1936, *Seven Types of Ambiguity*. London: Chatto and Windus.

Esslin M. 1965, *Absurd Drama*. Harmondsworth: Penguin.

Esslin M. 1969, *The Theatre of the Absurd*. New York: Anchor.

Figlio K. 1988, 'Oral History and the Unconscious'. *History Workshop Journal* 26: 120–32.

Finley M. 1963, *The Ancient Greeks*. London: Chatto and Windus.

Fish S. 1980, *Is there a Text in this Class? The Authority of Interpretative Communities*. Cambridge, Mass.: Harvard University Press.

Floud R. 1984, 'Quantitative History and People's History: Two Methods in Conflict?' *History Workshop Journal* 17: 113–24.

Fogel R. W. and Elton G. R. 1983, *Which Road to the Past?* New Haven: Yale University Press.

Foucault M. 1967, *Madness and Civilization*, trans. R. Howard. London: Tavistock.

Foucault M. 1972, *The Archaeology of Knowledge*, trans. A. Sheridan Smith. London: Tavistock.

Foucault M. 1973, *The Order of Things*. New York: Random House.

Foucault M. 1977, *Language, Countermemory, Practice*, trans. D. Bouchard and S. Simon. Oxford: Blackwell.

Foucault M. 1979, *Discipline and Punish*, trans. A. Sheridan. Harmondsworth: Penguin.

Foucault M. 1980, *Power-Knowledge*, ed. C. Gordon. Brighton: Harvester Press.

Fowler A. 1982, *Kinds of Literature: an Introduction to the Theory of Genres and Modes*. Cambridge, Mass.: Harvard University Press.

Fowler R. 1981, *Literature as Social Discourse*. Bloomington, Indiana: Indiana University Press.

Fowler R. 1986, *Linguistic Criticism*. London: Oxford University Press.

Fowler R., Hodge R., Kress G. and Trew T. 1979, *Language and Control*. London: Routledge and Kegan Paul.

Freud S. 1960, *Jokes and Their Relation to the Unconscious*, trans. J. Strachey. London: Routledge and Kegan Paul.

Freud S. 1968, *Introductory Lectures in Psychoanalysis*, trans. J. Strachey. Harmondsworth: Penguin.

Freud S. 1976, *The Interpretation of Dreams*, trans. J. Strachey. Harmondsworth: Penguin.

Frye N. 1957, *The Anatomy of Criticism*. Princeton: Princeton University Press.

Gallop J. 1982, *The Seduction of the Daughter*. Ithaca: Cornell University Press.

Game R. and Pringle A. 1983, *Gender at Work*. Sydney: Allen and Unwin.

Gardner H. (ed.) 1972, *The Faber Book of Religious Verse*. London: Faber and Faber.

Giddens A. 1979, *Central Problems in Social Theory: Action, Structure, and Contradiction in Social Analysis*. London: Macmillan.

Gilbert P. 1988, 'Authorship and Creativity in the classroom: Rereading the Traditional Frames'. In Hart (ed.) 1988.

Giroux H. 1983, *Theory and Resistance in Education*. South Hadley, Mass.: Bergin and Garrey.

Goldmann L. 1964, *The Hidden God*. London: Routledge and Kegan Paul.

Goody J. and Watt I. 1968, 'The Consequences of Literacy'. In *Literature in Traditional Societies*, ed. J. Goody, Cambridge: Cambridge University Press.

Gramsci A. 1971, *Selections from the Prison Notebooks*, trans. Q. Hoare and G. Nowell Smith. London: Lawrence and Wishart.

Graves D. 1983, *Writing: Teachers and Children at Work*. Exeter, New Hampshire: Heinemann Education.

Graves R. 1961, *The White Goddess*. London: Faber and Faber.

Green J. 1984, 'People's History and Socialist Theory'. *Radical History Review* 28–30: 169–86.

Green M. 1987, *Broadening the Context: English and Cultural Studies*. London: Humanities Press.

Green W. 1988, 'Literature as Curriculum Frame'. In Hart (ed.) 1988.

Greenblatt S.J. 1980, *Renaissance Self-fashioning from More to Shakespeare*. Chicago: Chicago University Press.

Greene J. 1972, *Psycholinguistics*. Harmondsworth: Penguin.

Greimas A. 1977, 'Elements of a Narrative Grammar'. *Diacritics* 7: 23–40.

Griffiths P. 1987, *Literary Theory and English Teaching*. Milton Keynes: Open University Press.

Halliday M. 1976, *System and Function in Language*, ed. G. Kress. London: Oxford University Press.

Halliday M. 1978, *Language as Social Semiotic*. London: Edward Arnold.

Halliday M. 1985, *An Introduction to Functional Grammar*. London: Edward Arnold.

Harris Z. 1952, 'Discourse Analysis'. *Language* 28 (1): 1–30.

Hart K. (ed.) 1988, *Shifting Frames: English/Literature/Writing*. Geelong: Deakin University Centre for Studies in Literary Education.

Heath S. 1981, *Questions of Cinema*. Bloomington: Indiana University Press.

Hebdige D. 1979, *Subculture: the Meaning of Style*. London: Methuen.

Hegel G. W. F. 1920, *The Philosophy of Fine Art*. London: G. Bell.

Henderson H. 1958, *An Introduction to Haiku*. Garden City, NY: Doubleday.

Herodotus 1954, *The Histories*, trans. A. de Selincourt. Harmondsworth: Penguin.

Hill C. 1972, *The World Turned Upside Down*. Harmondsworth: Penguin.

Hill C. 1986, 'Agendas for Radical History'. *Radical History Workshop* 36: 30–2.

Hilton R. 1973, *Bondmen Made Free*. London: Methuen.

Hodge R. 1981, 'Transformational Analysis and the Visual Media'. *Australian Journal of Screen Studies* 11/12.

Hodge R. 1984a, 'Historical Semantics and the Meaning of Discourse'. *Australian Journal of Cultural Studies* 2 2: 124–30.

Hodge R. 1984b, 'Sémiologie de l'amour et du pouvoir'. In *Le Récit Amoureux*, ed. D. Coste and M. Zeraffe. Paris: Champ Vallon.

Hodge R. 1986a, 'Aboriginal Myth and Australian Culture'. *Southern Review* 19 3: 277–90.

Hodge R. 1986b, 'Cliché and Reality-control: the Modality of Duckspeak'. *Sociolinguistics* XVI 2: 35–44.

Hodge R. 1986c, 'Song as Discourse'. In *Literature, Discourse, Communication*, ed. T. Van Dijk, Amsterdam: Benjamin.

Hodge R. 1989a, 'Discourse in Time'. In *Text and Talk*, ed. B. Torode, Amsterdam: Foris.

Hodge R. and Kress G. 1982, 'Functional Semiotics'. *Australian Journal of Cultural Studies* 1 1: 1–17.

Hodge R. and Kress G. 1988, *Social Semiotics*. Oxford: Polity Press.

Hodge R. and Tripp D. 1986, *Children and Television*. Oxford: Polity Press.

Horner D. 1982, *English: Orthodoxy and the Eighties*. Canberra: Australian Association of Teachers of English.

Houlbrooke R. A. 1984, *The English Family 1450–1700*. London: Longmans.

Hudson J. 1978, *A Walmatjarri Grammar*. Canberra: AIAS.

Hudson L. 1967, *Contrary Imaginations*. Harmondsworth: Penguin.

Humphreys S. 1983, *The Family, Women and Death: Comparative Studies.* London: Routledge and Kegan Paul.
Hymes D. 1968, 'Sociolinguistics and the Ethnography of Speaking'. In *Language, Culture and Society*, ed. B. Blount, Cambridge, Mass.: Winthrop.

Ibsen H. 1961, *Hedda Gabler and Other Plays*, ed. and trans. U. Ellis Fermor. Harmondsworth: Penguin.
Ionesco E. 1965, *Amédée*, trans. D. Watson. In *Absurd Drama*, ed. M. Esslin.
Irigaray L. 1986, *Divine Women.* Sydney: Local Consumption Publications.
Iser W. 1978, *The Act of Reading: a Theory of the Aesthetic Response.* Baltimore: Johns Hopkins University Press.

Jackson R. 1981, *Fantasy: the Literature of Subversion.* London: Methuen.
Jakobson R. 1971, *Selected Writings.* The Hague: Mouton.
Jameson F. 1971, *Marxism and Form.* Princeton: Princeton University Press.

King N. 1983, 'Changing the Curriculum: The Place of Film in English Departments'. *Australian Journal of Cultural Studies* 1 1: 47–55.
Kress G. 1977, 'Tense as Modality'. *University of East Anglia Papers in Linguistics* 5: 40–52.
Kress G. 1982, *Learning to Write.* London: Routledge and Kegan Paul.
Kress G. and Hodge R. 1979, *Language as Ideology.* London: Routledge and Kegan Paul.
Kuhn A. 1984, 'Women's Genres'. *Screen* 25: 1.
Kuhn T. S. 1962, *The Structure of Scientific Revolutions.* Chicago: Chicago University Press.

La Capra F. 1983, *Rethinking Intellectual History: Texts, Contexts, Language.* Ithaca: Cornell University Press.
Labov W. 1969, 'The Logic of Nonstandard English'. Georgetown Monographs on Language and Linguistics, vol. 22.
Labov W. 1972, *Sociolinguistic Patterns.* London: Blackwell.
Lacan J. 1977, *Ecrits: a Selection*, trans. A. Sheridan. New York: Norton.
Ladurie Le Roy 1979, *Carnival in Romans*, trans. M. Feeney. New York: Braziller.
Laing R. 1972, *Knots.* Harmondsworth: Penguin.
Laing R. and Esterson A. 1973, *Sanity, Madness and the Family.* Harmondsworth: Penguin.
Lamb C. 1987, *Love in the Dark.* Melbourne: Mills and Boon.
Lamont W. and Oldfield S. 1975, *Politics, Religion and Literature in the seventeenth Century.* London: J. M. Dent.
Laslett P. 1971, *The World We Have Lost.* London: Methuen.
Lawson H. 1948, *Prose Works.* Sydney: Angus and Robertson.
Leavis F. R. 1936, *Revaluation.* London: Chatto and Windus.
Leavis F. R. 1948, *Education and the University* London: Chatto and Windus.

Leavis F. R. 1952, *The Common Pursuit*. London: Chatto and Windus.

Leavis F. R. 1972, *Nor Shall My Sword*. London: Chatto and Windus.

Leith R. 1983, *A Social History of English*. London: Routledge and Kegan Paul.

Lennon J. and McCartney P. 1971, 'Let it Be'. London: Northern Songs.

Lentricchia, F. 1980, *After the New Criticism*. Chicago: Chicago University Press.

Lévi-Strauss C. 1963, *Structural Anthropology*, trans. C. Jakobson and B. G. Schoepf. New York: Basic Books.

Lévi-Strauss C. 1966, *The Savage Mind*. London: Weidenfeld and Nicholson.

Lévi-Strauss C. 1973a, *Structural Anthropology 2*, trans. M. Layton. Harmondsworth: Penguin.

Long M. 1976, *The Unnatural Scene*. London: Methuen.

Louie K. 1986, *Inheriting Tradition*. London: Oxford University Press.

Lovelace R. 1931, Poems. In *Minor Poets of the seventeenth Century*, ed. R. Howarth, London: Dent.

Lukacs G. 1962, *The Historical Novel*. London: Merlin Press.

Lukacs G. 1963, *The Meaning of Contemporary Realism*. London: Merlin.

Lyotard F. 1984, *The Postmodern Condition*, trans. G. Bennington and B. Massumi. Minneapolis: University of Minnesota Press.

MacDowell D. 1978, *The Law in Classical Athens*. London: Thames and Hudson.

Major-Poetzl P. 1983, *Michel Foucault's Archeology of Western Culture*. Brighton: Harvester Press.

Malinowski B. 1965, *Coral Gardens and their Magic*. Bloomington, Indiana: Indiana University Press.

Marcuse H. 1964, *One Dimensional Man*. London: Routledge and Kegan Paul.

Mares P. 1988, ' "Personal Growth" as a frame for teaching literature'. In Hart (ed.) 1988.

Martin N. 1983, 'The Place of Literature in the "Universe of Discourse" '. In *Mostly About Writing*, New Jersey: Boynton Cook.

Martin W. 1984, *An American Triptych: Ann Bradstreet, Emily Dickinson, Adrienne Rich*, Chapel Hill: University of North Carolina Press.

Marx K. and Engels F. 1968, *Selected Works*. London: Lawrence and Wishart.

Marx K. and Engels F. 1974, *Werke*. Berlin: Dietz Verlag.

Marx K. and Engels F. 1978–80, *Collected Works*. London: Lawrence and Wishart.

Marx P. and Stuart C. 1983, *How to Regain your Virginity*. Sydney: Methuen.

Matthews J. J. 1984, *Good and Mad Women: the Social Construction of Femininity in Twentieth Century Australia*. Sydney: Allen and Unwin.

McDonnell D. 1985, *An Introduction to the Theory of Discourse*. Oxford: Blackwell.

McGuinness B. and Walker D. 1985, 'The Politics of Aboriginal Literature'. In *Aboriginal Writing Today*, ed. J. Davis and R. Hodge, Canberra: Australian Institute of Aboriginal Studies.

McLuhan M. 1964, *Understanding Media*. London: Routledge and Kegan Paul.

McLuhan M. 1962, *The Gutenberg Galaxy*. London: Routledge and Kegan Paul.
McQueen H. 1970, *A New Britannia*. Harmondsworth: Penguin.
Merrick L. 1988, 'Rethinking Popular Culture'. *History Workshop Journal* 25: 178–81.
Miller P. 1961, *The New England Mind*. New York: Beacon.
Monty Python 1971, *The Big Red Book*. London: Methuen.
Muecke D. 1970, *Irony*. London: Methuen.
Mulvey L. 1975, 'Visual Pleasure and Narrative Cinema'. *Screen* 16 3: 6–18.
Mulvey L. 1987, 'Changes: Thoughts on Myth, Narrative and Historical Experience'. *History Workshop Journal* 23: 3–19.
Murphy M. 1984, 'Telling Stories, Telling Tales: Literary Theory, Ideology and Narrative History'. *Radical History Review* 31: 33–8.

Neal J. 1980, *Genre*. London: British Film Institute.
Norris C. 1982, *Deconstruction: Theory and Practice*. London: Methuen.

Odmark J. 1986, *An Understanding of Jane Austen's Novels: Character, Value and the Ironic Perspective*. Oxford: Blackwell.
Ong W. 1982, *Orality and Literacy*. London: Methuen.

Passerini L. 1979, 'Work Ideology and Consensus under Italian Fascism'. *History Workshop Journal* 8: 82–108.
Peacock M. and Scarratt E. 1987, 'Changing Literature at A-level'. *Literature and History* 13 1: 104–14.
Pearsall, D. 1977, *Old English and Middle English Poetry*. London: Routledge and Kegan Paul.
Pecheux M. 1982, *Language, Semantics and Ideology*, trans. H. Nagpal. London: Macmillan.
Pechey G. 1985, '*Scrutiny*, English Marxism and the Work of Raymond Williams'. *Literature and History* 11 2.
Peirce C. S. 1965, *Collected Papers*. Cambridge, Mass.: Belknap Press.
Perkins D. 1985, *China: Asia's Next Economic Giant?* Seattle: University of Washington Press.
Piaget J. 1959, *The Language and Thought of a Child*. London: Routledge and Kegan Paul.
Piaget J. 1971, *Structuralism*, trans. C. Maschler. London: Routledge and Kegan Paul.
Plath S. 1968, *Ariel*. London: Faber and Faber.
Plath S. 1975, *Letters Home*, ed. A. S. Plath. London: Faber and Faber.
Poovey M. 1984, *The Proper Lady and the Woman Writer: Ideology as Style in the Works of Mary Wollstonecraft, Mary Shelley and Jane Austen*. Chicago: Chicago University Press.
Porter R. 1988, 'Seeing the Past'. *Past and Present* 118: 186–205.
Poster M. 1978, *Critical Theory of the Family*. London: Pluto.

Powell T. 1980, *The Celts*. London: Thames and Hudson.

Prince G. 1973, *A Grammar of Stories*. The Hague : Mouton.

Propp V. 1968, *The Morphology of the Folk Tale*. Austin: University of Texas Press.

Rabb T. and Brown J. 1986, 'The Evidence of Art: Images and Meaning in History'. *Journal of Interdisciplinary History* 17: 1–6.

Radway J. 1984, *Reading the Romance: Women, Patriarchy and Popular Literature*. Chapel Hill: University of North Carolina Press.

Reid I. 1984, *The Making of Literature: Texts, Contexts and Classroom Practices*. Canberra: Australian Association for the Teaching of English.

Reid I. 1987, *The Place of Genre in Learning: Current Debates*. Waurn Ponds: Deakin University.

Reynolds H. 1978, *The Other Side of the Frontier*. Townsville: James Cook University.

Rigney B. 1978, *Madness and Sexual Politics in the Feminist Novel*. Madison: University of Wisconsin Press.

Rimmon-Kenan S. 1983, *Narrative Fiction*. London: Methuen.

Roe P. and Muecke S. 1983, *Gularabulu*. Fremantle: Fremantle Arts Centre Press.

Rosen H. 1986, 'The Importance of Story'. *Language Arts* 63 3: 226–37.

Rosenblatt J. 1979, *Sylvia Plath: the Poetry of Initiation*. Chapel Hill: University of North Carolina Press.

Rosenblatt L M. 1970, *Literature as Exploration*. London: Heinemann Education.

Rosmarin A. 1985, *The Power of Genre*. Minneapolis: University of Minnesota Press.

Ruthrof H. 1981, *The Reader's Construction of Narrative*. London: Routledge and Kegan Paul.

Said, E. 1933, *The World, the Text and the Book*. Cambridge, Mass.: Harvard University Press.

Samuels M. 1972, *Linguistic Evolution*. London: Cambridge University Press.

Saussure F. de 1974, *Course in General Linguistics*. London: Fontana.

Scholes R. 1985, *Textual Power: Literary Theory and the Teaching of English*. New Haven: Yale University Press.

Schorer M. 1972, 'Technique as Discovery'. In *Twentieth Century Literary Criticism*, ed. D. Lodge, London: Longmans.

Schutz A. 1970–3, *Selected Papers*. The Hague: Nijhoff.

Shakespeare W. 1963, *King Lear*. New York: Signet.

Sharpe K. 1986, 'The Politics of Literature in Renaissance England'. *History* 71: 232.

Sherwood T. 1984, *Fulfilling the Circle: A Study of John Donne's Thought*. Toronto: University of Toronto Press.

Shlovsky V. 1965, 'Art as Technique'. In *Russian Formalist Criticism*, ed. L. Lemon and M. Reis, Lincoln, Nebraska: University of Nebraska Press.

Silverman D. and Torode B. 1980, *The Material Word*. London: Routledge and Kegan Paul.

Silverman K. 1983, *The Subject of Semiotics*. New York: Oxford University Press.

Slevin J. 1986, 'Connecting English Studies'. *College English* 48 6: 543–50.

Smith F. 1978, *Reading*. Cambridge: Cambridge University Press.

Smith J. 1984, *Taking Chances: Derrida, Psychoanalysis and Literature* Baltimore: Johns Hopkins University Press.

Snitow A. 1983, *Powers of Desire: the Politics of Sex*. New York: Monthly Review Press.

Sophocles 1968, *Antigone*, trans. F. Storr. London: Heinemann.

Spencer M. 1986, 'Emergent Literacies: a Site for Analysis'. *Language Arts* 63 3: 226–37.

Spitzer L. 1967, *Linguistics and Literary History*. Princeton: Princeton University Press.

Stannard D. 1977, *The Puritan Way of Death*. New York: Oxford University Press.

Steedman C. 1984, 'Battlegrounds: History in Primary Schools'. *History Workshop Journal* 17: 3–19.

Steiner G. 1975, *After Babel*. London: Oxford University Press.

Stone L. 1967, *The Crisis of the Aristocracy*. London: Oxford University Press.

Stone L. 1977, *The Family, Sex and Marriage in England 1500–1800*. Harmondsworth: Penguin.

Stone L. 1981, 'The Revival of Narrative: Reflections on a New Old History'. In *The Past and the Present*, London: Routledge and Kegan Paul.

Storry R. 1975, *A Short History of Modern Japan*. Harmondsworth: Penguin.

Strang B. 1970, *A History of English*. London: Methuen.

Taussig M. 1987, 'An Australian Hero'. *History Workshop Journal* 24: 111–33.

Theweleit K. 1987, *Male Fantasies: Women, Floods, Bodies, History*, Oxford: Polity Press.

Thomas K. 1971, *Religion and the Decline of Magic*. Harmondsworth: Penguin.

Thompson J. 1986, *Studies in the Theory of Ideology*. Oxford: Polity Press.

Todorov T. 1977, *The Poetics of Prose*. Oxford: Blackwell.

Trilling L. 1951, *The Liberal Imagination*. London: Secker and Warburg.

Turner V. 1974, *Dramas, Fields and Metaphors: Symbolic Action in Human Society*. Ithaca: Cornell University Press.

Underdown D. 1985, *Revel, Riot and Rebellion: Popular Politics and Culture in England 1603–1660*. Oxford: Oxford University Press.

Uspensky B. 1973, *A Poetics of Composition*, trans. V. Zavarin and S. Witting. Berkeley: University of California Press.

Van Gennep A. 1961, *Rites of Passage*. London: Routledge and Kegan Paul.

Van Ghent D. 1953, *The English Novel: Form and Function*. New York: Holt, Rinehart and Winston.

Vogel L. 1983, *Marxism and the Oppression of Women*. New Brunswick: Rutgers University Press.

Voloshinov V. 1973, *Marxism and the Philosophy of Language*. New York: Seminar Press.

Wade White E. 1983, 'The Tenth Muse – a Tercentenary Appraisal of Anne Bradstreet.' In *Critical Essays on Anne Bradstreet*, ed. P. Cowell and A. Stanford. Boston: Hall and Co.

Ward R. 1958, *The Australian Legend*. Melbourne: Oxford University Press.

Waters M. 1972, *Feminism and the Marxist Movement*. New York: Pathfinder.

Watkins E. 1981, 'Conflict and Consensus in the History of Recent Criticism', *New Literary History*, 12.

Watt I. 1957, *The Rise of the Novel*. London: Chatto and Windus.

Weber M. 1930, *The Protestant Ethic and the Spirit of Capitalism*. London: Allen and Unwin.

Weinsheimer J. 1979, 'Theory of Character: *Emma*'. *Poetics Today* 1: 185–211.

Wellek R. and Warren A. 1949, *Theory of Literature*. New York: Harcourt, Brace and World.

White H. 1973, *Metahistory: the Historical Imagination in Nineteenth Century Europe*. Baltimore: Johns Hopkins University Press.

Whitfield S. 1968, *The Making of Star Trek*. New York: Ballantine.

Whorf B. 1956, *Language, Thought and Reality*. Cambridge, Mass.: MIT Press.

Widdowson P. 1982, *Re-reading English*. London: Methuen.

Williams R. 1966, *Modern Tragedy*. London: Chatto and Windus.

Williams R. 1977, *Marxism and Literature*. London: Oxford University Press.

Williams R. 1986, *Keywords*. London: Fontana.

Wilson Knight G. 1957, *The Wheel of Fire*. New York: Meridian Books.

Wimsatt W. 1970, *The Verbal Icon*. London: Methuen.

Woolf V. 1931, *The Waves*. London: Hogarth Press.

Woolf V. 1945, *A Room of One's Own*. Harmondsworth: Penguin.

Wright Elizabeth H. 1984, *Psychoanalytic Criticism*. London: Methuen.

Wright Esmond 1986, *Franklin of Philadelphia*. Cambridge, Mass.: Belknap Press.

Young J. and Nakajima-Okano K. 1984, *Learn Japanese*. Honolulu: University of Hawaii.

Young M. 1971, *Knowledge and Control*. London: Collier Macmillan.

Zunder W. 1982, *The Poetry of John Donne: Literature and Culture in the Jacobean Period*. Brighton: Harvester Press.

Index